PENGUIN BOOKS

A DIFFERENCE IN THE FAMILY

Helen Featherstone is currently Assistant Professor of Education at
Wellesley College. She has taught courses on aspects of Special Education at Harvard.

A
Difference
in the Family

Living with a Disabled Child

by **Helen Featherstone**

PENGUIN BOOKS

PENGUIN BOOKS
Published by the Penguin Group
Viking Penguin Inc., 40 West 23rd Street, New York, New York 10010, U.S.A.
Penguin Books Ltd, 27 Wrights Lane, London W8 5TZ, England
Penguin Books Australia Ltd, Ringwood, Victoria, Australia
Penguin Books Canada Ltd, 2801 John Street,
Markham, Ontario, Canada L3R 1B4
Penguin Books (N.Z.) Ltd, 182–190 Wairau Road,
Auckland 10, New Zealand

Penguin Books Ltd, Registered Offices:
Harmondsworth, Middlesex, England

First published in the United States of America
with the subtitle *Life with a Disabled Child* by
Basic Books, Inc., 1980
Published in Penguin Books 1981
Reprinted 1982, 1984, 1985, 1986, 1987, 1988

LIBRARY OF CONGRESS CATALOGING IN PUBLICATION DATA
Featherstone, Helen, 1944–
    A difference in the family.
    Originally published: New York: Basic Books, c1980.
    Bibliography: p.
    Includes index.
    1. Handicapped children—Family relationships.
I. Title.
[HV888.F4   1981]   362.4′043   81-7315
ISBN 0 14 00.5941 5   AACR2

Printed in the United States of America by
Offset Paperback Mfrs., Inc., Dallas, Pennsylvania
Set in Palatino

The author gratefully acknowledges permission to quote selections from the following: *The Exceptional Parent* magazine; copyright © 1971, 1972, 1974, 1975,
1976, 1977, 1978; reprinted by permission of *The Exceptional Parent* magazine,
Psy-Ed Corporation, Room 700, Statler Office Building, Boston, Massachusetts
02117. *A Child Called Noah* by Josh Greenfeld; copyright © Josh Greenfeld, 1970,
1971, 1972; reprinted by permission of Holt, Rinehart and Winston, Publishers.
The Birth of Language: The Case History of a Non-Verbal Child by S. Kastein and
B. Trace; reprinted by permission of Charles C Thomas, Publisher, Springfield,
Illinois. *And Say What He Is: The Life of a Special Child* by J. B. Murray and
E. Murray; copyright © Massachusetts Institute of Technology, 1975; reprinted
by permission of MIT Press. *This Stranger, My Son* by Louise Wilson; copyright
© Louise Wilson, 1968; reprinted by permission of G. P. Putnam's Sons. *The
Siege: The First Eight Years of an Autistic Child* by Clara Claiborne Park; copyright
© Clara Claiborne Park, 1967, 1972; reprinted by permission of Little, Brown
and Company in association with the Atlantic Monthly Press. *Journey* by Robert
and Suzanne Massie; copyright © Robert Massie, Suzanne Massie, and Robert
Massie, Jr., 1973, 1975; reprinted by permission by Alfred A. Knopf, Inc.

CONTENTS

ACKNOWLEDGMENTS

THIS BOOK reflects the experiences, the insights, the hard work, and the good will of many people. I am grateful to all of them.

Over the past thirty years many mothers and fathers of disabled children have written books and articles about their family's experiences. Their eloquence first moved me to write about the way a child's handicap touches the lives of those around him or her. They taught me specific things about the way the experience feels to mothers, fathers, sisters, and brothers. They also showed me that in honestly describing their own pain, anger, fear, frustration, joy, and learning, parents help others they have never met; their example encouraged me to speak publicly about private matters.

After I had begun to write and think about families, I met a group of women who shaped my thinking decisively and contributed many of the stories that thread through this book. They were the mothers of the disabled children who went to school with my son Jody. I am deeply grateful to all members of the group for their willingness to share their feelings with others, and for the trust and generosity with which they allowed me to write about their lives.

Writing is usually a lonely business, but I have had so much support during the years of writing and revising this book that I have not found it so. My students at Harvard listened thoughtfully as I talked to them about what I was learning about families, and directed me, through their questions, to issues I had neglected. My colleagues and former teachers, David Cohen, Courtney Cazden, and David Riesman, read an early draft of the first chapter and encouraged me to go on with the project. Jane Stevens, Leslie Bedford, Mary Jane Yurchak, Ruth Shir, Sally Locke, and Stanley Klein read parts of the manuscript and contributed valuable comments and suggestions.

A fellowship from the Bunting Institute of Radcliffe College (formerly the Radcliffe Institute) gave me time and a place for writing, and supportive colleagues with whom to share ideas.

A number of pediatricians took time away from busy practices to talk to me about their own experiences with disabled children and their families.

Susan Smith and Carrie McLeod typed the early drafts of the manuscript, cheerfully enduring illegible handwriting and an atmosphere of crisis. Elizabeth O'Meara typed the final draft and tied up administrative loose ends, encouraging me with enthusiastic comments and sacrificing her evenings and weekends to my tight schedule.

My editors at Basic Books, Martin Kessler, Phoebe Hoss, and Julia Strand, took immense time and trouble with the manuscript, showing me ways to focus my sometimes diffuse thinking and tighten my prose.

My gratitude to all these people is immense. But I owe my family even more. My son Jody has shown us all what it means to love someone who is different. Both my wise daughters have talked thoughtfully about how it feels to live with a handicapped brother. Both have patiently endured the endless round of deadlines, postponing outings and even conversations while I rushed to complete another set of revisions. Liza, who is older, has also read parts of the manuscript, corrected my errors, edited my prose, commented thoughtfully on my ideas, and encouraged me to talk about "the bad feelings as well as the good." Reiko Nishioka, an honorary member of the family for the last six and a half years, has repeatedly sensed our need for extra help, and stepped into the breach.

Without my husband Jay there would have been no book. He has believed in the project from the first and encouraged me to take the idea seriously. He has read the manuscript at every stage of writing and revision, until he knew it almost by heart. He has edited, corrected, suggested, and responded with contagious enthusiasm to the ideas and the stories. He has cheerfully assumed more than his share of household duties so that I could write. He has taken care of me.

A Difference in the Family

Introduction

FAMILIES stir our passions as nothing else can. It is no coincidence that the best stories—from *Hansel and Gretel* to *War and Peace*—are about families. Love and anger, pride and guilt, fear and exhilaration, loneliness and warmth, all are the stuff of the stories each of us weaves out of our individual lives in a family.

In this book I describe the pain and other feelings—both good and bad—that come with membership in a particular sort of family. I focus on the family with a difference, the family of a handicapped child. I am also concerned with families in general and with how they endure any serious trouble.

Because my theme is the way that children's difficulties shape the lives of those around them, I have not struggled for a definition of disability. We all know what the word means, yet each of us hesitates before applying it to a particular child or adult. At seven my son Jody cannot walk or talk; he is disabled by anyone's definition. But what about my friend's daughter, who runs and laughs and reads but cannot breathe easily in a dusty room or visit a friend who owns a dog? Or my student's Aunt Ethel who cannot hear much but reads lips so competently that "no one considers her handicapped"? When does a little boy stop being "difficult" and become "emotionally disturbed"? Actually, it hardly matters how we label these people. Their limitations will touch the lives of their sisters and brothers, their mothers and fathers. The troubles and pleasures of these families are my subject.

I

When I was twenty-five, a friend told me that her brother had been killed in a motorcycle accident two years earlier. She said, "Nothing bad had ever happened to me before." I turned this statement over in my mind for a long time. What could she mean? Bad things happen to everyone—even to the luckiest people. Two years later I learned that my newborn son was blind; on that day I remembered her words. Now I understood them. I knew that nothing bad had ever happened to me before.

Jody was born in late June 1972, while my husband Jay and I watched in exhausted amazement. Our older child, Liza, was then three years old. Although the baby was a month ahead of schedule, we felt no special concerns about him, because he weighed in at a healthy six and a quarter pounds and looked beautiful. We took him home after four days, infatuated with ourselves and our two wonderful children.

Nine days later the world fell in: the doctor who had delivered Jody called to say that routine examination revealed a placenta infected with a disease called toxoplasmosis. Many women have this disease during pregnancy and bear totally healthy children. I was less lucky. Over the next year we learned that Jody was blind, hydrocephalic, and retarded, that he suffered from cerebral palsy and from seizures.

Each week after that first telephone call brought new calamities, until we were almost numb with the pain. A specialist examined Jody's eyes and told us that they were seriously damaged: Jody would see little, if anything, of our world. Two weeks later the pediatrician noticed that his head was growing too fast. Another specialist confirmed the suspicions of the first doctor: fluid was accumulating inside Jody's skull, pressing against his brain. The infection had obviously spread beyond his eyes. Probably his brain was damaged, too.

For the next eighteen months I felt as though I were living in a hospital. The shunt that relieved the pressure inside Jody's head became blocked and then infected. Ordinary colds carried him to the brink of death. Even when he was healthy, he needed a lot of medical supervision.

When I was not visiting hospitals and doctors, I was trying to soothe a miserable baby. Jody cried most of the time, the anguished wail of a colicky infant. He rarely slept, and of course we did not sleep much either. I felt sorry for him, and perhaps even sorrier for myself. I am not certain that I had the energy or the imagination to feel sorry for Liza and Jay, who certainly suffered as much as I. Jody did not learn to sit or crawl, or bat at toys, or reach toward sounds. He changed so little that I stopped believing in development. I thought he would cry forever. I wondered whether his life held any chance of happiness. I wondered whether it was worth living.

During his second year Jody's spirits improved. He cried less and smiled more. A friend came to live with us, and Jay and I began to get more sleep. The balance of pain and pleasure gradually shifted, until we could see Jody's existence as pretty happy. We began to make room in our lives for other concerns: we took more care of one another and tried to help Liza with the difficult adjustment to a difficult little brother. I got pregnant. Somehow the thought of this new life cheered us all.

When Caitlin was born, fat and healthy, in the fall of 1974, I felt as though I had turned a corner. Jody's problems became an element in my life, rather than the dominant motif. With a thriving infant in the house, our family felt healthy again. Like the baby herself, we began to demand more out of life. Keeping pace with her, we grew. Bad times still came and went, but not all crises centered on Jody. Emotionally we were returning to the mainstream, although we still faced special problems. We were knitting Jody, and our new identities as mother, father, and sisters of a severely handicapped child, into the fabric of an ongoing life.

II

When Jody was born, I was finishing a doctoral dissertation on the impact of different sorts of preschooling on the development of young children. Because we desperately wanted Jody to learn and grow despite his devastating handicaps, I began to investigate a related area: the field of special education. I looked at schools, talked to people, and read books; I learned about good programs, new and old. As we struggled to help Jody and ourselves, we saw that two sorts of special education were evolving in our house—his and ours. Jody needed special help in order to learn; living with Jody taught us, his family, special lessons. It created new pressures and forced us to examine ourselves more closely than we ever had in the past. Jody altered our lives and our perceptions of what matters. We saw the world differently because we loved him and shared his home. Liza, Caitlin, Jay, and I were getting our own "special education."

This book is about that education. It is about us, and people like us, more than it is about Jody, because Jody remains partly a mystery. He cannot talk. He cannot see. He cannot move about and explore the world. He cannot even play with toys, although he can smile and laugh and enjoy treats. It makes me sad to write this, but it is almost impossible for us to imagine his world. Perhaps for that reason I am more aware of the ways Jody has reshaped our understanding than of the ways we have shaped his. This book reflects these concerns. It is about how it feels to belong to a family with a disabled child. It is mostly about being a parent of such a girl or boy, but I have thought and written about the difficulties confronting brothers and sisters. My own family's experience provided the seed. The experience of other people fed my ideas.

Slowly the world is beginning to hear about disability from the disabled themselves. But because the children I know are very young and very disabled, they have not begun to talk about how they see their own differences. They do not, therefore, figure here as speakers on their own behalf. This book is really about their families.

Libraries are full of books and articles about families of disabled children. Professionals—mainly psychologists and social workers—write most of these. Some advise parents on ways to help their children and themselves. Others reach a professional audience, reporting the results of studies and clinical observations.

Psychologists and social workers generally bring two strengths and two weaknesses to the tasks of advising parents and describing their experiences. As for the strengths, many of these professionals have received some training in thinking about feelings and human behavior and in evaluating evidence; most have also worked extensively with parents and children and thus may have learned to see common themes and to set individual responses in some larger perspective. On the other hand, a professional sees each family from a certain distance, and his or her* understanding is in some sense theoretical. He watches, he listens, and he makes inferences. Inevitably, such an observer lacks an insider's view. Perhaps this very distance generates the second problem: many doctors, teachers, social workers, and psychologists focus so intensively on parents' vulnerability that they miss their strengths. Many also surrender to an impulse to blame all family problems on parents.

Sympathy allows some professionals to bridge the gap in their experience. Jerry Jacobs's compelling study of fourteen families served by a school for mentally retarded children (1969) describes the search for professional help with eloquence, insight, and compassion. Jacobs seems almost to have stepped into the skins of the women he interviewed. Other professionals stand at a greater distance from their informants but still manage to broaden our understanding of what family members go through. Frances Grossman's study of brothers and sisters of retarded children (1972), Ethel Roskies's work with parents of children with thalidomide deformities (1972), and Robert Edgerton's interviews with retarded men and women (1967) come to mind. All combine rich and compassionate portraits of individuals with sensible comments on general trends. Erving Goffman (1963)—a particular hero of mine—punctuates brilliant theoretical analysis of the impact of difference on people's lives with moving quotes from stigmatized, sometimes handicapped people. At the other end of the stylistic spectrum, Ray Barsch (1968) presents statistics on child-rearing practices of parents with disabled children in Milwaukee in

---

* Disabled children, parents, and professionals come in both sexes. Nonetheless, it is my publisher's policy to follow the traditional use of a masculine pronoun for an individual of either sex in the general sense. Throughout, I have used "his or her" as much as possible and have otherwise tried to avoid the problem.

the early 1960s. His analysis of hundreds of interviews includes many interesting observations about the prevalence of particular complaints, practices, attitudes, and expectations.

Family members have created a smaller literature, based on different sorts of "data." Writing in the first person, mothers, fathers, sisters, and brothers tell the story of their own experience with disability. Each of these writers knows in intimate, sometimes heartrending detail how it feels to live with a particular handicapped child. They know the strains, the fears, the hopes, and the compensations. Countless parents have written eloquently of their own experiences. I think first of Clara Claiborne Park's extraordinary reflections on her attempts to help her autistic daughter (1967); of Josh Greenfeld's candid descriptions of life with his brain-damaged son Noah (1972, 1978); of Robert and Suzanne Massie's harrowing account of eighteen years with hemophilia (1975); and of Emily and John Murray's journals (1975). There are many more such stories. Some fill only a few pages in the *Exceptional Parent*—a marvelous magazine for families of the handicapped—while others tell of a longer family journey.

The strengths and the weaknesses of these first-person accounts mirror those of the professional literature: every book I have read has helped me to taste someone else's pain and joy and to feel the textures of another life; none has compared one family's experience with that of another, or fitted it into a larger perspective.* The people who write these stories—the vast majority are parents—are atypical in certain ways: each one has managed to preserve some sort of margin in his or her life, for without private time no one can write anything longer than a shopping list; most have vanquished a good part of the misery that once threatened to engulf them. We cannot generalize from these accounts to the larger population of parents of handicapped children. But if we read with sympathy—and an occasional dash of skepticism—we can learn a great deal about the way certain human beings have felt in particular situations.†

In this book I seek to combine two traditions: the intensely personal narratives of parents, and the broader, more "objective" work of scholars and professionals. I start, of course, with myself and my

* Charles Hannam's study of eight families of mentally retarded children is an exception. Hannam's oldest son has Down's syndrome, and his own family's story introduces his discussion of other parents' experiences.
† These books are discussed at greater length in the afterword.

family. I know more about the strange symphony of my own feelings than I will ever know about anyone else's inner life. I have watched our family longer and more curiously than I have watched any other collection of human beings. I begin to judge an idea by asking whether it makes sense in the context of my own life and in that of my husband and children. Here I can judge new connections by feel. My own experience has helped to form the grid through which I listen to other people's stories.

I try to marry my own intimate knowledge of "exceptional motherhood" with the analytic tools I have gotten from professional training. I draw on the experience of many people. For all its limitations, the professional literature has illuminated some interesting connections for me. The testimony of individual parents has shaped my thinking decisively. I have found some of this testimony in published material: in autobiographical books and articles, in letters to the *Exceptional Parent*, in interviews. The rest comes from people I know personally.

Three years ago Jody's school organized a support group for mothers. I joined this group at the outset and participated, keeping careful notes, for two and a half years. (I describe my methods at greater length in the afterword.) We met for a morning every other week to discuss our children, our worries, and our lives. We continued to see one another even after our children moved on to other programs. These women became my friends; from them and with them I learned much of what I believe about families, and about people's response to tragedy, disappointment, and difference. I was very glad that they allowed me to share with others their struggles, their triumphs, and their insights.

While working on this book, I taught courses in special education at Harvard. Most of my students were experienced teachers. Some were the mothers, fathers, sisters, brothers, and grandparents of a handicapped child. They talked and wrote about their experiences, responded to the ideas I put forward in class, and helped me to recast my thought on families.

All these witnesses—professionals, family members, mothers from the group—appear in the chapters that follow. I have changed the names of the latter but left their stories as they themselves told them. I have quoted from written accounts: these can be distinguished by their citations. And of course my own recollections thread through every chapter.

III

In reflecting on their child's disability, parents talk about four things: their own unhappiness; their family; professionals; the road to recovery. These themes are my central concerns here. Chapters 1 through 4 describe four sorts of pain: fear, anger, loneliness, and guilt. Chapters 5 and 6 explore some of the ways a disability can alter the family unit. I have concentrated on strains in a marriage, and on the difficulties that brothers and sisters face and the compensations they find. Chapter 7 focuses on an important group of outsiders: the professionals who serve the child. Chapter 8 talks about the way parents rebuild their lives, the stony path to what families, professionals, and handicapped people call "acceptance."

Many writers invoke the notion of stages to describe parents' changing responses to a child's handicap. Certainly these stage models tell a part of the story: people do change; many follow rather similar paths; for the most part, life improves. I think, however, that most stage theories oversimplify a complex and diverse process. Just as not all dying people pass through Elisabeth Kübler-Ross's well-known stages—denial, anger, bargaining, depression, and acceptance— mothers and fathers of the disabled travel in many different directions when they move beyond despair. This is presumably why theorists argue about the number and the character of the stages. (Contrast, for example, the schemes of Richmond 1973; Baum 1962; and Klaus and Kennel 1976.)

Families grope toward their own solutions. What works for one may be unacceptable to another. Victories, when they come, are hard won and intensely personal. Few people find shortcuts, or detours around unhappiness. Nonetheless, most parents quite rightly resist any interpretation of their lives that would convert them into objects of public pity. Like the disabled themselves, they want their achievements recognized; they have not given up; they are, they keep insisting, "leading a life."

I admire the purpose and the ingenuity with which parents and children forge a good life out of imperfect materials. I admire their refusal to succumb to accident or biology, their determination to maintain their own dignity. I could have written a celebration of the energy and resolution of the many families I know and know about. Instead, however, I have emphasized the adversity that families confront. Indeed, in most of these chapters I explore textures of certain sorts of pain. I have focused on the difficulties for two reasons. First, because they come at the beginning, when most parents need a lot of help, companionship, and insight. Second, because I myself have been moved by the eloquence and sincerity of parents, brothers, and sisters who have chosen to share their unhappiness. In this often relentlessly upbeat culture it takes courage to confess to personal despair.

IV

I have written this book to help anyone closely involved with a handicapped child or children to build bridges linking his or her own experience with that of others, as I and my family have done. I quote from many sources because I want my readers to hear the often-eloquent voices of mothers, fathers, sisters, and brothers talking about their feelings as members of a family with a difference.

Parents need these bridges for two reasons. First, many individuals in such families endure their own feelings in desolate solitude. Parents battle fear, sorrow, exhaustion, anger, loneliness, and guilt without ever really knowing how many others travel the same path. In order to rejoin the human race, they bury their unhappiness and put on a brave face in public. When they venture out to work, the supermarket, the hardware store, or the PTA, they see others who are conscientiously papering over their own despair.

The voices of other parents can bring a measure of comfort to each of us on our lonely islands of unhappiness. If we as parents are no less miserable, we are at least less alone. Sometimes others can do more than dilute our loneliness. They can teach us about our own lives. Listening to their sometimes shocking voices, we hear echoes of our own experiences, reflections of feelings that we may have hidden even from ourselves. Because they are at a distance from us, we can see these feelings more clearly. We find connections we miss when we examine our own souls.

People who are not parents need bridges of understanding: the professional, in order better to serve families in difficulty; the brother or the sister of a disabled child; the handicapped person himself, or anyone who has gone through difficult times in childhood; and finally, the "ordinary" person in an "ordinary" family—for all families are ordinary in that all share the same concerns to a greater or a lesser degree.

Each child is different; no child's future is assured; and all parents fear for themselves and their children. All families must learn to deal with anger, both justified and unjustified; with uncertainty; and with the inevitable. Raising children, especially when they are small, is a lonely business, perhaps especially for mothers in the industrial West. Guilt for a child's unhappiness and shortcomings plagues parents of every stripe, whatever they may say to friends and relatives. Even the best-endowed child strains his or her parents' relationship. A disability only intensifies the strain, as it does other family problems.

I stress the parallel between disability and relatively ordinary family ills for two reasons. One is to correct the view of those who perceive beleaguered parents and children as saints or heroes, outcasts or freaks. The second is to show families with disabled children that their difficulties differ only in degree from those of other families. In coping with their extreme situations, such families share with all families the heroism of coping with whatever life offers.

If I have a message, it is this: All the members of a family are immensely vulnerable to one another. The pain of one child's disability reshapes every life in unexpected ways. Nonetheless, individuals endure. Each learns ways to live with pain, to alter, and even to banish much of it. Each experiments with different ways of being. Each makes a life—often a good one—out of a difference in the family.

Chapter 1

Fear

IN TELLING the story of a child's disability, parents often begin with fear. Fear often arises long before their son or daughter earns any sort of official label, before the school or the doctor identifies an important difference. Over the years fears change—in content, in quality, in intensity. Time does not usually banish them altogether, because the family of a disabled child must live with a special degree of uncertainty. Parents agonize about the limitations that the handicap will impose and about the world's response to difference. They worry about their child's future, about themselves, and about their other children. Brothers and sisters wonder anxiously about the place of the handicap in their own lives and about their future responsibilities.

"There Must Be Something Wrong"

Often fear presents itself as an inner dialogue. Two voices argue inside one head. The first sounds a warning note. It may say, "Amy never smiles at me, or studies the leaves the way her sisters did. There must be something wrong with her." Or, "Sylvia is two months younger than Andrew, but she's already crawling. Why doesn't he move around more?" Disquieted, the mother begins to contemplate some sort of action. Then a more reassuring voice answers the first: "It's okay. Andrew was a month premature. He's bound to seem a little slow at first. Dr. Spock says normal children develop at different rates." As long as each voice retains some credibility, the dialogue continues, but time usually silences one or the other. Normal children *do* learn at different rates; a spurt of development eventually reassures the mother or father who worries unnecessarily about disability. Alternatively, a doctor may confirm the parents' blackest suspicions.

Each family has its own story, its own versions of the inner—and sometimes outer—dialogue. Diane Kovacs remembers comparing her son Josh with the other toddlers at the park. She remembers her concern about his slowness, and the reassurances offered by friends, relatives, and doctors. Unable to persuade anyone else to acknowledge the validity of her doubts, she felt stuck. She needed to know what was really wrong before she could either help Josh or begin to face his limitations. Finally she found a doctor who told her the truth. "I left his office in tears, but I also was free now to proceed to something, to gain some control over the situation instead of feeling like a helpless victim" (Kovacs 1972). No longer divided internally, Diane Kovacs could muster all her resources for the battles ahead.

Professionals and parents talk about "denial"—unwillingness to believe a diagnosis—as a part of the adjustment to disability. It is true that mothers and fathers sometimes deny the extent of the tragedy. I think we can best understand this process as part of the search for truth—as one half of the inner dialogue. Hoping to reassure themselves, parents collect facts and observations that buttress their hopes. At the same time they watch warily for symptoms, for surer indications that something is wrong. Karin Junker, whose third child, Boel, seemed subtly different from her older brother and sister, describes her efforts to settle nagging doubts. Unable to formulate her suspicions, she observed Boel constantly—"spying" she called it, remembering the covert, anxious intensity with which she watched her daughter, even in sleep. "It was a sort of sly hunt for symptoms, of what I didn't know" (Junker 1964, p. 38).

Relief from this faceless anxiety comes to some families fairly speedily. In other households, years pass before either voice subsides into silence. Even a diagnosis may leave many questions unanswered.

My husband and I learned that Jody's eyes were badly damaged when he was two weeks old; the doctor told us that the infection that had scarred his retina might have invaded his brain as well. For months we worried and wondered: Would Jody be retarded, and if so, how seriously? Would he see at all, and if he could, how much? We watched him nervously, searching for the answers to these questions. Hope battled with despair. I remember one evening when he was about four months old, and I had brought him into our bed for the late evening nursing. As we sat silently, he turned his head toward us, apparently watching our faces. My pulse raced: I realized with a shock that I partly wanted to believe him blind, because I was using his blindness to "explain" the delays I had already noticed. If he could actually see, I would have to accept the doctor's judgment that he was retarded.

The uncertainties of the earlier period inspire a special terror: the panic of acknowledged powerlessness. Parents cannot prevent what they fear, because it has already happened. Thus, they worry whether their baby is blind—or retarded, or deaf—not whether he will be. They have to direct their efforts to learning the truth, rather than to changing it.

At the moment of diagnosis a disabled child may differ little from his peers. A mother, concerned by her baby's failure to crawl, learns at a neurological consult that he has cerebral palsy. A father observes a curious indifference to noise in his otherwise alert toddler. These symptoms cause few problems in the present. But fear looks to the future.

Parents are numbly, despairingly miserable when they learn of the disability—more unhappy often than they have ever been before; yet the road ahead looks bleaker still. As the years go by, the disability will grow more conspicuous. Often during the early period only a skilled clinician can discern a problem, and even he may require a laboratory test to confirm the diagnosis. In a few years even the un-tutored eye of a preschooler will find the child deviant. If things are hard now, surely, reasons a parent, they will be worse later.

Fears for the Child

The first anxieties may be the most concrete. Is there some sort of treatment for this problem? Can my child lead a normal life? Parents of a deaf girl worry about speech, lip reading, and communication with strangers. A new mother thinks of all the experiences that her blind baby will miss, and wonders whether ears and hands can ever guide him adequately in an invisible world. The father of a cerebral-palsied girl contrasts a drab, lonely, wheelchair-bound life to the opportunities that await able-bodied young women. Whatever the handicap, almost all parents worry about ultimate independence and the quality of their child's adulthood.

Very young children spend most of their time within the protected confines of the family. Still, parents worry about the day when their disabled child will move out into the community, for school, play, and work. If "mainstreaming" (participation in an ordinary classroom, as opposed to a special one) and independence seem likely, parents agonize about the social impact of difference. They worry that other people will avoid or victimize their child, that bosses will discriminate against him when he grows up, that unkind words and glances will bruise him as he struggles to negotiate the world of the able-bodied.

None of the small victories that help to cheer such parents through an ordinary day brighten their vision of the distant future and its imagined difficulties. Cynthia Gordon, for example, trembles when she contemplates her daughter's adolescence and adulthood. Laurie is four now. She was born with a spinal defect and cannot yet walk by herself, although she is learning to get around with a walker. Cynthia feels that the worst problems will come later. "People tell me things will get better, but I don't see how they can." She dreads the inevitable decisions: Ought Laurie to go to the local public school, for example, or would she thrive better in a special setting? Cynthia knows that as the years pass, Laurie will grow more conscious of her own differences. "Right now it's mainly me who feels it," Cynthia has told the mothers' group. "But as she gets older, I'm worried whether kids will tease her, and how she'll feel when they run off to play and she can't. Right now they all run off, and she's left sitting by herself in the corner. I feel bad for her, but she doesn't seem to notice."

For more severely handicapped children—the severely and profoundly retarded, the autistic, and those with multiple disabilities—the issues are different. When life-long dependence seems inevitable, the prospect of an institution darkens the horizon. Sherry Golden, whose three-year-old son Jamie is so severely handicapped that he may never learn basic self-help skills, contrasts the decent life that she and her husband have built with the unspeakable scenario they may not be able to avert:

Sometimes I think I will die from hurting to think of his future without us. For now he has love, good health, happy times and lots of work (therapy) to do. What does he have to look forward to if he cannot improve, but a bed with bad smells and only a dimness of life around him? (Golden 1974)

Few people have visited a public facility for the retarded or disturbed, but we have all read about such places. Their horrors are vivid to the parents of a child who may someday have nowhere else to go. In the privacy of families and support groups many mothers and fathers whisper, "I hope to God he dies first."*

Our sense of the future imparts meaning to our present activities. The possibility that a child will end his days in loveless custodial care mocks a parent's efforts to teach him skills and nourish his spirit. Josh Greenfeld, whose son Noah is autistic, talked to another parent about what lay ahead; after surveying the possibilities, they agreed: "Most of us, for all our hopes and dreams, are still fattening up our children for the inevitable institutional kill" (1972, p. 180).

Each member of a family is vulnerable. Children depend on their parents' love and care; parents rely on children's decency and well-being. Brothers and sisters shape the circumstances of one another's lives in a hundred small ways. Certain disabilities force the recognition of this vulnerability by provoking—or threatening—constant crises. An epileptic boy and his family worry about convulsions and public response to them. The father of a retarded teenage girl fears sexual involvement, rape, and pregnancy. Suzanne Massie, whose son Bobby suffers from hemophilia, trembles in anticipation of the next

* Parents are not the only ones haunted by the threat of an institution. Mary McCracken, in a moving account of her first year as a teacher of emotionally disturbed children (1973), speaks of being goaded perpetually by the fear that if she failed to help them grow, her charges would end up in the filthy, lifeless back wards of the state hospital.

bleeding episode. She limits Bobby's activities, trying to avert crippling damage to his joints. The crises come anyway; she is helpless to prevent them:

> There is nothing to do but learn to live with fear, in constant dread of the unknown. Such a way of life does strange things to the personality. Fear can grip and dominate you until you are unable to move in any direction. A person living with hemophilia can finally become paralyzed with fright, like a rat in a maze who has met with an electric shock at every innocent-looking exit until finally he simply turns frantically in circles, afraid to try any more doors. . . .
>
> During a crisis, I was possessed by a strange tense calm. I could fight. I *knew* what had to be faced. Such a strange feeling of release would suffuse me! It made me feel guilty sometimes. I would breathe a sigh of relief; it was only a knee. I knew about knees. The bad time was *after* the crisis, that apprehensive waiting for the next blow, wondering what it might be, from what direction it might come.
>
> It is late at night that raw panic comes. And despair. Lying in bed, sleepless, I could feel my heart pounding fiercely in my chest, dominating the stillness of the night. Waves of anxiety rolled over me. My hands were clammy. Where? What? When? When?
>
> Exhausted by my thoughts, finally I would sleep—only to be pursued by nightmares. Always in these dreams, Bobby, or one of the girls, is out of reach and dying. I try to reach them, but I cannot. My limbs are heavy and I cannot lift them. I see Bobby lying on the sand at the bottom of a great, deep dry well. I cannot go down. Or, I am caught in an elevator and he is falling off the top of a building. Or I have lost Susy and I search the streets and she is gone. When I woke from these dreams, covered in sweat and weeping, I would lie in the dark, shaking for hours, sometimes until dawn. These nightmares were so real that I would have to force myself to go into the children's bedroom to see if they were still there and even when I saw them and heard them breathing, I did not believe. (Massie and Massie 1975, pp. 173–174)

Suzanne Massie's nightmares sound very much like the bad dreams that terrify small children. These images of powerlessness remind us that people who love a person with hemophilia are vulnerable in some of the same ways a child is. Alien forces control their lives. Although they must act in a terrifying drama, they have little control over the script. Parents of such children feel that they have gained the power of adulthood only to lose it again through an accident of biology.

Fears for Ourselves

A child's disability raises the specter of his parents' old age, declining strength, and death. Even normal children exact a heavy commitment of time, energy, and emotion. But ordinary parenting follows a natural cycle that respects our mortality. When parents are young and healthy and energetic, children require vast amounts of exhausting physical care. As both grow older, this demand tapers off, and eventually the children grow independent. Parents hope and expect that by the time they die, their sons and daughters will no longer need overseeing judgment or physical care.

A severe disability disrupts this natural order, extending a child's dependence beyond a parent's strength, health, even lifetime. A disabled child forces parents to think of their old age in ugly, dismal terms.

I remember, during the early months of Jody's life, the anguish with which I contemplated the distant future. Jody cried constantly, not irritable, hungry cries, but heartrending shrieks of pain. Vain efforts to comfort him filled my nights and days. One evening when nothing seemed to help, I went outside, intending to escape his misery for a moment, hoping that without me he might finally fall asleep. Walking in the summer darkness, I imagined myself at seventy, bent and wrinkled, hobbling up the stairs to minister to Jody, now over forty, but still crying and helpless. Parents' thoughts linger on the costs—human as well as monetary—of raising such a child, and on the probability that they will ultimately fail to provide all he needs.

Many mothers and fathers look forward to a time when their children are grown and leading their own lives. They hope to regain then some of the freedom they gave up to become parents. If a child is seriously disabled, this hope seems remote. Lucy Forest, whose son Christopher was one of the most severely retarded children in Jody's school, returned often to this thought:

I look at the people down the street. Their kids are fifteen and eighteen, and now they can just get in the car and take off when they want to. I mean, just go out for a cup of coffee, or whatever. And then I think, "When will that ever happen for us?" We'll always have to be thinking of Christopher. . . . We'll never have that freedom.

Uncertainty about a child's prospects can twist disagreeable moments into grotesque caricatures of the future. When development is terribly slow or atypical, no one knows for sure how it will proceed. It is easy to imagine the future as an endless rerun of the unbearable present with a script that leaves no room for parents' personal dreams:

What a night! Noah was up all of it. Two urinations, two b.m.'s, four diaper changes in all. And the period in between, he bounced and jumped and chirped.

Obviously Noah isn't making much headway; he has become more and more lax in his toilet training. And when I project, all I see is a sleepy life of never-ending diaper-changing for us all. (Greenfeld 1972, pp. 106–107)

Fears for Love

Along with the terrifying questions about a child's long-range prospects and our own mortality come concerns for ourselves as parents. We wonder about our own capacity to love our child—or to love what he may become. Inspecting a prospective school, parents encounter the shocking reality of their child's likely future.

We visited the nearby school for retardates, a red-brick building set on the side of a hill, like a bunker. There is little space. In a railroad-flat setup they have three classes: younger children, older children, and adult retardates. The classes for the children look like happy bedlams, mongoloids running around, kids screaming, their muscles twitching. We came in time to watch one of the adult retardates celebrate his birthday: the singing of "Happy Birthday," the blowing out of the candles, the serving of the ice cream and cake. Of course, they were all like children, those close-eyed, sweetly vacuous heads. I almost cried. I refused to imagine that Noah, my son, belonged in such a place, with such a group. (Greenfeld 1972, p. 74)

Perhaps the worst part of an encounter like this is the parent's emotional response to the children. He finds himself recoiling from them; noticing this reaction, he wonders whether he could care for his own child if she or he became like these others.

Most of us know that some of the love we feel for our children is selfish. We love them in part because they enhance and ornament our lives. We wonder whether we will be able to love a child who deviates from all our dreams.

But Rusty. We had in that month's time learned that what Rusty had was probably Hurler's syndrome. We had learned that Hurler's is a progressive, degenerative disease that most often makes its victims deaf, blind, dwarfed, crippled, hunchbacked, deformed, desperately retarded, with damage to many internal organs—most critically, the heart.

Rusty was still Rusty. The only thing that had changed in the month of our research was our knowledge, our fear, and his complexion—now grotesquely covered with chicken pox.

Two A.M. was the hardest. At that time, I nursed Paul while all the rest of the world slept. My poxy children whimpered and fretted, and when Paul was sated, I pattered from Fred to Rusty to change, comfort and caress each of them. And I feared. And I prayed.

Those two A.M. feedings and prayers are the foundations even today, ten years later, of my only certainties.

Picture Rusty. He is four years old, tall and sturdy. His hair is red, though it has been variously described as orange and pink. Strawberry blond is probably technically correct. His eyes are big and bright with life, and tonight also with fever. Freckles splash across his nose and spill here and there onto his cheeks. His skin is so soft that rubbing his back soothes me as much as it does him. His skin is pretty to the eye, and to my fingers it's like talc on down. This night he doesn't look himself. He looks distorted and disfigured with chicken pox and a runny nose, and I am fighting panic because in the half-light of predawn I find myself seeing—not my Rusty with the chicken pox, but a grotesque nightmare of Rusty caricatured into the pictures we have seen in the medical journals of "children with Hurler's." We've learned the disease is sometimes called "gargoylism" and in my mind's eye is a Chagall mix of artistic medieval gargoyles, medical prognostications, and the image of a beloved four-year-old with chicken pox.

How will we love him when he is transfigured into that?

How will we care for him when he becomes what I am seeing?

What will we do? What will he be? What will we all be? (Green 1975)

Maxine Green raises the fundamental questions. As parents we need to love our children as much as they need that love. To fail here seems unthinkable, unforgivable. Yet when we glimpse caricatures of their futures in the anonymous faces of handicapped adults, doubts assault us: "How will we love him when he is transformed into that?"

Parents of disabled children share the usual reactions to disability. A few have always had warm, protective feelings for the handicapped. Others feel threatened, uncomfortable, or even repelled in their presence. Having a disabled child almost inevitably changes the most negative attitudes (of course it does not always banish them altogether), but embarrassing memories can add a particular poignance to a parent's fears for his child's future. In our mothers' group Rosalyn Gibson remarked that she and her husband now owned her parents' house—the one in which she had grown up. A retarded woman lived nearby with her mother and father—as she had since she and Rosalyn were children together. Although this woman was approaching thirty, she looked and acted like an eleven-year-old. Memories of her childhood troubled Rosalyn: all the neighborhood children, "including me," persecuted the retarded girl cruelly, calling her names, taunting her, and even assaulting her physically.

How can a mother expect the world to deal tenderly with her child when she once shared many of the attitudes she now seeks to eradicate? Guilt often magnifies fears.*

Mixed feelings toward the child himself can generate special concerns too. Few mothers and fathers manage to love all their children all of the time. Yet most of us believe almost magically in the power and constancy of love—especially a mother's love. Margaret Drabble's heroine, Rose Vassilou, is perhaps typical of mothers everywhere, as she struggles to understand why she worries so constantly about her sturdy, and unarguably normal, son Konstantin.

. . . she did not worry about Marcus and Maria. They would come to no harm, there was nothing in her that could harm them, she loved them so, their faces and their voices, that she could never harm them, she could transport them to the Pole or enclose them in a cellar and they would not be harmed, because of her love. With Konstantin (and this was the truth of the matter) it was different, because there had been a time when she had ceased, almost, to love him, when he had become unacceptable, in some way, to her, when his growing self (repelling kisses, suspicious, ungainly) had been impossible to indulge. They had quarrelled then, he and she (at the worst time, before she made her mind up to divorce Christopher, before the end, worn out with the two demanding babies, unable to cope with an articulate, complex, sulky growing boy)—they had bickered and quarrelled, and she had ceased, secretly, briefly, ceased, physically, to love him. She had stopped going in to his bedroom when she went to bed, to see him asleep. She had ceased to love as she had once loved. The spirit bloweth whither it listeth, with vicious negligence and malice. She had learned, now, to love

---

* The newly disabled are also vulnerable to these memories. Erving Goffman, for example, cites the case of a colostomized adult who, remembering how annoyed he used to feel when he smelled an odor in a public place, was sure that he himself now offended the young people on the bus. (1963, p. 34)

him again, she loved him again passionately, yearningly, but she would never cease to worry about that gap, that space of time when she had quietly, wearily failed him. (Drabble 1972, p. 149)

A handicapped child generates just as many mixed feelings as a cranky, defiant six-year-old. An uneasy consciousness that one sometimes fails to love this especially vulnerable little person can intensify realistic concerns. Reluctance to acknowledge the uneven texture of affection creates a vicious circle of fear and guilt.

Brothers and Sisters

For other family members the issues are somewhat different. With rare exceptions, brothers and sisters of a handicapped child are even more uncertain than their parents about the nature and extent of the handicap, and its implications for their own lives. Immaturity and inexperience lead to unexpected—and sometimes fundamental—misunderstandings. A sibling's special relationship to a disabled child gives rise to special concerns.

When they are still quite young, able-bodied brothers and sisters wonder whether the disability will compromise their own health in some way. They may worry about "catching" the handicap, as one might catch a case of chicken pox. Even when a little girl learns that her brother's blindness or retardation will not spread to her, she may still feel vulnerable. For example, a mother explained to her four-year-old daughter that the new baby's problems came as a result of his "getting sick" before he was born (prenatal rubella); for months the little girl worried that her own head colds might have disastrous consequences.

As they grow older, children wonder about a sister or a brother's future. At eight my older daughter observed, "I hear lots and lots about disabled children, but I don't know anything about handicapped adults. What happens to them when they grow up? What will happen to Jody?" Her question startled me into a new look at my community. I realized Liza was right. Recent changes in state and federal education laws have brought handicapped children increasingly into the schools and before the public eye. However, many handicapped grown-ups remain largely invisible—hidden in homes, sheltered workshops, and state institutions. Looking around them children may wonder whether the handicapped ever grow up at all.

Just as parents worry about old age, able-bodied children think about their own adulthood. Some wonder where ultimate responsibility for a disabled brother or sister lies. Do my parents expect me to take charge when they no longer can? Will I be able to care adequately for a disabled person, or find a husband (a wife) who will agree to share this job? How will this sister (this brother) shadow my own grown-up life?

Finally, children worry about becoming parents. Some wonder whether they carry a defective gene that threatens the health of their own unborn children. Fortunately most of these fears are groundless; parents and physicians can reassure many young people. Nonetheless, those who have grown up with a difference in the family know that accidents and diseases strike with terrifying randomness. Memories of their parents' unhappiness may darken their own dreams of family life.

The Role of Others

Most fear arises naturally out of the circumstances of the handicap. Some is generated unnecessarily by friends and professionals who want to persuade parents to behave in a certain way. People who believe that institutionalization serves the best interests of parents and child often paint an excessively pessimistic picture of a disabled child's prospects. The doctor who urged Helene Brown to give up her infant daughter asserted that "this child will be a vegetable. If you spend the rest of your life taking care of her, she'll never recognize you" (Brown, 1976, p. 34). (By contrast, the neurologist who encouraged the Browns to take Karen home assured them that she would be handicapped only by a slight limp. Neither prediction came anywhere near the mark.) Other parents tell similar stories.

My own responses to such bleak predictions are mixed. On the one hand, I have learned from my own experience and from conversations with other parents that fear itself is an enemy. It can, as Suzanne Massie eloquently explains, paralyze and enervate parents so that they can scarcely act at all. Those who stir up unnecessary fears may unwittingly push parents over the edge of reason. (For example, several mothers told Jerry Jacobs [1969] that inaccurate predictions had led them to think about killing their newborn babies.) On the other hand, professionals, friends, and relatives usually tell their frightful tales in good faith. In many cases they hope to persuade conscientious parents to institutionalize a young child, and they choose an argument designed to lessen parental guilt: this step is necessary for the good of those you love. Few who disagree with the ultimate goal—institutionalization—will applaud the method. Yet perhaps the wisdom of the tactic depends in part on its result: if parents do place a child, a dark view of his developmental potential may help reconcile them to a difficult choice; if the child stays at home, the effect of this pessimism may be less benign.

Parental fears are debilitating; they are not usually neurotic. Friends, professionals, and family members who try to dispel them often fail because the fears are so firmly grounded in reality. A parent's grim image of available residential care, for example, often reflects reality only too accurately. Burton Blatt, former Commissioner of Mental Retardation in Massachusetts, has vividly documented the hellish existence that the back wards of some state institutions offer the retarded (1973). Robert Edgerton's careful interview study of fifty-one "graduates" of Pacific State Hospital (1967) indicates that the view is as bleak from within as from without. Professional observations corroborate parents' fears that hard-earned developmental progress can erode in the impersonal atmosphere of an institution.

So it is with other fears. Josh Greenfeld writes of his son Noah: "Later he will be a grotesque, but now he is beauty in its richest, most fleeting sense" (1972, p. 72). Experience only confirms such a perception. Visiting a model preschool for autistic children, I was struck by the children's beauty and appeal and by the enthusiasm of the staff. The upstairs classrooms housed older children; I wanted to blame the depressing effect there on poor curriculum and staffing, but actually the teachers had furnished the rooms with attractive and appropriate materials and had worked hard to fashion a good program. The children, however, had lost their otherworldly charm; they were now simply psychotic adolescents. The hopes of parents and teachers had faded along with their baby fat.

Getting Better

Despite the grim realities, most parents do find that their fears diminish with time. Looking back, some mothers and fathers feel angry at professionals who failed to show them that the future need not be as bleak as it looked. Like Claire and Joseph Canning, whose daughter Martha has Down's syndrome, they believe that their grief would have been more bearable "if just one person had come to us to tell us that despite our sadness there was hope, that this was not the end of the world, but rather a challenge . . ." (1975, p. 9).

These parents are correct, of course. Every family has a right to information, professional support, and counseling. But even the wisest words leave many fears untouched. In the early months of Jody's life our pediatrician told us that things would never be so bad again. He was profoundly right, but I did not really believe him at the time. Jay and I knew, even at the outset, that other families had endured the same tragedy sturdily, that some had found it an impetus for growth. In our pain, however, we believed that those others who had written books, talked on television, and impressed friends and neighbors were fundamentally different from ourselves. Their brave words and smiling faces reproached our own disarray and misery instead of encouraging us.

If the image of other survivors fails to alleviate fear, what will? Time and experience have helped me much more than wise counsel. When I learned Jody was blind, I was shocked. I wept for the perfect baby I had lost, for the sunsets he would never see, for the four-year-old who would not be able to play outside unsupervised. But in a few days I learned to live with the idea of blindness, to believe that if he were "only" blind, he could have a rich, rewarding, and independent life. I lived in terror of retardation. It would be a year, the doctor said, before we could judge his development. I thought of the retarded children I had seen in special classes—their vacant expressions, their agonizing clumsiness, their "different" look. I could not imagine myself the mother of such a child. I thought I would have some sort of a breakdown before it happened. This baby I could and did love, but I felt incapable of loving a "retarded" child.

Actually, of course, the dramatic moment of the breakdown never occurred. As the months passed, things were both worse and better than I had imagined. Reality was worse: the baby had to cope with cerebral palsy and seizures, as well as with retardation and blindness. He was hydrocephalic. His shunt blocked often; family head colds brought him to the brink of death. He was hospitalized seven times in the first eighteen months of his life. Within the year I would have given worlds for the hope that he would one day walk and talk like the bumbling special-class children of my earlier nightmares.

Although outer reality was worse than my most despairing fears, my own inner reality—my feelings about my child and our family's life together—got better. As I became used to coping with today, as I watched myself rush a baby blue with seizures to the hospital, cope with the fears of an older child, and stand fast under what seemed an endless rain of blows, I became less afraid about tomorrow. My fantasies always seemed so far off the mark that they lost their power. I came to believe that the only thing I knew for sure about the future was that it would not be as I imagined it.

I think something similar probably happens to other people. Life with a handicapped child rarely follows anticipated patterns. Fears ease as experience discredits fantasy, as mothers and fathers learn that the actual problems of raising their child differ from the ones they had imagined. Similarly, small victories over private demons reassure parents about their own ability to raise their child. Linda Davidson, for example, worried about her dealings with the outside world. Even the decisions about Marianne's school transportation troubled her deeply. One day Marianne became so sick that Linda, all on her own, had to summon the police and get them to rush her and her child to the hospital. Everything went wrong, but she coped: she got Marianne the necessary medical attention. In retrospect she felt reassured: "One thing I have learned in the [mothers'] group is to assert myself. I really asked for what I wanted. I used to just stand there quietly, thinking the doctor knew best." As Linda saw herself handling the worst that life could deal out, she grew more confident and less afraid. Through slow stages she learned to recognize herself as a competent mother of *her* handicapped child.

As time passes, both parents gain a measure of control, even though important parts of their child's life and future remain beyond their reach. They know a good deal more about their child's disabilities than they did at first; they no longer wait, bound and gagged, for the ax to fall. If they worry about the school placement they can talk to the teacher. In a medical crisis they know which doctor to call. They have learned to navigate in the sea of experts and services.

Changes in attitudes toward handicaps, increased visibility of the disabled, and new public services also help allay parental fears. During the long ice age of special education, when attitudes and services changed slowly or not at all, parents could almost see their child's future laid out years in advance—often a bleak vista. During the 1970s a disabled child's educational opportunities changed dramatically. Most children are now eligible for more schooling, at an earlier age, in a more normal setting. These changes can temper a parent's fear by rendering a few of his nightmares obsolete.

The last thing to be said about fear is that it often wears an impersonal face. One mother remarked that, as she tried to cope with what the doctors told her about her retarded daughter's future, she began to feel "that all the unpleasant descriptions and pessimistic opinions embodied in the diagnostic process had nothing to do with this nice baby that we'd had at home since June and liked very well" (J. Bennett 1974). A diagnosis raises the specter of a faraway future in which the child is grown—and transformed into someone frighteningly alien. The continuing experience of living in the present teaches parents that changes occur slowly, that the child does not suddenly become the stranger they fear—the tragically deviant or dependent adult. He remains a person his mother and father know intimately and care for in many, if not all, ways. He will probably never look to them like the dimly remembered figures from the special class, the psychotic adolescents on Ward Three, or the illustrations in a medical text. As they slowly realize this truth, they worry less about their capacity to love their child—and less about the attitudes of strangers.

Suzanne Massie speaks of the way most people play with the future, dreaming, making plans, building castles. One of the horrors of hemophilia, she says, is that it makes a mockery of this innocent pastime. Disappointments come to seem inevitable, diabolically fixed, when a bleeding episode shatters each anticipated pleasure.

Few disabilities throw as many ugly surprises as hemophilia; yet many parents of children with other problems find that after a while they, too, resist the impulse to live in the future. Several mothers in our group felt that as they learned to focus on the present, they grew happier with themselves and their child. They spoke of the importance of "taking one day at a time," offering this maxim to one another like an amulet.*

Living in the present represents a hard-won personal victory. Most of us were raised to keep our eyes on the road ahead. We went to schools that justified long hours of dreary, mind-dulling drill and memorization by citing our future needs for skills. We sat quietly, walked in straight lines, and completed history assignments because these activities led to good grades and good jobs. As adults we continue to work and plan for a brighter tomorrow. Some of this is, of course, necessary and appropriate. Our short-term and our long-term interests may not coincide, and sometimes the long-run has to come first. Nevertheless, a life in which the future (or the past) overshadows the present can be deadening. Many people need to shift the balance more toward the here and now and concentrate on improving the quality of their daily experience. For parents of disabled children, who must fight against fear, this is even more critical than it is for the rest of humanity.

* Professionals who have not themselves fought free of crippling fears sometimes misunderstand parents' efforts to safeguard the quality of their daily life. This issue can feed into the tension between parents and professionals. Teachers often complain that parents are too present-centered. This means that they do not follow up on the teaching and discipline initiated in school, that they "take the easy way out." One special class teacher, for example, described the experience of teaching a twenty-three-year-old retarded woman to tie her shoes. The new achievement excited her student's parents; they thanked the teacher profusely. Delighted, she offered to show the mother and father her techniques, so they could teach their daughter other skills. Their lack of enthusiasm disappointed her. She pointed out that although it took time to teach these self-help skills, it saved time in the long run.

Her remarks reminded me of Rosalyn Gibson, who told the group that she still spoon-fed her blind three-year-old because the alternatives created such chaos. Meanwhile, the teachers encouraged Nancy to feed herself at school and urged Rosalyn to follow their lead. Like the other teacher, they spoke of time saved in the long run. Rosalyn thought about the family meals ruined by flying food and recrimination, and the long hours of clean-up. Probably a child needs both perspectives: someone who cares for the realities of today, the quality of life in the present; and someone who pushes for change and growth.

A case study of a workshop for retarded adults (Nemzoff 1977) illustrates the impact of this sort of conflict on a developing institution. The professional staff of Pleasant Valley Workshop pushed for new policies that would send retarded adult workers out into the community for jobs and recreation. Many parents objected vigorously. They worried that community hostility and personal failure would hurt their children; they worried about the physical dangers hidden in the workaday world. After years of agonizing about the future they preferred a program that safeguarded the *status quo*, allowing them to concentrate on other aspects of their lives. The professionals, by contrast, wanted to challenge the retarded workers and themselves, to see signs of growth. In the cautious, conservative program that satisfied parents, they felt they were "stagnating."

Chapter 2

Anger

Disability visits an extraordinary, cosmic injustice on a child and his parents. The behavior of other people—ranging from neighbors to school boards and professionals—compounds the family's miseries. Only a few parents rage aloud at the inequities of fate or berate their fellow men for insensitivity, bias, and indifference. Still, most have good reasons to feel angry.

Rage rarely bubbles up alone. Usually it mingles with other feelings. An angry person feels hurt, frightened, disappointed, miserable, or desperate *and* furious—all at once in a swirl of emotion.

In our diverse culture, among families, social classes, and ethnic groups, widely different—and rarely explicit—rules govern the expression of anger, a situation that can generate misunderstanding and ill feeling. (To many people shouting sounds downwardly mobile.) I reached late adolescence without ever seeing my mother and father get angry with one another. I felt uncomfortable when my friends' parents argued, as they often did. If my parents felt mad, I did not know it.

Perhaps in consequence, I do not tolerate anger well. As a parent I battle a tendency to interfere in arguments between children, to overreact to outbursts. If anyone I love is angry with me, I feel both wounded and furious. If I am mad, I sometimes disguise my feelings with a joke. Yet I have changed over the last few years. I admire friends who argue comfortably with their husbands and wives, and I have come to see that the most serene surface can cover smoldering rage. Many people accept anger more matter-of-factly than I do, but others share my feelings. For them, as for me, anger is a social and personal problem.

Nearly every family has implicit rules about who is allowed to feel angry with whom, as well as about how each expresses the feeling. Again, culture and upbringing obviously influence these rules, sometimes in baffling and contradictory ways. I hate being angry with my husband or children. When I do feel mad, I fear that if I say so, I will escalate the conflict. Perhaps it was out of this fear that I used to try to ignore rising annoyance. When I did speak, the effect was like dropping a stone into a pot of superheated water: my anger boiled up and over, with terrifying force. The more I said, the angrier I got. The force of this accumulated rage dissipated slowly. When the smoke cleared, I often regretted the things I had said. Thus, for me, the issue of anger tangled with the issue of control.

Current fashions in child rearing and self-help urge us to deal with our feelings in an open way. This is good advice, as far as it goes. Anger, however, poses special problems, three of which have particular relevance to families of disabled children. First, the honest expression of anger usually evokes a response—often more anger. The resulting barrage of accusation and counter-accusation can leave everyone scarred. Second, all of us find ourselves in situations where it is impolitic to express irritation; sometimes it even seems wrong to *feel* mad. Third, we sometimes feel irrationally—and unjustly—angry. In these pages I shall talk first about the side of anger parents discuss most comfortably, and then about anger's darker side.

"I Feel Like I've Been Ripped Off"

John Kennedy used to say that life is unfair, that one's sense of justice is constantly outraged by what actually happens. Because this is true, because we have only to look around us to see evidence of the arbitrariness of the universe, parents sometimes feel that it is absurd to be angry about the disability itself. Yet, at another level it seems absurd not to be. Our parents, our teachers, and our culture raise us to believe that if we work hard and behave decently, our lives will work out better than if we do not. Many of us apply this doctrine more or less successfully for years.

A child's disability flies in the face of much that families, school, and experience teach us. We have not changed. We still work hard to meet our obligations to parents, children, employers, and friends. Suddenly disaster strikes our carefully constructed world. What could be more unfair?

In the mothers' group Lucy Forrest described the ways in which she and her husband planned and prepared for their baby in the months before his birth. They bought a new house, attended prepared childbirth classes, and practiced the breathing routines conscientiously. Together they would welcome their child in the delivery room; together they would bring him to a new house. Suddenly everything went wrong: the baby was microcephalic; an ambulance rushed him from the delivery room to another hospital. The doctors concealed the grim prognosis. At 6 A.M. on the last day of Lucy's hospital stay, a pediatrician broke the official silence: he announced that Christopher was profoundly retarded and would never function above the level of an infant. Later, after describing to the mother's group her sorrow, anger, and despair, Lucy summarized her husband's response: "Kevin keeps saying, 'I feel like I've been ripped off.' "

Even parents who feel obscurely responsible for the disability may feel angry. I believed that Jody's toxoplasmosis was my fault. While I was pregnant I had read an article that linked this obscure disease to birth defects, suggesting that infection might come through contact with cats or uncooked lamb. I had conscientiously overcooked my meat after that (I give cats a wide berth anyway), but as I searched for explanations I remembered an occasion on which I had slipped up: a friend had served us a rare, juicy shishkebob and I had gobbled it up hungrily, without a second thought. Perhaps I had gotten toxoplasmosis then—no one could be sure because, like many adults, I had never had any symptoms of illness. At any rate, I had gotten it somewhere, and as a result Jody was handicapped.

In retrospect I felt I had not taken the threat of disease seriously enough (I knew toxoplasmosis did not affect one baby in a thousand). Even as I took precautions I rebelled, thinking, "For heaven's sake, if you run around dodging meteorites, you'll end up in the funny farm."

32

I see myself as spontaneous and informal, poorly organized and forgetful—two sides of the same coin. The disease seemed a judgment on my life and character. So I felt responsible: I felt that Jody's disabilities had come about through my oversight or, even worse, as a natural consequence of the way I am. At the same time I was angry: perhaps I had been careless, but the punishment was wildly out of proportion to the crime.

Like Lucy and her husband, I shake a fist at the cosmos. Neither of us personalizes the object of our anger: life, that obscure opponent and ally, has violated the rules; life has ripped us off.

For parents with religious convictions, the injustice of disability poses more serious problems. It is one thing to shake a clenched fist at life and another thing to challenge God. Robert Massie states the questions as many religious people may feel them: "If a healthy child is a perfect miracle of God, who created the imperfect child? Why would God create imperfection? Especially in a child? Especially in our child?" (1975, p. 14).

These questions trouble even confirmed atheists. Most of us have pondered them before reaching adulthood: related problems often provoke adolescent religious crises. A child's disability resurrects old, often unresolved questions. Massie says nothing in his book about feeling angry. Perhaps his mind does not work that way; or perhaps anger clashed too directly with his religious convictions for him to feel comfortable expressing it.

In a mother's account of a conversation with her physically impaired daughter, we can sense the difficulties parents and children may face when they find themselves blaming God:

From the time Michelle was old enough to question her birth defects, we have always answered, "You were born this way. God made you." And the answer was sufficient.

But recently she asked, "Why did God make me with no feet and two fingers?"

"We don't always know why God does things, Michelle."

"Well, I wish I was like everyone else. Anyway, God is not like this. How would He like it?" (Ouellett 1976)

Few parents blame the cosmos aloud. Everyone knows that *some* children have birth defects. And as one mother points out, the bitter question "Why me?" must always flip itself over eventually to the equally reasonable, "Why not me?" (Green 1975). Acknowledging this fact, mothers and fathers judge their own rage to be childish or absurd. For religious parents anger poses a heavier problem: it cuts them off from a powerful sustaining force in the moment when they most need support.

Anger at Other People

The original disability is only the first occasion for anger. Plenty of others follow. For one thing, the reactions of other people to the child and his handicap often hurt parents in all sorts of ways.

I remember the tears of my father-in-law and the reluctance of my mother-in-law to visit me in the hospital when Jeff was born. I remember the hurt and the anger I felt as my mother rattled on about what she and a friend had for dinner the night before and how hot and humid it was in the hospital. She talked about going to the beach, while all I could think about was whether our baby would live.

I was shocked when my mother-in-law demanded to know, "Who signed for that baby's operation?" Ignoring my bewildered silence, she pressed on with unconcealed hostility. "Someone had to sign."

Then I finally dredged up, "I guess Carl did. I don't remember who did. . . ."

"You have burdened my son for life," she said. (Pieper 1976)

Few grandparents express themselves with the cruel directness of Elizabeth Pieper's mother-in-law, but probably all feel the private pain of disappointed dreams. It is, as Mrs. Pieper points out, their loss, too. As parents of greater seniority and longer experience, they may see more clearly than their children how radically a child's defect will alter family life. The mother and father of a handicapped child need comfort and understanding as they cope with confusion and disappointment. Naturally many are infuriated when their own parents withdraw to mourn or, worse, strike out at them in anger.

Jay and I were lucky: our parents were able to put aside their own grief for a while, to comfort and support us. Not everyone is capable of this restraint.

As the child grows older and his disability sets him off from other children, family members may encounter hostility, fear, and cruelty. One mother recalls a conversation with her able-bodied children:

One day after school Chris confronted me. There was a white line around his mouth. He suddenly looked very small and vulnerable for eight years old.

"Mom," he asked, "what is a vegetable?"

I knew immediately what was coming. In spite of my intentions always to give honest answers, I heard myself stalling, "Vegetable? Oh, you know, peas, carrots. . . ."

"No. Not that kind! You know what I mean! The kids on the bus said my brother is a vegetable."

"It's just a word." Suzanne, then ten years old, broke in. "It's a word some of the kids use when they want to hurt you or be mean and nasty. Like dumdum, rattlebrain and . . . ," she swallowed, "retard."

"Do the kids say things like that?" I wished I hadn't asked. Their faces told the whole story. (Leaf 1975)

Here the disabled child himself inspired hostility, although the cruel remarks wounded his brother and sister. Sometimes outsiders accept the child but expect unreasonable sacrifices of his parents. Lucy Forrest described to the mothers' group the ways that neighbors and strangers had helped her and her husband Kevin to implement a demanding treatment plan for Christopher. Volunteers came in daily to "pattern"* the little boy; contributions helped the family finance bimonthly trips to a distant clinic. But this support, given freely during the early months when the Forrests devoted every minute to their baby, almost evaporated when they started to pick up the threads of their previous life. Specifically, when Lucy began to repaper their new house, some of the volunteers acted shocked and even hostile. Their reaction wounded the young couple; they felt that the world exacted a heavy price for its sympathy, asking that they devote their entire lives to their hurt son and give up pleasures others take for granted.

The Forrests' experience touches on the larger issues of services for disabled children, which can lead to immense anger, bitterness, and heartache. In the past, families of severely impaired children found little help in the public sector. Parents without a lot of money had to depend on luck and charity to meet their child's educational, medical, psychological, and therapeutic needs. Services have improved startlingly in recent years; most dramatically, federal laws now guarantee an appropriate education to all children, regardless of disability. Still, parents and children in many areas continue to require services that either are not there or exist only in a form that mocks the hu-

---

* A controversial treatment for children with brain damage developed by the Institutes for the Achievement of Human Potential in Philadelphia.

manity of all concerned. The horrifying quality of residential facilities for the retarded hurts parents deeply, by demonstrating how little the larger society values these children. In many cases this hurt turns to anger.

There is something in this society that doesn't want to see the true face and feelings of the disabled person—a force of illogic, fear and indifference that wants to keep him or her hidden except for the token cripple who appears annually on a stamp or seal designed to wring our collective hearts and appease our collective consciences until next year. And it's always little children they bring us, to feed the fantasy that they will all get well and there won't be any crippled adults to claim our attention and care.

But what of my son . . . If the march of all those dimes won't keep him out of an institution when our arms are too old and weak to hold him what will? What will guarantee him a life that is at least pleasant and decent, if not full, active and rewarding? (Golden 1974)

Even when services exist, parents and other community members may disagree about priorities. Barbara Sullivan of our group angrily reported a neighbor's comment: "You know, Barbara, you're pretty lucky to have Luke picked up in a cab every day, with the government paying for it." Whatever this woman intended to convey, one message came through clearly to Mrs. Sullivan: "My taxes are paying for your taxicabs, and I resent it."

Anger at Professionals

The medical profession is the largest single target of parental anger. Parents complain, first of all, about the manner in which their doctor (or doctors) presents the initial diagnosis. "Hardly anyone," writes Janet Bennett, "is pleased with the way she found out about her child's handicap" (1974). Parents complain about the doctors' reluctance to believe them and to respect their burning desire to know what is really wrong. Parents complain about cowardice and equivocation. They complain that doctors swing from one infuriatingly unrealistic extreme to the other. They complain that hospital staffs treat them without tact, consideration, or even common humanity. I could cite instances from nearly every volume I have read. One story will do.

Robert and Suzanne Massie took their infant son to a major hospital to learn why he had continued to bleed after a routine blood test.

The hospital personnel treated us with that blend of condescension and coldness that I have now learned to know well, and to hate. They took Bobby away. No one would explain what was happening or what was going to be done to him. Mysteriously, they said only, "We are going to take some blood." He was taken from my arms, my roly-poly jolly baby, and rolled away down the hall. Then, chillingly, I heard from far down that hall some terrible screams. I was filled with panic. The screaming went on and on. We asked what was happening. "They must not be finished yet," was the curt answer. After nearly an hour, I was so agitated that Bob said, "I'm taking you downstairs so you don't have to hear it anymore." We went to the cafeteria. When I came up I could still hear his screams; by now they were hoarse. Beside myself, ignoring the nurses who called after me, "You can't go down there," I ran down the hall in the direction of the noise and into a room filled with other babies in cribs. I found Bobby, still screaming, exhausted from crying so long. He was all alone. I snatched him up, rocked him, and kissed him. In a few moments his crying stopped. I found out later that the procedure itself had taken only ten minutes. They had taken blood from the jugular vein and then dumped him back in his crib, leaving him to cry, although we had been only a few yards down the hall and could have calmed him quickly. It was the first of many such experiences. In the years ahead I was seared by the lack of understanding, the lack of compassion—yes, the cruelty—that comes from the rigid and arbitrary rules practiced in some of the best hospitals we have. Even now, when I think of this moment, I am filled with a terrible rage.

A day had gone by. We still knew nothing. Increasingly alarmed, we hovered over the head nurse's desk, asking anxiously, "But can't you tell us anything? What is the matter with him?" The head nurse would put on what I call now the head-nurse smirk and say, "Oh, no, there is nothing I can tell you. I think you will want to wait to hear what Doctor has to say." I particularly loathe nurses who use that expression, Doctor, without a name.

So we went on waiting. Doctor did not come. In this case, Doctor was one of the most renowned hematologists of New York Hospital. Neither he nor any of his assistants ever took a moment to call the head nurse's desk to give us a word of advice or hope. The agony of waiting by terrified parents was simply not considered. We tried to get in touch with Doctor himself; we were put off by secretaries. Over and over again the same cold phrase was repeated, "Wait." My mother arrived and kept vigil with us.

On the evening of the second day we were still waiting in a stifling, overheated waiting room with hospital green walls and antiseptic furniture of cheap chrome and plastic. I smoked cigarette after cigarette. Bob was exhausted. It had been his first day on the new job. He had just joined us again. Suddenly a man entered. It was at last the long-awaited Eminence, "Doctor," himself. He was wearing a gray suit, and his eyes looked down

at the floor as he hurriedly came in. There were no preliminaries. He announced coldly and matter-of-factly, "The child has classical hemophilia.
There will be compensations, you may be sure." And with these enigmatic
words, he turned on his heel and walked out. (1975, pp. 11–12)

Parents looking for diagnosis are frightened and immensely vulnerable. They have already suffered days, months, even years, of
agonizing doubt. They stand exposed and powerless before the experts. Indifference, condescension, or equivocation wounds them
deeply.

Personal experience has taught me that anger is not always pro-
portional to the crime. I can remember flashes of irritation that seemed
unjust to me even at the moment I experienced them. The epidemi-
ologist who diagnosed Jody's toxoplasmosis interrupted his explanation of the disease to assure me that my future children would be safe:
having been infected, I now carried antibodies that would protect
them. I knew he was pointing out one of the few bright spots in a
darkening sky, but I had not asked about my child-bearing future.
I remember thinking angrily, "I don't *care* about 'future children.' I
love this baby. Don't dismiss him as though someone else could replace him."

Another specialist terminated each consultation by telling me how
beautifully I was caring for my son. His reflexive evaluation irritated
me: he did not, after all, know enough about my mothering to make
an informed judgment. My objections seemed petty, since I knew he
meant well. Still, his words always reminded me of all the things I
was *not* doing.

Parents' anger, when expressed clearly and forcefully, can help
keep professionals honest and teach them the limits of acceptable
behavior. Some doctors apologize and change their ways when they
learn they have hurt a child or a family. Even when discussion brings
no resolution, the parent who complains appropriately avoids the
curdled taste of undigested anger. However, doctors command more
respect than parents, both in the agencies serving the disabled and
in the world at large. This great disparity in power shapes the relationship of physician to parent and reduces the likelihood of honest
exchange. Many parents seethe inwardly or complain to friends but
avoid confrontations with the professionals themselves. These mothers
and fathers worry about losing services or acquiring a disparaging
label. Their fears reflect reality all too well: organizations sometimes

take criticism as evidence of a parent's emotional disturbance (see chapter 7 for more on this situation).

Most of the anger I have talked about so far is justified. The original injustice is monumental—however much reason tells us that life is not just. Neighbors, relatives, and strangers can act thoughtlessly; so can professionals. I have been struck, however, by other aspects of a parent's rage. First, not all of it is reasonable or justified. Second, anger can distort and obscure other emotions. And third, although each of us acknowledges some anger readily, we may conceal from ourselves anger that is deeply felt but far less acceptable.

Oversensitivity

When people have been deeply and frequently wounded, they grow sensitive: words and glances can jar raw nerves even when no unkindness is intended. The mother of a boy with Down's syndrome describes an encounter with a new neighbor:

I used to feel that I had to explain Jim in some way to new people who saw him. Once I said something about him to a new neighbor, and she said that she had not noticed that there was anything wrong with him. "I just noticed that he was cross-eyed," she said. "My goodness," I thought, and I looked again. I had not noticed that his eyes really do not focus well. Since then I have not tried to explain Jim anymore. (Michaelis 1974)

To me this neighbor's comment sounds like a friendly effort to reassure the mother that her child does not appear to be all that different; crossed eyes fall within the range of ordinary problems. Yet Mrs. Michaelis's sensitivity is understandable in the light of the many hurts she has endured over the years: the woman who decided not to buy the house next door after she saw "him"; the mother-in-law who made sure Jim did not attend his uncle's wedding; the teachers who complained about the stains on Jim's teeth; the school principal who noted that "quite frankly, Mrs. Michaelis, parents are sometimes our biggest problem." When many people are hostile, it is hard to give others the benefit of the doubt.

All differences arouse interest. When they are out in public families must bear the weight of surprised stares and curious glances. Many parents feel angry at those who pay them this unwanted attention. Barbara Sullivan reports that when strangers gape rudely at Luke she counterattacks: "Who do you think you are, staring at us that way?" Although no one else in the mothers' group would express herself with equal force, most say they echo Barbara's sentiments inwardly.

I understand the hurt behind Barbara Sullivan's retort. Yet I sympathize with those who stare, because I find that my own eyes are drawn toward disabled children and their families. When I am with my son—whose handicaps are obvious—mothers realize that concern and fellow feeling prompt my interest. Our children's problems force a momentary bond; we speak or smile and pass on feeling a little less isolated. If I am alone or accompanied only by my able-bodied children, I try to conceal my curiosity. I am afraid of hurting tender feelings.

From time to time strangers ask me about Jody's difference. After I have described his problems, some respond with a story of their own. A supermarket checker spoke of her retarded niece, now sixteen years old, of the sorrow and guilt her sister had felt after the diagnosis, of the girl's unexpected progress in a special school. An older woman told me that her youngest daughter was mildly retarded, that she had lain awake night after night agonizing about this child's future. She never mentioned her concerns to friends, because she did not want the little girl to be labeled "retarded."

Generalizing from my own experience, I suspect that parents misunderstand some stares and whispers. A stranger's curiosity may reflect a concern that he finds difficult to express openly. Unfortunately, it can hurt parents by reminding them how different their child looks.

Not long ago Jody started a new school. On the first day I took him myself, intending to spend the morning. As soon as he was comfortably settled in the classroom I withdrew to the observation booth. The program pleased me, but after a few moments I realized that I felt depressed. Although my feelings made no sense to me, they evoked a memory. A year earlier I had interviewed a teenage babysitter. Caitlin and I liked him immediately, and his enthusiasm seemed to equal ours—until he met Jody. At that moment his jaw dropped; mumbling something about checking his afternoon schedule, he hastened out the door. Disappointment and chagrin washed over me. I hated to lose this bright, lively babysitter. But even worse, I suddenly found myself looking at Jody through adolescent eyes. I saw not the cheerful, handsome seven-year-old whom I care for every day, but a seriously deviant little boy who drools and makes strange, uninterpretable noises. The forgotten terrors of Jody's babyhood surfaced. I saw my son as I might have seen another seriously handicapped child seven years before. I realized that not everyone has changed as I have, and that not everyone would find our family as attractive as I do. Not a good moment.

Sitting in the observation booth at this new school, I felt something similar. This time I looked at my son as a new teacher might. I saw a little boy with severe cerebral palsy and no useful vision. I wondered why he had made so little progress in seven years, and whether he would ever develop rudimentary skills or move about unaided. I wondered whether I could have helped him more.

Familiarity and routine blunt our awareness of disability after a while. Without meaning to, a stranger can upset this internal balance, allowing us to see our child from a new angle; to fend off pain we may turn angrily on the outsider.

Mixed Feelings

As mental health professionals often note, anger is seldom a pure emotion: first, we feel sad, frightened, or disappointed; then we feel angry. This doctrine (like most psychiatric doctrines) can be carried to a point where it ceases to enhance understanding—sometimes anger overshadows all other feelings. Nonetheless, it makes a valuable point: almost any disagreeable emotion can turn into anger. Kay Katz, the mother of a little girl with the fatal degenerative illness, Tay-Sachs, recalls occasions when her own pain and misery begot rage:

It was particularly painful to see younger babies who could do more than Joann, or to see mothers in the supermarket reprimanding their kids. I wanted to scream at them, "Don't you know how lucky you are?" Christmas shopping, birthday cakes, school buses, bikes, jumpropes, all entered the category of what not to look at. And soon, I couldn't bear to look at little girls at all. (Katz 1975)

Fear, exhaustion, and despair transform themselves into impassioned and righteous fury. The wretched conditions in state schools for the retarded enrage parents partly because they affront cherished values, but more because parents tremble at the thought of their own child's future. The other reactions—fear, helplessness, hurt, or whatever—do not, of course, invalidate the anger.

Sometimes we are reluctant to face the feelings that lie behind rage —our vulnerability dismays us, and we concentrate on anger hoping to feel more forceful. Thus, I have in bad moments heard myself laying claim to anger I did not actually feel. As an undergraduate, for example, I received an unfavorable and obtuse comment on my senior thesis—a criticism that cut me to the quick. I had worked more seriously on my thesis than on any previous undertaking. I was in love with it; yet I doubted its worth. Since entering college I had wished (and pretended) to be above caring about grades and evaluation. Yet, of course, I was far from achieving this independence: as I read the anonymous comment, every critical word rang true to me, even though a second professor had written glowingly of my scholarship and insight. I hated my own response as much as I hated the criticism. How contemptible, I thought, to depend on the opinion of others. So in telling my friends of the incident, I pretended an annoyance I was too hurt actually to feel.

Although I think I am wiser now, similar episodes have occurred in the lifetime of my disabled son. When Jody was two and one-half months old, I took him to see the distinguished specialist who had diagnosed his hydrocephalus six weeks earlier. By this time Jay and I knew that Jody was blind; doctors warned that other problems might develop. We could only wait and see. I approached this examination nervously. After a thorough exam the doctor told me, gently and sadly, that my son would certainly be retarded, that there was "motor involvement" as well. Miserably, wishing now to regain the uncertainty of an earlier hour, I asked him how he could tell: which tests had Jody flunked?

"The Babinski reflex should have disappeared by age three months," he replied.

"But Jody isn't three months yet," I protested, feeling irritation and perverse hope rising together.

"Well," he said, "it should have faded. Three months is the latest we ever see it in normal infants."

"But he was a month premature," I argued.

"Still. . . ."

"Well, what else was delayed?" I asked.

"He did not turn in the right direction when I rang a bell," the doctor replied. "Normal infants orient to sound by this age."

"But he is blind," I said. "Surely that might change things."

"This is not a visual test."

Irritation tightened muscles in my chest and shoulders. I asked the doctor whether he knew that although sighted children reach for and grasp a visual stimulus by six months, normal blind babies don't even *try* to reach for a toy they hear—even a familiar toy with a known sound—before they are ten months old?

"No," he said, "I didn't know that, but it doesn't change my opinion."

When I described this interview later, first to my husband, then to my mother, I spoke of the frustration I had felt in the face of his certainty. My anger was not simulated: I was upset that someone who knew so little about the special problems confronting a blind infant would pronounce with such assurance upon my son's future. Nonetheless, I nourished my anger, hoping to distract myself from other, stronger emotions. Mostly I felt terrified and unfathomably sad. (I see this conversation differently now: in retrospect I am grateful to the doctors who shared their suspicions with me immediately, rather than waiting for time to remove all doubts.)

Anger at the Child

Although people sometimes embrace anger too readily—perhaps to cover other sorts of pain—on other occasions they may entirely fail to identify it. Certain kinds of anger can be exceedingly upsetting. Rereading a draft of this chapter, I realized with a shock that I had not even mentioned the fact that parents may feel angry at their own disabled child. Experience has taught me that such omissions usually mean something. But what? I am a parent myself. My children occasionally irritate and even enrage me, just as anyone else's do. I wish they did not, but I accept the situation as an inevitable outgrowth of group living and of the tangled web of love, identification, hope, and mutual involvement that make up family relationships. Yet I realize that, often as I scold my able-bodied daughters, I am rarely vocally or consciously angry with my severely disabled son. Rationally, this makes sense: since he is wholly dependent physically, unable even to change positions unaided, he cannot and does not annoy me in the way his sisters do. If his hair is uncombed, his shoes untied, or his face unwashed, the omission is mine, not his. He cannot procrastinate about getting dressed, wash his paint-covered hands in a sink full of spinach leaves, or insist that I search the house for a particular stuffed animal before turning out the light. Nevertheless, he can be a pain in the neck. He will reject carefully prepared meals with an expression of ultimate disgust. He sometimes awakens me at 2 A.M., laughing, gurgling, and calling out, when I yearn passionately for an undisturbed night's rest. Still, I do not get angry with him in the same way that I do with the others. I am less sure that his behavior is under his conscious control, less clear that anger makes any sense. This is reasonable; yet anger may at times have little to do with sense.

Turning from my own responses to the writings of others, I find a similar void: few parents talk, in interviews, in articles, in books, or in parent groups, about feeling angry at their disabled sons and daughters. Obviously these children can be as enraging as their more typical siblings—often even more enraging. But a handicap can make anger seem illegitimate or unfair, even if it fails to defuse the emotion altogether. Clara Park describes the fury mounting inside her as she watched her autistic daughter drench the floor with bath water, ignoring her mother's vehement "No, no." Elly was still a toddler then, and no one considered her abnormal—only "stubborn and obtuse."

I grew more angry than I have ever been with a child—so angry that I cannot recall it without shame. In my anger, I slapped my little girl's naked flesh again and again, until I could see the redness on her skin and she was screaming with pain and shock. I screamed myself. "No, no no. NO!" I don't know how often I did this—three or four occasions, perhaps, no more. Then it was no longer necessary. Elly understood nothing else, but she understood "no, no." I rarely had even to slap her hand, never to hit her hard. I did not have to scream. The words were enough.

And of course almost as soon as she understood the words, I came to understand that she might not have been able to help the behavior for which I had punished her. Everything was different after she came home from the hospital. It was years before I could get really angry with her again. (Park 1967, pp. 108–9)

Even though diagnosis did not change Elly's behavior, it altered her mother's response to it. Clara Park stopped feeling angry, because she saw Elly differently.

Barbara Trace, whose daughter Joan failed to develop language during the preschool years, describes a parallel journey:

On one particular occasion, Joan embarked on a rampage that surpassed all others. After unloading her toy shelves, she jockeyed up to the windows as usual. However, this time, she tore the curtains down and ripped them into shreds. When I went up to her room after naptime, she was surrounded by filmy bits of organdy. I was so furious at this wanton destruction that I spanked her very hard. She looked at me with an impassive expression on her face and did not even cry. Actually, the only time that Joan cried during a spanking was when it hurt her physically. This time, I apparently had not reached through her diaper clad bottom.

I was thoroughly miserable whenever I spanked her, and I did it infrequently. It actually accomplished nothing. After a while, it became abundantly clear that any form of discipline I administered, whether verbal or physical, was harsh and unjust.

My role, therefore, for the time being, was simply that of a caretaker. Although I was frequently hostile and angry at her, I tried to control myself as much as possible. I strove to deal rationally with this totally irrational human being. For the most part, I succeeded in remaining patient and calm. I loved Joan very much and felt great responsibility for her. (Kastein and Trace 1966, p. 33)

Observation taught Barbara Trace to question her own responses: neither words nor physical punishment seemed to touch Joan. Deciding that anger served no educational function, the mother schooled herself to greet irrational destructiveness with unruffled reason.

David Hundley is autistic. He is also severely allergic to a number of foods. His mother is a prisoner of his needs: just keeping him alive occupies her days and her nights. When her father died unexpectedly, Joan Hundley could not leave David to go to the funeral or visit her mother. She remembers with anguish that her father had been asking her to visit for months; she refused because of David.

David's complete dependence, his physical vulnerability, and his antisocial behavior cut his mother off from her family at a time when she needed it very much. She says she felt bitter and frustrated, but she does not say whether her anger found a target: "My depression lasted for months" (Hundley 1971, p. 49). I would guess that, resisting the impulse to blame David, she turned a seething rage inward, against herself.

Elly, Joan, and David make their parents' lives very difficult. But because these children do not willfully choose to disobey or destroy, anger at them may appear as senseless as anger at fate itself. When disability magnifies a child's vulnerability, parents feel they owe him total devotion, unqualified and unremitting love. It takes courage to face rage and resentment (the obverse of real commitment) and the guilt these feelings bring.

Sometimes the example of a friend or a child can help parents confront difficult feelings. When Andy Hamilton announced passionately, "I *hate* being retarded," his mother agreed inwardly. To herself she admitted, "I *hate* being the mother of a retarded child." After a friend remarked quite casually of her own disabled son, "You know, I can only bear to be alone with Billy for an hour at a time," Jennifer Hamilton decided, with surprise and relief, that she could learn to speak equally frankly. In an article in *The Exceptional Parent*, she wrote of wishing for her son's death, of the embarrassment she felt when he acted "retarded," of the boredom his repetitious conversation inspired in her, of her rage when he exploited her impatience. "My feelings on these occasions approach pure hatred" (Hamilton 1977). The letter columns of the magazine indicate that this list of grim admissions consoled at least a few other mothers and fathers and helped them to face their own less loving feelings.

Brothers and Sisters

Able-bodied children also have good reasons to be angry—at their handicapped brother or sister, at their parents, and at life itself. Like their elders, they may find that a handicap complicates natural annoyance:

I knew that my friends' younger brothers and sisters made messes and sometimes tore up books and toys, but nothing they did could compare with Mindy's constant destructiveness. If Mindy had been just plain bad I could have felt vindicated in the knowledge of her "badness." But Mindy was not "bad." She was deaf, and as yet without the skills of speech and lipreading. Part of me knew it was unfair to be angry with my deaf sister for filling my shoes with coffee. Still, in another part of me, the resentment lingered. (Hayden 1974)

Like Barbara Trace and Clara Park, Vicky Hayden must share close quarters with a very badly behaved little person. She, too, questions the legitimacy of her own rage: her sister's deafness excuses much mischief, and makes Vicky's fury seem in some sense "unfair."

Some sisters in her position conceal their irritation. A sense of fair play prevents them from cuffing someone more defenseless than themselves, or from shouting, stamping their feet, or even complaining. The intensity of their own anger can frighten them. They remain silent rather than expose ugly thoughts to public scrutiny. Sensing his parents' protective concern, a child wonders whether he can yell with impunity at his handicapped sister or brother. A perceptive mother or father can help by legitimizing reasonable anger. Fifteen-year-old Kevin, whose sister Catherine is multiply handicapped, speaks:

I used to be scared of getting steamed at her, like I didn't have the right to. But Dad set me straight on that one day. I'll never forget it. I'd brought over my friend, Chris, to go swimming and had left a notebook on the table in the kitchen and Catherine somehow got hold of it and ripped it up. She didn't mean to, but boy, was I hopping mad. But I just kept it inside, turning twenty shades of purple 'cause I thought Mom would let me have it if I yelled at her. Well, Dad saw me and told me that it was okay to be mad but that it was how I handled my anger that was important. It just kinda made me see that Cathy can do stupid things like anyone else around here. (Thornburg 1978, p. 22)

Listening to normal brothers and sisters talk about family life, I am struck by a paradox about disability. In the world outside the family, in school and in the neighborhood, children long to fit in, to resemble everyone else. In these contexts a disability, or even a sibling's disability, stigmatizes them as different. Inside the family, however, each child wants to be special. Each needs assurance that he occupies a unique place in the family circle. Here disability confers a certain advantage, a passport to special attention, recognition, and privileges. In consequence, many able-bodied brothers and sisters remember a childhood tinged by jealousy and resentment.

Mindy's achievements always met with animated enthusiasm from our parents. In contrast, it seemed Mother and Daddy's response to my accomplishments was on the pat-on-the-back level. I was expected to perform well in every circumstance. I wanted my parents to be enthusiastic about my accomplishments too. I didn't want to have to beg for praise. I didn't want to be taken for granted. I wanted to be noticed. (Hayden 1974)

Brothers and sisters sensibly observe that normal family rivalry can excite the same passions. This perception seems to help in two ways: it reassures a child about frightening feelings. And it "normalizes" the deviant sibling a little by pointing up his resemblance to other people.

There are no simple answers to anger, no leakproof double-duty trash bags for disposing of unwanted feelings. Those of us brought up to avoid scenes—a large fraction of the human race—find that, as we try to cast off the chains of habit and express anger and disappointment more forcibly, we often create new problems. If we feel uncomfortable with gentle folk who never raise their voices or speak ill of their neighbors, those whose anger erupts in frightening outbursts repel us even more. Both children and adults search for some middle way that allows them to handle anger without destroying bonds, hurting other people, cultivating hypocrisy, or seething inwardly.

A child's disability intensifies this dilemma. Parents are faced with many serious grievances—the disability itself, the attitudes of others, the misuse of professional power, and the irritating behavior of the handicapped child—and various pressures constrict the expression of their anger.

Anger creates problems. It is also a vigorous response to distress. The rage that shocks or embarrasses bystanders may fuel a mother or a father's energies in unexpected ways. As a poet says, a healing anger cleanses the mind. In this psychiatric age we are so used to thinking of anger as a problem—an "issue"—that we forget that it is a resource, too. Its function is perhaps most obvious in troubled people who seem completely without rage or rancor. I think, for example, of John Frank, whose book about his severely retarded son came out over a quarter of a century ago. Frank is a lawyer of considerable distinction, the protegé of several Supreme Court justices. With great simplicity, and without perceptible bitterness, he tells the story of his son's birth, illness, diagnosis, and institutional placement. He records the early misdiagnoses without criticism, seeing them as part of the doctors' search for answers. He escapes the impulse to lash out at friends and professionals who urged him to remove Petey from his home, and praises instead their "rare perception and feeling" (1951, p. 92).

Considering the ways in which anger cuts people off from one another, I expected to find Frank's evenness refreshing. Yet I closed *My*

Son's Story feeling drained and depressed. The anger most of us taste as we negotiate a course for our disabled child swamps some other emotions and, in so doing, fuels our energy and quickens us to action. Anger keeps us fighting. Turning on the doctor who belittles our decision to keep a severely disabled child at home, we forget our hurt and sorrow. We take a stand and raise ourselves to defend our own, like a mother bear with cubs. Suddenly we feel more angry than sad, and we welcome a rush of heat and energy. With the anger gone, sorrow and irretrievable loss stand bleakly outlined against a gray sky.

From people like Frank one learns the true dimensions of tragedy, the heartbreak of loss without agent or villain. Angrier parents teach equally important lessons. I first met Elizabeth Black at the introductory meeting of a new mothers' group. Strangers to one another and to the school, most of the women tread warily. Not Elizabeth. She was too angry to conceal it or to tolerate the silver linings that others were attemping to spin for themselves.

Rosalyn Gibson introduced herself and outlined her daughter Nancy's problems. With tears in her eyes, she described new uncertainties that had surfaced in recent weeks. Toward the end of the meeting she observed that someone had once comforted her by observing that God never gives you more troubles than you can bear. Elizabeth Black begged to differ: "I don't even believe in God, but sometimes I look up and tell Him that I hate Him." She raised a clenched fist heavenward.

Most listeners—including me—flinch inwardly when Elizabeth dares to make a scene with the Almighty. Anger at God, or fate, makes fundamental emotional sense, however, and may liberate parents from pettier resentments. Whether or not a mother can find someone to blame, she is entitled to feel furious as well as unhappy—entitled to celebrate that rage, if possible.

Not long ago Elizabeth Black took her daughter for an evaluation. Listening to her describe Kim's response to the test battery, the little girls' comical way of holding a bottle, and her ingenious strategies for disposing of unwanted food, I realized how much Elizabeth enjoys her daughter; she savors her accomplishments and toddler wisdom. She still shakes her fist at heaven, but her voice vibrates with pride and pleasure. Her anger is vigorous and lively, part and parcel of her love for Kimberley.

Chapter 3

Loneliness

PAIN of any sort isolates. A special loneliness is the most pervasive theme in the stories told by parents with disabled children.

This loneliness is nourished from within and without. The fear and anger I described in earlier chapters contribute to it. Fear cuts people off; many have difficulty sharing dark fantasies. Even when they do manage to speak, others often respond awkwardly. Anger isolates us in even more obvious ways. We can get little comfort from the person who makes us mad, and excessive rage alienates others as well. Even friends withdraw if our sensitivity grows beyond a certain point: anger, whether spoken or concealed, creates awkwardness.

The two most prominent ingredients of a parent's loneliness are difference—his own and the child's—and isolation. The disabled child is unlike other children. He is marked in some important way, even if the difference is not immediately apparent. His mother, father, sisters, and brothers live in a family that reflects that difference; their consciousness of difference makes them feel very much alone on some occasions. Failures of other people to understand their special concerns intensify the problem.

Disability may isolate families in a variety of ways. Most concretely, it often interferes with ordinary social activities. Young children always complicate their parents' efforts to get out of the house, whether to a Laundromat, a park, or a movie. A disability adds to the difficulty of organizing expeditions and recreation. It also creates invisible social barriers. Many people feel awkward with pain and difference. They avoid a disabled person and sometimes his or her family as well. Even where people remain in close proximity to one another—as in the family itself—communication may suffer. Certain feelings are difficult to discuss. Many disabilities—like deafness, blindness, cerebral palsy, and retardation—block some of the avenues of communication.

In the Beginning

The birth of a handicapped child sets his parents off from others. If the diagnosis of disability is made in the delivery room or the hospital nursery, a mother, for example, finds herself cut off from the other mothers on the obstetrical ward. She cannot share the happy inconsequential chatter about birth weights, labor, and nursing woes without a sense of heaviness and hypocrisy. Her heart simply is not in it. Unable to join the instant community of the maternity ward, she turns to family and friends. Unhappily, they may avoid her in embarrassment. One young mother reported that for the first week after her baby's birth she saw no one but her husband and mother. When she called friends who had promised to visit her, they muttered uncomfortably, "Well, we heard that there were problems. . . ."

If the tragedy is less obvious, people retreat in subtler ways. Pearl Buck angrily recalls the false comfort offered by friends who suspected her daughter's retardation before she did. Their reassurances, successful at the time, led her to question the quality of their friendship later: "To this day I cannot understand their shrinking. For to me truth is so much dearer than any comforting falsehood, so much kinder in its clean-cutting edge than fencing and evasion, that the better a friend is the more he must use truth" (1950, p. 14).

Other parents describe similar experiences, sometimes tracing in retrospect their own contribution to the general uneasy silence. Tragedy creates awkwardness on every side. Widows and divorced people also complain of sudden isolation. It takes social skill and courage to ease other people's embarrassment; stricken parents are not in a position to minister to the rather secondary anguish of professionals, friends, and relatives.

During the initial period parents are so swamped by their own turbulent emotions, by changes in their vision of the world and their own future, that few worry about loneliness. In the months, years, and even decades that follow, however, as they try to meet their children's changing needs and design a reasonable life for themselves and their families, most parents do at times feel isolated. They express this loneliness very variously.

Some feel shut out by the physical limitations that the disability imposes on family activity. Others suffer most deeply from a personal and internal sense of their own family's uniqueness: they feel most bleakly alone when they glimpse Madison Avenue's image of the grinning, healthy "typical American family" in a commercial for life insurance. A third group are wounded by the lack of understanding they encounter in the wider world—or even among family and friends.

The Tyranny of Mechanics

A child's disabilities set real physical limitations on a family's outside activities. The woman who might otherwise have worked part-time stays home to care for her blind daughter. Knowing the importance of early learning, she hesitates to entrust the little girl's education entirely to a nursery school. The child's limitations may circumscribe family recreation as well.

The simple mechanics of feeding, transporting, and caring for a disabled child rule out many things that other families take for granted. If parents fail to overcome some of the barriers to participation in what might be called mainstream pleasure, the resulting sense of isolation can poison their lives. The bitter loneliness expressed in this letter to the *Exceptional Parent* is a warning:

We have a twenty-six-year-old retarded daughter and for at least fifteen years my husband and I have not been able to "have a date." We really want to and have tried every source we know, but we cannot find anyone to stay with our daughter, everyone has a million excuses, but it all boils down to the fact that they don't want to be bothered.

I guess being an exceptional parent means really going through life alone with no caring or showing any human kindness. Our wish is that we could "have a date" just the two of us, but we can't find anyone at all to stay with our daughter. (Schult 1975)

Some parents go to heroic lengths to enjoy ordinary pleasures. A woman whose two sons are confined to wheelchairs with muscular dystrophy undertook a cross-country camping trip with her family (Strickland 1974). The horrendous mechanical problems of such a trip would daunt most of us. Reading her story and looking at the picture—the boys in the water, supported by their mother and sister, the family camped somewhere along the seven-thousand-mile way— I felt exhausted. I wondered where these parents found the energy to change two disabled boys, bring them to the beach, and support, instruct, and reassure them in the water after hours on the road. Then I thought about this mother's daily routines. I tried to imagine her shopping, cooking, cleaning, visiting friends, taking the children to a restaurant. How lonely and excluded she would feel if she took the path of least resistance, caring for them at home and asking her husband to deal with the outside world. My dream of a vacation is rest and recreation. This trip gave Jo Strickland's family something they needed more: a sense of breaking through the barriers that shut them off from the world.

Abandoned pleasures can come to represent a world lost with the disability. "You know," reflected Rosalyn Gibson, near the end of a mothers' meeting, "I've been thinking about our family. It seems like we just don't have as much fun as we used to before Nancy was born." It is more difficult to get out; when they do go somewhere Nancy, who is blind, spoils much of the fun. Rosalyn sadly described their trip to the state fair. "Everyone had a marvelous time. I feel horrible saying it, but it was because Nancy was sick. She felt so terrible that she only wanted to be left alone. She just sat quietly in the stroller without making a fuss, and we saw everything."

The winter Nancy was three, Sunday afternoon hockey games became a symbol of frustrating compromise. Rosalyn enjoyed the outing immensely when she had time to concentrate on the game, but Nancy usually made that impossible. She got cold quickly, having discarded both mittens in order to feel things with her hands. And she was bored as well, since she could neither see the game nor wander around exploring. Naturally she protested, and soon everyone shared her misery. To avoid this fiasco, Rosalyn and her son Charles took turns staying home with Nancy. This reasonable "solution" blitzed family outings.

Over the summer the Gibsons "went into hock" and bought a luxurious camper. Now they all attend the games together. Nancy stays in the camper, on one of the beds, where, warm and safe, she enjoys listening to the television and playing with her toys. The older children take turns checking on her and getting warm. The family has scored a small but important victory over isolation.

A Difference in the Family

A personal consciousness of difference contributes to loneliness almost as palpably as do physical barriers. Just as not many children are like the exceptional child, not many families resemble his or her family. This conversation between Annette Oulett and her daughter Michelle is a shocking reminder that loneliness is partly a matter of just being different:

I was tending three pots on the stove and tossing a salad for supper one evening when Michelle came into the kitchen. "When I'm grown up, if I have a baby will she have no feet and two fingers like me?" she asked. . . .

"No, Chell, I don't think your baby would be born without feet like you. She'd probably be just like Marc and Suz." Then, as I drained the cooked potatoes, I thought to ask, "How would you feel if your baby was born just like you?"

"I'd like it," she said.

"Oh?" I said. "Why?"

"Because then she'd be just like me!"

Well, I'd never thought of that before. To an adult, Michelle's answer that she would like her baby to be just like her sounded selfish, even shocking. But I can remember as a child daydreaming about finding my twin—someone just like me somewhere in the world. How much stronger this feeling must be for Michelle who's never seen anyone just like her. She's seen other children with artificial arms or legs but never anyone with a congenital anomaly identical to hers. Never anyone who was born "just like me." (Ouelett 1976)

Parents of children with unusual disabilities speak of a similar longing to know someone "just like me." They often go for years without seeing a child like theirs or meeting a parent who has faced the same diagnosis. Through the *Exceptional Parent*, Susan Diaz sent out a "desperate plea" for contact with other parents of children with a problem called "tuberous sclerosis." She received thirteen replies in six months: each one expressed astonishment that there was actually someone else somewhere in the world facing the same dismal set of problems (Diaz 1974).

I was twenty-seven when Jody was born. In the next two years it seemed as though all my close friends bore new healthy babies. I watched these children sadly. They were so alert. They learned and changed and grew. They beguiled me with their smiles, and waving arms, and fat bottoms. *This* was the sort of baby I wanted, I thought disloyally. One who would bat at mobiles, pull my hair, throw peas on the floor, and wear out the knees on his overalls. Seeing the good fortune of others, I ached at our loss. I almost wished something would happen to one of these perfect children, so that a friend could share my heartache. And, of course, I hated myself for these feelings. I loved Jody, didn't I? How could I want to trade him for some other baby? How could I wish misfortune on the friends I loved? It was all too awful, and I felt lonelier than ever.

I stopped feeling that way after Caitlin's arrival. Here at last was the baby I had dreamed of for three years, the baby who grew and fattened, and went at life with gusto. I was content with my lot. It seemed to me that children were the only real wealth, and that our three were very beautiful. I could rejoice again in my friends' children, and admire their accomplishments without ambivalence. Actually I enjoy babies more than I did before Jody's birth; he has taught me to see their development as a special sort of miracle.

Unhappiness itself is alienating. Not only because people shun the unhappy—they really do—but also because misery resents other people's happiness. In our culture today, a good deal of sadness lies concealed under studiedly cheerful visages. The unhappy person often concludes, quite wrongly, that he or she suffers alone.

Parents speak of the difficulty of surviving holiday seasons and festival times. Every American knows how Christmas is supposed to look: Two proud parents watching, arms locked, while healthy, beaming children frolic under the tree among stacks of shiny toys and new clothing. Unhappiness, poverty, or deviance are all but immoral during the Christmas season. Like the poor, the non-Christian, the single, and the sad, parents of disabled children feel the strain. They recall other, happier Christmases. They compare themselves to the jolly family they see advertised everywhere. They confront the difficulty of finding suitable toys for their disabled child. They watch their nieces and nephews playing together, and feel the isolation of their disabled child more poignantly.

Because a handicap causes unusual problems, parents often find that others do not understand their concerns or even their pleasures. Mr. Davis, whose son Christopher has Down's syndrome, describes to Charles Hannam some of the things that annoy him most: Christopher likes to dangle bits of string, watching them swing to and fro. He grinds his teeth. And he spits. "We go up the wall . . . and what is more people will say to you, 'Well, you know, that's nothing,' but after months and years of listening to it, it is a lot" (Hannam 1975, p. 77). Those who assure Mr. Davis that his son's habits are "nothing" probably hope to hearten him. Unwittingly they confirm his feeling of alienation, his conviction that parents of ordinary children cannot understand his feelings.

In the preceding chapter I wrote about the wounds that parents sustain at the hands of strangers, neighbors, friends, professionals, and even family members. Incidents that provoke anger lead to a sense of isolation as well: a parent who is insulted or patronized feels cut off and lonely as well as hurt. As I said earlier, loneliness and anger reinforce one another: hurt, angry people are often prickly and difficult to befriend. Social ineptitudes cut them more deeply.

> In conversations with other employees in the firm, my references to the fact that Sally was retarded were usually met with, "Why don't you put her away? Why should you be burdened with a child like that?"
>
> My retort was instant and sharp: "I'll never do that. Who do you think you are that you can play God? You have no right to decide what I should or should not do with my child. If that's the way you feel, I don't need you as a friend."
>
> Dead silence. Nothing more was said on the subject at all. And I began to avoid social contact of any sort because I was tired of hearing "Put your child away." (Schult 1975)

In a world where few people share their experiences, parents look to professionals for understanding as well as practical help. Under favorable conditions a professional can reach out to parents and children, making them feel understood and cared for.

We love this man who told us our child was going to die. How is this possible? There was never a limit to the amount of time he would spend with us. In his soft voice he explained what was happening to her and encouraged us in the way we were taking care of her. He talked to her during his examinations, handling her gently, respecting her life and our love for her. Where he gets his understanding I do not know, but it is precisely what is desperately needed by parents like us. (Katz 1975)

Most parents eventually find at least one professional who understands and appreciates them. Many tell of other encounters that magnify their sense of isolation.

Why should this be so? An irreversible disability poses serious difficulties for doctors as well as parents. Physicians are trained problem solvers. The hope of curing people lured them into medical school. Activists by temperament, many work sixty hours or more each week. The disabled child frustrates their impulse to help; neither driving energy nor vast clinical knowledge does him much good. Parents often feel that their disabled child is just another face to the overworked clinician (the doctor's behavior can reinforce this impression), but I think that many physicians go through a silent mourning of their own.

Perhaps the most significant obstacle to mutual understanding between parent and professional is the most obvious: neither has had the chance to stand in the other's shoes. A physical therapist who had, after years of professional practice, adopted a cerebral-palsied boy, gave me a good example of what this means. She said that her experience as a parent had dramatically affected her professional behavior. "Before I had Peter I gave out [physical therapy] programs that would have taken all day. I don't know when I expected mothers to change diapers, sort laundry, or buy groceries." As a parent, she reported, she often neglected physical therapy in favor of trips to the park. Parenthood taught her about limitations on time, energy, and emotional resilience; it showed her the complex trade-offs inherent in rules whose values she had never previously questioned. For example, the only sitting position that frees Peter's hands endangers his vulnerable hips. As a professional she had warned parents to forbid this "W" position; as a mother she saw that Peter benefited socially, intellectually, and emotionally from the many activities it permitted. Life with Peter increased this physical therapist's insight into parents' priorities and problems. It is the rare professional who steps into the exceptional family's world at the end of the day.

Cutting Oneself Off

After a few wounding experiences, some parents find themselves withdrawing from contact with the wider world. Conscious of their own vulnerability, they avoid situations that might increase their pain.

Rosalyn Gibson recalled her response to one bruising encounter after Nancy's premature birth. Before the little girl came home from the hospital, the doctors explained that her gag reflex had not yet developed, and she might choke. Rosalyn kept the crib mattress elevated as they suggested, but she knew that that might not be enough. "I was a wreck, worrying about everything that could go wrong, watching and checking her night and day." One day a friend stopped by to visit, and Rosalyn poured out her anxieties. Her friend urged her to calm down: "These children don't generally live very long anyway." Rosalyn froze, unable to speak. "I wanted to shout, 'No! That's my baby. She's completely healthy, she's going to be fine. She just has this one problem now, because she's so little'. . . . I never poured out my heart to anyone again."

Perhaps getting comfort is a learned skill. We have to know where to go and how to describe our need. Otherwise we get hurt. No one can know what feelings prompted Rosalyn's friend to speak as she did; perhaps her remark was clumsy rather than callous. I feel that friends, seeing our—the parents'—misery, "take sides" in a strange way, in order to protect us against "wasting" our lives, against the life we seem to have chosen. They love us; seeing the misery our child has brought us, they almost hate him. They offer an alternative they hope will guard us against broken hearts and tired bodies. In so doing, they may hurt us without meaning to, by increasing our worries and convincing us that no one else cares about our child or understands our concerns. This was what happened to Rosalyn. She needed reassurance and comfort. When her first experiment backfired, she retreated from intimacy, convinced that on this subject, at least, friends can hurt as much as they help.

Cynthia Gordon told the mothers' group that she fights against the impulse to withdraw from contacts. Her daughter Laurie has a spinal cord defect called "spina bifida" that has delayed her walking and slowed down her growth. In the early years Cynthia dreaded meeting new people. A trip to the shopping center seemed formidable; she wondered how she and Laurie would respond when strangers stared or asked questions. Even among people she knew Cynthia felt alone. Returning from a long-planned reunion with several old friends, she reflected that Laurie's handicap had shadowed all her pleasures. The other children played together while the adults talked, but Laurie could not keep up with the group. Cynthia watched her drag herself slowly across the room in her friends' wake or sit quietly with the grown-ups while the others played. She ached for her daughter, even though Laurie looked comfortable enough.

"I wonder whether sometimes people wouldn't rather not see our handicapped children. Nobody says anything, but I wonder whether they don't wish that we had left them at home with a babysitter." Realizing the dangers of withdrawal, Cynthia pushes herself over the threshold, beyond the sanctuary of her home. Time and determination are on her side. When the world is basically friendly, as Cynthia's seems to be, the first efforts to meet it are the hardest. Successful encounters breed confidence and break the vicious circle of fear, withdrawal, and isolation.

Other parents find themselves in a further tragic bind: they hesitate to identify themselves and their child with disability. Anne Gibson (1972) wrote that she had been unable to read about retardation for the first twelve years of her son's life. This reaction is by no means uncommon. When my son was six months old I checked several issues of the *Exceptional Parent* out of my local library and read them from cover to cover. With each page my gloom deepened. Although we already knew that Jody's development would be retarded, we could not predict the severity of his handicaps. Looking ahead, I identified passionately with every mother who wrote to describe her family's troubles. Each story was sadder than the last. I lived each life with the writer as though it were my own. Up until that day I had sustained myself with the hope that Jody's mental handicap would be mild—that he would learn to walk and talk and even go to school. Now I saw the peculiar poignancy of mild retardation; I learned that a mother suffers special pangs for the child who understands and struggles against his own difference. Suddenly I felt at a loss: what was there to hope for? My husband pointed out that reading about retardation seemed to depress me. Months passed before I looked at the *Exceptional Parent* again.

Parent groups can evoke a similar response. Lucy Forrest, Patricia O'Conner, and Linda Davidson all agreed that a mothers' meeting could leave them feeling very low. During the first year, when wounds were fresh, hearing about other people's pain helped in some ways; it often depressed them as well. Thursday after Thursday, Linda Davidson went home and cried. Mrs. O'Conner skipped most sessions altogether, knowing that if she arrived feeling sad, she would be totally miserable by the time she left.

No one can read about a child's disability or talk to other parents without confronting the past and the future. These encounters stir up fear, uncertainty, anger, and unfathomable sorrow. If the pain is too great, parents naturally avoid it.* Sadly they may cut themselves off from contacts and knowledge that would help break down the sense of isolation—settings where they could give and receive mutual understanding, where their situation might seem more ordinary.

Sisters and Brothers

I have spoken, up to this point, about the ways in which a child's handicap can isolate his parents. Parallel forces operate in the lives of able-bodied brothers and sisters. Heavy babysitting and child-care responsibilities can cut them off from their peers (Frances Grossman's [1972] data suggest that this happens more often among poor families than among affluent ones). Like his parents, a child may find that a consciousness of his family's difference prevents him from feeling ordinary. Inwardly he echoes the eight-year-old who concluded, "I'll never be really regular, because our family will always be different."

Schoolyard attitudes intensify the problem. The young often subscribe to the doctrine of guilt by association and ostracize those known to have a "weird" family member. If they feel pressure—internal or external—to include the disabled child in their play, other kids may leave them alone. As a young adult, Victoria Hayden remembers how some of these factors added up, for her, to a lonely childhood:

Mindy's "differentness" rubbed off on me in the eyes of my playmates. I was the sister of "that deaf kid." Mindy was a "drag" for me and my playmates. She was difficult to communicate with, wild and stubborn. I was

---

* This problem is not limited to parents. Erving Goffman (1963, p. 37) discusses the ambivalence with which many of the handicapped themselves view others in the same position.

often excluded from neighborhood games because of my sidekick. And then there was the unwritten family rule that I was to leave with Mindy whenever my playmates made fun of her. They often did mock her, of course, and we would leave—except for one time which to this day gives my conscience no rest, when I joined in. I lost many playmates by having to side with Mindy. I felt neglected by my family and shunned by my peers. I was a very lonely little girl. (Hayden 1974)

Even when they realize that a child's difference may come between family members and the wider world, parents and professionals hope that it will draw family members closer to one another. In the long run it often does; but in the early years powerful feelings can interfere with mutual support within the protected circle of a loving home.

As I stressed in earlier chapters, able-bodied children often avoid discussing feelings and fantasies related to a handicap. A friend of mine asked her daughter for her first memories of a disabled person and was startled by her vehement reply: "Bobby and I thought you and Daddy were cruel to make us visit Uncle Joseph." The old gentleman had cerebral palsy. He was hard to understand and, to them, funny looking. The children's fear and embarrassment seem natural enough; yet ten years elapsed before either admitted any of these feelings to their mother. Another woman remarked sadly that her older daughter, who seemed to share willingly in the care of her handicapped brother, admitted considerable resentment and guilt when she was grown and married herself; she never mentioned these feelings during childhood and adolescence (Wakefield 1978, p. 28). Rosalyn Gibson of the mothers' group reports that although five-year-old Martha wonders about Nancy's future—"When she's bigger like me, will she be able to see?"—the older children ask no questions. Childhood can be a lonely time, even for the best adjusted. All children stage inner dramas that would astonish their parents and teachers. They share their perceptions of the handicapped even less readily than they reveal their feelings and fantasies on other subjects. Measuring their own turbulent thoughts against the well-meaning pieties of civilized adults, they conclude that some thoughts do not bear inspection.

The able-bodied sibling may, then, endure many of his feelings alone and without support, even when parents are tactful and eager to help. Conscientious, sensitive parents often have conscientious sensitive children; seeing how pushed and saddened their parents already are, such children hesitate to burden them further.

Isolated Parents

As children protect parents, so parents often protect one another. I remember that during Jody's infancy I found it an enormous relief to talk to friends rather than to family. Jay and I shared much of our sorrow, fear, and fatigue. Yet our fates were so bound up together that I hesitated to tell him how close I sometimes felt to despair. We depended on each other as we never had before. When I was delayed at the hospital, he imagined me in an auto accident; when he returned ten minutes late on his bicycle, I was sure he had been killed. Knowing this, how could I raise the specter of the breakdown that occasionally seemed imminent? With my parents it was almost the same. They needed to believe I was strong, was coping; my despair would have fed theirs.

Friends were different. They loved us, felt sad for us, cared and helped in many ways. But they did have their own lives, and I could speak to them of my anguish without worrying that I struck at a faith essential to their survival. In a curious way love and concern enforce a certain reticence: the very consideration and sensitivity that help to hold a family together may set parents and children apart from one another.

Consider the absolute solitude in which John Frank decided to institutionalize his infant son. Concern for his wife's health and sanity occupied the first place in his thoughts; yet he made the decision without consulting her. He agonized alone. Before mentioning placement to his family he conducted a six-month long search of available facilities and corresponded with St. Rita's, where he eventually placed John Peter. Frank's circumstances were to some extent exceptional. His wife was pregnant, and her physician said that the trauma of separation—or decision—might endanger the unborn child. Yet although the pregnancy delayed discussion of the issue of placement, Mr. Frank's lonely decision was made before its onset. In matters of great importance, most of us struggle alone. We seek information and confirmation from others more often than we actually reason together. Of course, Mr. Frank had to persuade his wife before he could actually place Petey, but sharing this final responsibility is very different from sharing the misery, the guilt, and the doubt that surely assailed Frank at every step along the way to decision. The process of persuading and being persuaded can be as isolating as the silence that precedes it. At last, Frank suffered a nervous breakdown. In the aftermath of his collapse, he told his wife that he wanted Petey placed in an institution. Shaken, she acquiesced:

We have never, from then until now, discussed her thoughts about it. I had always supposed that she bowed, not to please me, but to save me from strains greater than she thought I could manage. We have always tried to look after each other. (Frank 1951, p. 150)

Husband and wife strive to care for one another; paradoxically, they do so in solitude.

Even when parents make decisions together, they come to the experience of "exceptional parenthood" as fundamentally different people. In our family each person feels the pain of Jody's disability in his or her own way. When Liza was younger, she used to complain about the smell of Jody's food and his way of eating it. He cannot chew properly, so he still eats baby purées. If he does not like the menu, the food dribbles down his chin, soaking his bib and his shirt. Caitlin complains less about this mess than about the way Jody screams when he is changed or washed. If he disrupts a peaceful dinner, she reproaches him heatedly.

To me the hardest part of living with Jody comes with the steady drizzle of guilt about things not done, approaches not pursued, games not played, efforts not made. Jay has fun and shares jokes with Jody, but resents the constraints—real, symbolic, and imaginary—Jody puts on the family's freedom. (Then again he both richly enjoys the other children and chafes at the restraints they impose.) Our concerns are all different because we are different people and have carved out different niches in Jody's life.

The Search for Support

A sense of loneliness reflects more than the realities of the situation— the lack of understanding friends, the vivid sense of difference. It is also a function of our absolute need for concrete help and psychological support. When a person's life is changing in dramatic and unexpected ways, when he awakes each day to confront demands he cannot adequately meet, that need seems boundless. Jane Lazarre, in an autobiographical account of her own painful adjustment to motherhood, describes the terrible isolation in which she tried to understand her own feelings about her (quite normal) son in the first months after his birth:

One of the mothers in the group called me at home one morning. Benjamin had not slept well for five nights. Every evening just as James and I sat down to dinner, Benjamin would commence his "period of irritable crying," shrieking in clear agony for three hours. We would take turns walking him, rocking him, singing to him, but usually nothing worked. The three hours had to pass miserably and then, exhausted, he would fall asleep for a while. For most of the interminable day while James was in school, I would walk Benjamin again, trying to quiet his pain.

"Isn't being a mother the most wonderful thing you have ever done?" the woman asked me that morning on the phone.

"Not really," I answered, holding back tears. "Actually it is quite miserable and exhausting," and I put my hand over my mouth so I would stop before it was too late.

"Oh, don't say that," she said maturely.

So I didn't. And I stopped going to the group. I was becoming convinced that I was the only mother in the world who had such hateful feelings toward the child I loved so intensely, who wished over and over that it had never happened, who, finally, could understand those women I had met when working for the Welfare Department who had burnt their babies' arms, beat their faces, killed them. But I would never breathe a word of such vicious identification, I decided. I would hide my true feelings in order to avoid the terrible looks which say, I am not like you nor have I ever been. (1975, pp. 77–78)

So it is with parents of disabled children. The very intensity of one's need for support, love, understanding, and concrete help can make a circle of friends seem narrower than it actually is. Suzanne Massie describes the desperation she felt in the middle of the night as she waited, rigid with fear, for Bobby's next bleeding crisis.

Statistics tell us dryly that suicides are most frequent in those dark hours before morning. How I longed for a human voice! But it is unthinkable to call anyone in the middle of the night. Certainly not after 10:00. One's best friend . . . well, perhaps 11:30. But at 2:00? Who could be so good-tempered? Yet that is when, do what you will, the fear comes over you. What will be next? Will he fall? Will it be serious? Can I stand it? What happens if I can't? And the girls? What if something should touch them?

Sometimes, when Bob was away and I was alone, nearly overcome, I would go and stand by the phone, trying to find the courage to dial a number, running over in my mind the friends I could count on. And I would decide there were none. I leaned my head against the wall, banging it silently, and would sob until I exhausted myself.

Once I even put my head in the gas oven. But I chickened out. (1975, pp. 174–75)

Mrs. Massie's loneliness is nearly absolute. Few parents face what she has faced. Most find that as they learn to live day by day their fears ease and they sleep more tranquilly. As they find more reliable sources of support, they need them less desperately. As the match between what they need and what they get improves, they grow less lonely.

For solitude and difference do not, by themselves, spell loneliness. On many occasions we parents rejoice in empty rooms. The lucky among us pay more than we can afford for remote summer cottages, out of earshot of other vacationers. We congratulate ourselves on being different, on setting our own standards, and avoiding the pressures toward conformity. However, we do need human contact, care, and sympathy. We need the reassurance of knowing that others share our feelings. If we cannot find comfort and understanding when we need them, we feel lonely. Perhaps it is only a passing twinge, gone in the next instant, as we turn to other things. But if, like Suzanne Massie, we find ourselves alone in the dark confronting unrelenting terror, without either a hand or a human voice, then our loneliness swells, like a sinister genie billowing out of a bottle.

Fighting Loneliness

Some remedies suit only particular individuals: participation in a YWCA exercise class, rapprochement with a sister-in-law across the street, a bout of psychotherapy. Other solutions win more adherents and deserve mention here.

First of all, many parents derive immense encouragement from other parents in the same boat. Just knowing that such people exist lessens the sense of isolation. Solid contact with the wider world of those concerned with the disabled can make an even greater difference. Parents find that joining a local chapter of the National Association for Retarded Citizens, United Cerebral Palsy, or a similar parent association can change their lives. They become actors instead of victims. The chance to meet other parents with the same concerns and problems, the shared work and sense of accomplishment, the opportunity to give and receive help, all chip away at loneliness. (There are, of course, other results of parent associations—their concrete accomplishments and real services—but the community they create for the lonely and hurt may be just as important.)

Parent-support groups that meet regularly to talk can help even more. Catherine Lederman, reflecting on her time in our mothers' group, concluded that this was the one setting that freed her to describe her feelings with total honesty. To the rest of the world she played a role. "I was acting, starring in a movie about myself." In a small group of other stricken parents, with the encouragement of a social worker who shared their fate as mothers of handicapped children, she could be herself. In different words, other parents echoed her feelings: The rest of the world does not really want to hear about your problems; even if you tell them, they will not understand what it is really like. Here in the group you can be honest, expose your sorrow to others who share it, and receive comfort. "The group," says Barbara Sullivan definitively, "has helped us all."

Parent associations and groups are not for everyone. Many people are too exhausted from caring for their own families to commit themselves to work for the larger population of handicapped children. Not joiners by temperament, they recoil from activities, newsletters, and meetings. A support group is formidable in other ways. The thought of exposing private fantasies and family problems to the scrutiny of others repels some parents; many would agree with the father who objected, "Talking doesn't solve anything."

Limited contact with other parents may also help. Leo Buscaglia (1975, p. 115) tells of a parent education workshop that he ran in California some years ago. Invitations were issued to all the parents of disabled children in the area, and six hundred showed up. At the end of six evening sessions, featuring lectures, movies, and slide shows, Buscaglia asked the parents to specify what they had found most helpful. Over 85 percent wrote that the most valuable part of the experience was learning that so many other parents had disabled children.

The magazine *Exceptional Parent* offers parents another sort of opportunity to learn that others share their problems and pleasures. Many, many parents write to say how much this forum means to them.

Any sort of contact with other similarly situated parents can lessen the sense of isolation. Nonetheless, parents spend most of their lives among normal people, and relationships within the community shape their daily experience. As I observed in the preceding chapter, friends, relatives, neighbors, professionals, and strangers may offend without meaning to. Hurt, tired, and frightened, parents draw back. Later, as they recover from the initial shock, they learn to make allowances for the awkwardness of others and to discern the warm impulse that lies behind some clumsy gestures.

The issue of accepting helps illustrate my point. Any tragedy involving children stirs many hearts. People offer the child's parents various sorts of help, ranging from toys and money to babysitting. Parents respond to these gestures in a variety of ways.

Catherine Lederman observed that she always felt indignant when someone offered her gifts. She said that she worked hard to keep her head above water, to avoid depressing the people around her. She thought she was coping well, and she wanted no pity. Offers of help carried an unwelcome commentary on her efforts. Whatever she actually replied, she felt like saying, "What do you mean? We're doing okay. We don't need anything."

Barbara Sullivan responded very differently when the Jaycees in her community sent Patrick fifty dollars to buy Luke a special car seat. As the seat cost only thirty-two dollars, she called to find out where she should send the remaining eighteen. The donors urged her to keep the money and buy Luke something special for Christmas. Barbara said that the gift had moved her very much, "because it means that there are some really good people out there, people who care."

In a culture that emphasizes independence as vehemently as ours does—we may act kind like Rousseau, David Riesman says, but we all talk mean, like Hobbes—offers of help that go beyond ordinary courtesy often meet an ambivalent response like Mrs. Lederman's. Nonetheless, recognition of the concern and fellow feeling behind such gestures sustains many parents and convinces them that they are not alone.

The loneliness of the disabled and their families is a political as well as a personal problem. Poor services and bigotry isolate the disabled and their families. Educational and legislative changes of the last decade have brought the problems of disability into the public eye and have improved attitudes and opportunities. Some parents feel far less lonely when they see other people struggling to help children like theirs, and learn that at last their children have legal as well as moral rights to services.

Changes in schools matter immensely. In the recent past, handicaps kept many children out of school, isolating them and their families. The children missed the opportunity to meet and play with others their own age. Child-care responsibilities cut many mothers off from work, adult company, and congenial activity. Local and federal legislation now guarantees every child an appropriate education in the "least restrictive environment" possible. Seriously handicapped children move out of homes and hospitals into programs with other boys and girls. The more mildly affected proceed from special placements into regular schools and classrooms.

"Mainstreaming," as this process is called, changes children's lives in practical ways. At its best it also improves attitudes on all sides. Able-bodied children learn that their disabled peers are more like them than different. The disabled gain confidence in their own ability to make it outside the narrow world of home and special class. Parents feel less isolated and apprehensive as they see their children participating in the universal rite of public schooling.

Of course, it does not always work this way. Barbara White interviewed learning-disabled children who divided their school hours between resource room and the regular class. She reported that although the children with minor disabilities preferred to be with normal classmates, those with more obvious differences said they liked the separate setting better. This second group found integration difficult and, when observed, showed a higher proportion of "negative interactions" in the normal classroom than they did in the resource room.* Remembering my own schooldays, I do not find these data astonishing: children rarely overlook difference, and they can be very nasty to each other. If mainstreaming were easy, the special class would not have been invented in the first place. I believe that exposure and integration will in the long run improve attitudes toward the disabled, just as they have for other minority groups. If

* Personal communication.

schools supplement the mandated changes with imaginative educational programs that help able-bodied children to understand disabilities and cope with their own responses to the unfamiliar, they will avert a good deal of transitional pain.

The media also exert a potent force on social attitudes—and register changes with considerable sensitivity. There are now retarded and handicapped children on *"Sesame Street,"* while disabled detectives outwit able-bodied criminals on prime time. (These latter often upset parents and special educators by providing a too rosy version of disability, but they may at least help broaden the public vision of what disability means.) Fictional and documentary programs about the disabled have become almost commonplace.

Improvements in schools and public buildings permit the disabled and their families to participate more freely in the world around them. Movies and television programs remind viewers that disability shapes the lives of people much like themselves, that good health carries no manufacturers' warranty, that "normal" people are what activists in the disability movement call "TABs," the temporarily able-bodied (Kleinfeld 1979). These changes in the public realm help ordinary families to step into the shoes of those who live with disability.

Not long ago Liza, Caitlin, Jody, and I wound up a morning of shoe shopping and library browsing with a trip to the post office. Since the building lacked a ramp, Liza and I carried Jody's wheelchair up the front steps. Lamenting the architectural taste of an earlier era—the love affair with long flights of stairs—I heaved open the heavy door and gazed in horror at a second rampless staircase, longer and steeper than the first. Fortunately a young mother offered a hand. As we deposited the wheelchair on the top step, she glanced down at her own two healthy daughters and then at Liza and Cait. Following her gaze, I noticed how similar our families looked. Perhaps she did too. "Now I see the point of all those ramps," she said. "I mean, I've been on crutches lots of times. Steps were a problem, but I always knew it would end. Watching you I suddenly thought how it must be to cope with the problem day after day."

Such moments allow parents to see themselves as pioneers and teachers instead of as outsiders.

Chapter 4

Guilt and Self-Doubt

O
UR CHILDREN are our achievements. We work countless hours caring for them; we weep over their troubles, their sicknesses, and their failures; and we cudgel our brains for solutions to their problems. Parenting—especially mothering—is hard work. When children are beautiful and happy, a mother does more than rejoice: she takes credit:

Our children were intelligent, responsible and adaptable. They were also— quite irrelevantly—beautiful, with a pink-and-gold beauty which seemed to belong not to the real world but to the illustrations of old-fashioned story-books. I luxuriated in their beauty; it seemed to me that I had un- accountably given birth to two princesses and a prince. As I looked at them, remembering my own bespectacled childhood, they seemed a special and continuing miracle. It is our eyes that we believe. Irrationally, it was their beauty, with which I had had nothing whatsoever to do, that summed up my pride in them. It shone around them, an astonishing, almost palpable fact, as if to symbolize their less superficial successes, their intelligence and their affection.

That year, the year of Elly's beginning, a friend had visited us, one with whom we had long been out of touch. A man with a gift for intimacy, he formulated a single question to bring us close again: "Tell me," he said, "what have you done in the past five years of which you are most proud?"

He, a man of considerable attainments as a scientist, was proudest of his successful psychoanalysis. I was proudest of my children. (Park 1967, p. 16)

The whole culture supports a mother in the opinion that her children are what she has made them. Whether from upbringing, Freud, or *Family Circle*, most women learn this lesson thoroughly by the time they are grown.

This notion may support a young mother through the broken sleep and frequent loneliness of her first child's infancy and toddlerhood; it usually backfires eventually. If a mother takes full credit for the toddler's glowing smiles and precocious syntax, whom does she blame for the schoolboy's nightmares and inefficient study habits? The old Boston politicians have a saying: If you take credit for the sunshine, then you're going to have to shoulder the blame for snow. If home-baked cookies and maternal serenity shaped the confident kindergartner, what transformed him into a sullen unwashed teenager? No one knows for sure the contributions of nature and nurture to development, but in the current state of public opinion, most conscientious mothers feel either guilty or smug. The smug certainly exist, but they seem to be in a minority.

What about fathers? They are, I think, both less and more vulnerable. On the one hand, children figure somewhat less prominently among the supports to a man's self-esteem. More men than women work outside the home; they usually put in longer hours, earning more money and more prestige, than women do. They spend correspondingly fewer hours alone with their children, consciously molding and teaching them.

The mother, with fewer outside resources, is particularly vulnerable when a child is handicapped. Even if she has a good job, her happiness and her sense of achievement rest far more on her children's physical and emotional perfection than does her husband's. In this way she is obviously at a disadvantage. Yet in another way she may be fortunate: she is more likely than her husband to realize just how shattered she is.

Most mothers know that much of their self-respect depends on their children. The mother of older children has felt her emotional barometer rise and fall with the vagaries of each child's development, has noticed how mad and sad she is when a child fails to measure up to society's standards or to her own.

71

Participants in a mothers' group thus discuss, without a startling sense of novelty or revelation, the fear that their children's handicaps are somehow their fault. Their self-esteem has plummeted, and they know why. This realization scarcely solves the problem, but it may put them ahead of their husbands. My own impression (based on the accounts of parents and on countless conversations with them) is that while the father of a handicapped child usually recognizes the practical problems of care, his wife's suffering, and his own sadness, embarrassment, rage, and even despair, he is less attuned to the possibility that his own self-confidence has suffered. And maybe it has not: in the eyes of the world, a man's major accomplishments *are* outside the family. Nevertheless, some fathers do report feelings of guilt. I would guess that self-doubt nags others as well.

Explaining the Handicap

Learning of a child's handicap can threaten a parent's sense of adequacy. Most obviously vulnerable are the mothers of children whose problems are seen as emotional. Child psychiatrists, pediatricians, and teachers look to parents' behavior and attitudes for the source of children's emotional disorders. They transmit these views directly, through books about disturbed children,* and indirectly, through popular child-rearing manuals. Birch and Chess (1965) describe the ways in which doctors' failure to acknowledge that children do differ in temperament leads many parents of normal children to agonize guiltily about relatively harmless behavioral aberrations. The popular culture of television and the movies reflects and reinforces professional opinion.

Up until quite recently, for example, many doctors and psychologists linked infantile autism to maternal inadequacy. Bruno Bettleheim states uncompromisingly that "the precipitating cause of infantile autism is the parent's wish that his child should not exist" (1967, p. 125). Beatta Rank (1955) saw "immature and narcissistic" women behind the facade of apparently well-adjusted mothers. Leo

* See, for example, Virginia Axline's *Dibs in Search of Self* (1964) and Dorothy Baruch's *One Little Boy* (1952).

Kanner (1949, 1954) painted equally chilling portraits of the "cold, humorless perfectionists" who brought him their autistic children during the 1940s and the 1950s.* These writings and many others in the psychiatric tradition inflict quite unnecessary suffering on parents: recent research has altered the climate of professional opinion so dramatically that few serious investigators still award environmental factors sole responsibility for infantile autism.

The point is broader than autism. Recent evidence also suggests that biochemical factors contribute to schizophrenia; no one knows what future experience will reveal about other psychiatric problems. Even in the newborn nursery, children differ radically in their levels of activity and irritability and in their basic responses to life. Parents of large families know that no two babies respond in the same way even to similar environments: each child shapes his world even as it shapes him. Newer research† documenting this process indicates that a welcome change in medical thinking may be in the making. Even so, parents should continually and energetically remind themselves that no one knows much about the causes of most emotional disorders, and that they can make good use of a psychiatrist's suggestions without jumping on the guilt wagon.

It is easy to understand why the parent of an emotionally disturbed child feels guilty or inadequate, but a similar reaction from the mother of a blind or brain-damaged child puzzles many people. To me, having lived through guilt and self-doubt, it makes intuitive sense. Our children are, as I have said, wondrous achievements. Their bodies grow inside ours. If their defects originated *in utero*, we blame our inadequate bodies or inadequate caution. If, like Mrs. Park, we accept credit for our childrens' physical beauty (and most of us do, in our hearts), then inevitably we assume responsibility for their physical defects.

The world makes much of the pregnant woman. People open doors for her, carry her heavy parcels, offer footstools and unsolicited advice. All this attention seems somehow posited on the idea that she is creating something miraculously fine. When the baby arrives imperfect, the mother feels she has failed not only herself and her husband but the rest of the world as well.

* Kanner did not assume that parental coldness caused autism, however. He believed at the outset and continued to believe that autism was an "inborn autistic disturbance of affective contact" (1973, p. 184). He saw the parents as "successfully autistic adults" (1954).

† See for example, Thomas, Chess, and Birch (1968).

Soon this diffuse sense of inadequacy sharpens. Nearly every mother fastens on some aspect of her own behavior and blames the tragedy on that. The mother of a child with cerebral palsy recalls the night following the diagnosis:

Mike and I didn't mention Debby as we went to bed that night. Too hurt to cry, too frightened to talk, we spent those hours struggling with our separate guilts.

I relived every moment of Debby, from my first problems of pregnancy through the hours of labor, up to the moment of her birth. What had I done wrong? How had I hurt my baby? During the fourth month of pregnancy I started staining slightly. Under doctor's orders I stayed in bed for two months. Should I have stayed in bed? Maybe Nature knows best, and I was wrong to challenge her decision. No, no, then I wouldn't have Debby, and a hurt Debby is better than no Debby. Perhaps I could have postponed the birth for just a couple of weeks, and then Debby would have had enough strength to withstand the trauma of labor.

I thought about my doctor. Why hadn't I gone up North to the obstetrician who had delivered our other children? Why hadn't I insisted on a Caesarian section when I knew that the birth was taking too long and things weren't going right? Why did I give in to pain and agree to medication?

Mike, too, was tossing around in his bed. "Fine doctor I am," he said to himself. "I have magic hands for every one else, and with my own family I'm helpless. There I sat in the hospital, nobly minding my own business, while the cells in my daughter's brain were dying off from lack of oxygen. Couldn't I have done something then? Why didn't I foresee the problem and insist that a Bennett machine and a respirator be available? Maybe I could have saved those few crucial minutes that caused this lifetime injury."

Utter nonsense, but this is what we thought that night, and this is what we have let ourselves think over and over again. (Segal 1966, pp. 18–19)

The story is much the same if the problem originates after the birth. Marianne Davidson contracted meningitis at the age of three weeks. Describing the illness in our mothers' group, her mother recalled that the baby had taken her 4 A.M. bottle well but seemed "a little funny." When Marianne slept past eight o'clock that morning, Linda Davidson went to check on her and found her feverish and limp. Linda called the doctor who suggested she bring the baby into his office at one o'clock. But the Davidsons recognized that Marianne was seriously ill and rushed her to the nearest emergency room by police car. Their good sense and courage (it takes courage to defy a doctor's advice) saved Marianne's life: the doctors told the Davidsons later that few infants survive this form of meningitis. As an outsider,

I congratulate the parents on their watchful eyes, quick thinking, and acute sensitivity to their baby's need. But because the disease damaged Marianne's brain, Linda Davidson blamed herself: "If only I had thought to take her in at four, perhaps she would have had a better chance."

Fathers may torture themselves too. As his autistic son approached his third birthday, Josh Greenfeld strained after explanations for the little boy's increasingly strange development; he wrote in his journal:

Shit! I wish we had not induced him. But all the pieces fit together: born early, a vomiter rejecting external reality, a furtive laughter, delayed emotional development. And my vanity. I thought that by marrying outside my race that bad genes—the diabetes on my father's side, the mental illness of cousins on my mother's side—could be eliminated. Instead I have further scattered bad genes. (Greenfeld 1972, p. 54)

To a childless or a serene disposition, all this self-blame may seem farfetched. Yet the accounts I have quoted here come from people who are actually coping well, who are aware of their feelings and able to describe them. Many others fare far worse.

Some lucky parents weigh the facts, balance them against their intuitions, and decide whether guilt makes any sense. Most people struggle in vain for such a level-headed perspective. Mothers in our group sometimes commented that though they judged other women's guilt senseless and self-defeating, they could never shed their own. Even when everyone admits that guilt defies rationality, it often persists, frustrating parents and professionals alike.

In these pages, and in the conversation of exceptional mothers, the concept of guilt merges with a diffuse sense of inadequacy. Perhaps this is why a mother so often fails to eradicate guilt—because it blurs into a general feeling that if her child is not okay, she herself is not quite right. Leah Ziskin remembers that her daughter's retardation transformed her image of herself: "I felt I had become a completely different person. . . . I felt I was nobody." Intellectually she saw that she had much to be proud of: she had completed an exacting medical training and managed to practice pediatrics part-time while tending two healthy sons and a good marriage. But none of these accomplishments mattered after Jenny was born. "All I knew at this point was that I was the mother of an abnormal and most likely retarded child" (Ziskin, 1978).

People feel guilty when their mistakes hurt someone else. They feel inadequate when they have tried to do something and failed, or when the problem grows out of what they are rather than what they did. Thus, Marilyn Segal and Linda Davidson feel guilty, each suspecting that her own oversight has caused her daughter's handicap. Other mothers—especially, in my experience, mothers of handicapped only children—wonder whether they *can* produce a normal child. They do not know where they went wrong, but their child's disability has convinced them that they are not as good as other women. To them, motherhood is a biological as well as a social achievement.

The Daily Grind

And so, in a variety of ways, the origin of a disability poses a threat to a parent's—and especially a mother's—self-esteem. If a mother bases part of her self-respect on her children's adequacy—on the product of her parenting—she bases another part on her day-to-day success in responding to the demands of others. If, over a typical day, she meets most of her children's needs and her own, fulfilling her responsibilities however she sees them, it helps her to feel good about herself. But even in the absence of obvious external problems—disability, poverty, widowhood, divorce—many women find this sense of adequacy hard to come by.*

The needs of young children are boundless. Society judges a mother's performance harshly yet provides her with few unambiguous guidelines and no support. When the preschooler in the supermarket shrieks for candy, every onlooker knows how to handle him, but each has a different idea. The young mother may mirror the ambivalence of public opinion. With conflicting messages from Dr. Spock,

* In the last ten years many college-educated women have written about the difficulties and frustrations of full-time mothering. Myra Ferree's study of working-class mothers suggests that even low-status jobs may give a solider sense of achievement than housework and child care. Ferree (1976) asked 135 working-class mothers—74 employed, the rest at home full time—to evaluate their performances both as homemakers and as employees. A majority (57 percent of the housewives, 67 percent of the employed women) judged themselves "not very good" at homemaking. All of the employed women felt that they were good at their work; a majority rated themselves "extremely good." Only 7 percent of the housewives described their performance in equally glowing terms.

Parent-Effectiveness Training, and Grandma, how is she to act? In this confusing state of affairs, success is all. If she silences her child quickly and peaceably, she feels adequate and triumphant. If she does not, she may judge herself a failure. Lacking clear guidelines for her own behavior, the contemporary American woman must judge her mothering by its results. Since children are complex and changeable, success is often in doubt. Even in an era when a woman inherited a tradition of motherhood from her own mother and grandmother, Freud referred to parenting as one of three impossible careers (the other two were being the leader of a nation and being a psychoanalyst).

The mother of a handicapped boy or girl faces even larger difficulties. Her child's needs are often more numerous, more taxing, and more insistent than those of able-bodied peers. In addition to appropriately timed helpings of food, sleep, approval, love, discipline, encouragement, and surveillance, the child may require physical therapy, transportation to distant schools and medical people, and special home teaching. Care and therapy tax the mother's time and energy. Tasks like dressing, bathing, and toileting, which most children manage unaided after the first few years, may challenge a disabled child for a long time. Each specialist will suggest a few (perhaps small) things the mother can do at home. By gradual increments, the program grows beyond what is doable.

I remember the day when the occupational therapist at Jody's school called with some suggestions from a visiting nurse. Jody has a seizure problem which is controlled with the drug Dilantin. Dilantin can cause the gums to grow over the teeth—an effect that is especially likely if the gums are irritated by either poor hygiene or erupting teeth. The nurse had noticed that nearly all the preschoolers at the school suffered from this overgrowth, and recommended, innocently enough, that the children's teeth be brushed four times a day, for five minutes, with an electric toothbrush. The school suggested that they could do this once on school days, and that I should try to do it the other three to four times a day. I trotted out a valid and convenient excuse: Jody's dentist had advised against an electric toothbrush.

Although I tried to sound reasonable on the phone, this new demand appalled me. I rehearsed angry, self-justifying speeches in my head. Jody, I thought, is blind, cerebral-palsied, and retarded. We do his physical therapy daily and work with him on sounds and communication. We feed him each meal on our laps, bottle him, change him, bathe him, dry him, put him in a body cast to sleep, launder his bed linens daily, and go through a variety of routines designed to minimize his miseries and enhance his joys and his development. (All this in addition to trying to care for and enjoy our other young children and making time for each other and our careers.) Now you tell me that I should spend fifteen minutes every day on something that Jody will hate, an activity that will not help him to walk or even defecate, but one that is directed at the health of his gums. This activity is not for a finite time but forever. It is not guaranteed to help, but "it can't hurt." And it won't make the overgrowth go away but may retard it. Well, it's too much. Where is that fifteen minutes going to come from? What am I supposed to give up? Taking the kids to the park? Reading a bedtime story to my eldest? Washing the breakfast dishes? Sorting the laundry? Grading students' papers? Sleeping? Because there is no time in my life that hasn't been spoken for, and for every fifteen-minute activity that is added, one has to be taken away.

Life with a handicapped child is often like this. Perfectly valid needs must be denied simply because few people can do everything. "Many times," said the physical therapist I quoted before, "we skip the physical therapy and take the kids to the park." Some days that choice seems wise and right; some days it does not.

Even when a mother manages all the routine care that specialists recommend, other things may reproach her. Lucy Forrest says that every time she sees Christopher lying on the living room floor she thinks, "Gosh, I'm terrible. I really ought to stop this [whatever she is doing] and play with him." Her younger daughter sometimes plays alone or with other children. She looks for what she wants, goes to her mother when she needs her, learns as she plays. Although this child needs lots of attention, she can also be involved and learning while her mother concentrates on other tasks. Christopher does not seem to learn on his own. If his afternoon goes by without direct adult stimulation, Lucy feels it has been wasted. In one sense, laundry and house cleaning matter much less than a child's learning. Yet these tasks have to be done—and sometimes they give a greater sense of accomplishment than another half-hour of play with an unresponsive child.

A miserable or withdrawn child undermines a mother's self-assurance in a particularly insidious way. Rosalyn Gibson, for example, scarcely trusted her own judgment at all for a while. Nancy's puzzling development and general unhappiness had worn away her confidence. She found herself demanding advice and reassurance constantly, even in simple matters. She remarked in the mothers' group that some of the suggestions she got from others were so obvious that she felt like an idiot for not having thought of them herself.

As she watched Nancy's teacher, her frustration and confusion grew. Mrs. Simpson was strict with the little girl and "did things right"; perhaps in consequence, Nancy performed better for her than for her mother. Rosalyn was gentler than the teacher. She hesitated to push her daughter for fear of jeopardizing their relationship, but she felt that she had "bought" Nancy's devotion with her own "softness." Nancy's affection for Linda Simpson hurt and puzzled her. Sometimes Rosalyn felt that she was not much of a mother to her youngest daughter: "A mother should be more than just someone who cooks your meals, cleans up, gives you a bath, and is there when you hurt yourself," she said. "A mother answers your questions, provides guidance, and teaches you." Rosalyn could do that for her older children; with this little one she never felt entirely sure.

All parents face the question of how far to protect their children, how much independence to allow, where to set limits. The parent of the disabled child feels this tension even more insistently. Parents hold two sometimes incompatible goals: to arrange their child's world so that he feels, and is, as normal as possible, and to protect him from harm. Physical disability and sensory loss (blindness, deafness) pose a threat to any child's social and emotional development. Knowing the stigma that difference carries, parents wish to set their child off as little as possible. On the other hand, disability usually requires special sorts of protection. Annette Ouelette, whose daughter Michelle was born without legs, worried about whether the little girl could maneuver in the rocky terrain at day camp (Ouelette 1977). Betty Pendler suffered agonies of indecision before allowing her twenty-year-old retarded daughter to travel the New York subway alone (Pendler 1975). Suzanne Massie worried each day over the proper balance between protection and independence for Bobby. At home she could watch him surreptitiously, guarding his safety without emphasizing his difference. As he grew older, he needed more freedom. Each day brought difficult decisions: Should he climb trees? Sled? Ride a bicycle? Should he play with aggressive children or only the meek and mild? There was no way to be sure, especially since he sometimes bled for no discernible reason.

So we often guessed wrong, and when we did there was no one to blame but ourselves. Why couldn't we have foreseen? Why did we permit that? And who was to absolve me from the sense of guilt and failure. No one. Simply, it was necessary to begin again, to risk again, to try again to roll the boulder up the hill. (1975, p. 96)

Balancing the demands of the child's (and the family's) normal life against the demands of the disability may be the hardest task of all.

Parental Omnipotence

So far I have talked about two categories of threat to a mother's (and a father's) self-esteem: the disability itself, and the difficulty of being an adequate parent to any child, particularly an exceptional one. Parents and professionals cooperate to create a third problem, which I call the fantasy of parental omnipotence. This notion holds parents (or mothers) responsible for the reactions of everyone—the disabled child himself, his family, the policeman on the corner—to the disability. Whether this idea originated with parents or with professionals, it has gained many enthusiastic adherents in both camps. Here two mothers discuss the attitudes of neighborhood children:

MRS. P: It all fits in the parents' attitudes themselves. If you have doubts, you reflect your doubts in your attitudes. I've come across many parents who have an extremely difficult time in the neighborhood with their child, even though their child is probably nowhere near as retarded as mine. I almost feel it's because they set an attitude in their neighborhood of being a little embarrassed about the situation or self-conscious about it.

MRS. K: I agree. This is very important. The parents' attitudes carry over to other children and to the neighborhood, too. (Klebanoff, 1971)

Professionals reinforce these common views and insist that the mother's attitude shapes the disabled child's adjustment and the attitudes of the rest of the family.

The emotional and special parts of your child's makeup, his attitude towards himself and the world in general, his relations with other people, his frame of mind, and his behavior can be shaped. Here is where you are the key person.

Your child will take his cue from you. If you consider his handicap an overwhelming calamity which makes life not worth living, so will he. If you are bitter against an unjust fate, he will be too. If you make his handicap the focal point of his life and yours, he will use it with self-centered bids for sympathy to tyrannize over you now, and over others later. If you measure his accomplishments and progress against those of other children you not only increase your own anguish, but also put an additional strain on him.

But if you place his handicap in proper proportion to his assets he will do the same. If you, unshaken in your faith or philosophy, accept it calmly, so will he. If you do not make it the excuse for overindulgence and special privileges, it will not occur to him to do so either. If you gauge him only by himself he, too, will be spared many distressing comparisons. In short, your child's contentment and emotional health are a reflection of yours. (Stern and Castendyk 1950, pp. 12–13)

There is a germ of truth in these glib formulations, but they grossly oversimplify reality and thus injure everyone involved. Of course, parents need to regain a sense of control over their own lives; they do not need to hear that every problem is their fault.

The notion that the world, like a magic mirror, reflects the parents' own deepest feelings for their child compounds a fourth problem: the reaction of the other children in the family.

Conventional wisdom holds that if parents deal with a child's handicap in an open, loving, matter-of-fact manner, brothers and sisters will follow suit:

Very early I spoke very freely to Paul of my hurt, hostility, and anxiety about having a retarded child. And very early I urged him to express his feelings freely to me. So, when he was seven years old, he requested that I not include Lisa when I picked him up at Sunday School because he couldn't handle the stares. This openness has resulted in his including her voluntarily in many of his social activities.

I knew I had "passed" the test when Paul told me he had to write an autobiography (he was in sixth grade) and he included in it: "I have a sister, who is retarded, and she is lots of fun." (Pendler 1975)

Professional advice reinforces this theory:

What about the other children? How will brothers and sisters feel toward the handicapped child?

This, again, depends to a very great extent on the attitude of the parents. If the parents treat the handicapped child in as natural a fashion as his condition permits, then his brothers and sisters will think much less about the situation than if the mother hovers over the handicapped child in constant tension and excitement. If the parents have really accepted the infirm child with all his limitations, the brothers and sisters are more likely to accept him. (Egg 1964, p. 49)

It is not hard to imagine that in this climate of opinion a mother may be devastated by self-accusation if her older children's grades fall, if they openly reject the baby, or if they act tense, dependent, and immature. Her self-confidence, which seemed already at rock bottom, may drop even lower.

Brothers and Sisters

Meanwhile, brothers and sisters struggle with self-doubt. Some feel apologetic about their own good health, wondering whether they ought to have been stricken instead. Others worry about jealousy: They resent the extra attention paid to the disabled child, but regard their feelings as disloyal and unfair. After all, they are lucky enough to enjoy good health and unimpaired faculties. How could they begrudge their sister the help she so obviously needs? And then there is the issue of behavior. If the disabled child seems more vulnerable than others his age, brothers and sisters may feel guilty about normal teasing and fighting. Guilt does not obey the laws of reason: although not one child in ten thousand has done anything to cause a brother or sister's handicap, many feel obscurely responsible. Children who have fantasized the death or the disappearance of a new infant sometimes blame themselves when a disability comes to light. One little girl sat on her baby brother's head hoping to stop his constant crying; later she supposed that she had injured him permanently. When a thirteen-year-old developed epilepsy, her older sister tormented herself with unanswerable questions: "Why her? Why not me?" They had always been close friends and looked much alike. It seemed as though the younger girl were taking some unfair rap for both of them.

Disabled children require even more adult attention than do ordinary ones. Their limitations try the patience of any normal brother or sister. Yet, as I emphasized in chapter 2, the disability can undercut normal anger by "explaining" irritating behavior and justifying special attention. Since no one can turn anger on and off like an electric lamp, many children feel guilty about their rage and resentment, and about the occasions when they vent their frustrations on the disabled child himself. The world seems to expect them to love their vulnerable brother or sister with special intensity. They often feel that they do not measure up.

Praise and Blame

The exceptional family stands in a strange, and at times rather sad, relationship to outside opinion. Guilty, unsure, unprepared, and lonely, both parents and children long for understanding, reassurance, and approval. In the war against inner demons, they turn to others. I remember my struggles during Jody's earliest years. We had to decide whether to keep our difficult baby at home or to look around for a good residential school. Many things played into this momentous decision, but I remember, quite uncomfortably, that one factor was the opinion of other people. I was afraid that the world would judge me a rejecting, inadequate mother if I let Jody live somewhere else. If there was one person left in all the world who opposed placement, I did not want to do it. I paid no attention to a phalanx of friends and relatives advising institutional care: I figured I was doing more, not less, than they advised.

The whole situation recalled a problem that had troubled me as a child: the problem of the hero. Most of us, I reasoned, are neither heroes nor cowards, and no one judges us in these terms. We are ordinary people. Yet suppose I, an ordinary person, am walking alone beside an icy, isolated river and see someone drowning. I have two options: I can jump in and try to save him (risking death myself), or I can agonize on the shore. In the first case I am a hero; in the second, a coward. There is no way I can remain what I was before—an ordinary person. As the mother of a profoundly retarded child, I felt

I was in the same position: I had to look like a hero or a coward, even though actually I was still an ordinary person.

The question of what people would think came up in another context as well. There is a place in Philadelphia that claims to have a cure for brain injury. Their "cure" is highly controversial, and all of Jody's doctors expressed a good deal of skepticism. They were surprised and disappointed that we, who were so "intelligent," would be taken in by what they saw as fanciful promises. Their good opinion was important to me—more important than I liked—and I wished desperately to go to Philadelphia without their knowledge. I would be happy to tell them about the program later when they marveled at Jody's unexpected progress.

In the end, for quite unrelated reasons, Jay and I canceled our appointment in Philadelphia, and I was rather relieved to escape the doctor's disapproval. Months later, a friend told me excitedly about a child who was progressing on this program and asked why we did not try it. I felt depressed for days: I wanted everyone to agree with, support, and admire all of my decisions.

Criticism hurts. In the mothers' group Barbara Sullivan recalled the discomfort she felt as she sat in the hospital next to Luke's crib while he recuperated from pneumonia:

He was black and blue, like a little junkie, from all the needles. And he's so thin. I was sure all the people going past thought I abused him. They looked at me so strangely, and then at him. I kept covering up his legs so no one would see them.

Many parents find themselves doubly vulnerable: although the world's criticism wounds them grievously, its admiration fails to soften their harsh self-judgments. They hunger for reassurance but recoil from praise, in a self-defeating double standard.

Mrs. Johns greeted me warmly and glanced down at my boys. Her eyes rested first on Rusty, now visibly showing signs of the retardation that had just begun to mark his features and his manner. She responded to Fred (as who cannot!) but could hardly fail to notice the hearing aid receiver in each ear and little harness in which he wore his aid. Then she met my eyes and said, with genuine compassion, "I know you just love them all the more. . . ."

When Mrs. Johns said to me, "I know you love them all the more," she spoke from her own strong commitment to children who need more love. But I wanted to hit her! I didn't though, because I was raised to be a lady, and ladies don't hit people. I think I said something like "No, Ma'am, I don't. I can't love them any more, but I love them as much." (Green 1975)

Why did Maxine Green wish to hit Mrs. Johns? Even after reading the rest of the article, I am not sure; but it seems to me that when Mrs. Green heard the words of tribute, she felt she had been misunderstood in some basic way. Mrs. Johns brushed against a sensitive nerve: how does a mother love a child who is tragically, devastatingly different, a child who shatters her most cherished visions of the future? Mrs. Green has agonized over this question (see chapter 1) and doubted her ability to love a deformed, retarded Rusty. Mrs. Johns's formulation, however sincere, ignores the complexity of love. Praise of this sort can set the recipient off from the rest of humanity, by celebrating imaginary virtues. It can magnify a mother's guilt, convincing her, once again, that whatever outsiders say, she is less than she ought to be.

Praise can isolate its recipient in another way, by seeming to stand in for the help and the genuine connection that the parent really wants.

Yes, we worried when Bobby played with other children, but we wanted him to have friends. Yet fewer and fewer mothers permitted their children to play with him. Oh, it wasn't a mean, overt cutting off. Simply, they were "busy" or Tommy had other plans—unfortunately. "So sorry, maybe tomorrow." Occasionally, I would run into one of the neighborhood mothers at the supermarket and she would say, "Oh, you know we'd love to have Bobby, but I would be afraid my little Johnny might hit him or something." I kept hoping they would ask, "Is there a chance he might come? Is there something I should know when he does come over?" But they didn't. It was easier just to cut him out, and then to add, "Really, I think you're so wonderful. I just don't know how you do it." (Massie and Massie 1975, p. 96)

In such a context praise seems less genuine tribute than a cheap and sentimental substitute for real help.

The voices of others touch each of us most deeply when they echo our own convictions about ourselves. When guilt and self-doubt plague us, critical voices strike a responsive chord, while the admiring ones sound hollow and empty. Before we can draw comfort from a friend's tribute, we have to learn to trust ourselves. Fortunately, many parents do discover ways to cope with guilt and buttress sagging self-esteem.

Rebuilding

A lucky few rebuild with the very bricks that smashed their world in the first place: the work of caring for a handicapped child nourishes their confidence. In journeying from doctor to school, they learn a lot about disability, about disease, about services, and about children. Watching themselves endure pain and fight for services, mothers and fathers learn about strengths hidden deep inside themselves. When their efforts rehabilitate a hurt child, they feel justifiable pride.

Even when a child progresses slowly, his care may enhance a mother's self-confidence. Barbara Sullivan, of the mothers' group, and her husband Patrick work with Luke every day; most of his accomplishments have come through their patient efforts. (When transportation difficulties kept him out of school for several months one winter, his progress astonished the teachers.) Luke's handicaps are severe, but he responds cheerfully to family and teachers. Experience has taught Barbara to see herself as the expert on her son. She knows that she understands his needs and manages his care well.

However, as I have said, the daily care of many handicapped children erodes self-confidence instead of fortifying it. Most parents need more conscious strategies for winning back what they have lost. Some wage an ongoing rearguard action against guilt, routing it one place, succumbing to its torments somewhere else. Catherine Lederman fights this slippery opponent by watching for ways in which she is punishing herself without benefit to anyone else.

Ellie Lederman's retardation was diagnosed early, and she entered the early-stimulation program at Carver School before her second birthday. When she turned three, she moved to a special classroom in her own town. In theory, the change offered her mother more freedom, since Ellie spent more time in school each day. In fact, Catherine seldom ventured out of the house; she wanted to be available in case Ellie got sick or had a seizure. She had not worried before. She had believed that the people at Carver and the doctors at the nearby hospital could handle any crisis, but she was not sure about the staff of the new school and stuck close to the phone most of the time Ellie was away.

As she described her problem to the mothers' group, she began to question her judgment. In fact, the teachers at the new school were well trained and highly experienced. They probably knew as much about treating seizures as any one had at Carver, and a nurse and a hospital backed them up as well. After acknowledging these facts, she paused, grinned slowly, and then asked, "Hey, is that the guilt?" She decided that she had been punishing herself for sending Ellie away for a larger part of the day and for enjoying her new freedom.

Most of us pass through adolescence with the idea that the first twenty years of life are for learning, and that once we grow up, we will pick a role or occupation and settle into it. We see adulthood as a time for accomplishment rather than for development, a time for being rather than becoming. This, at least, was my vision. Experience has modified my ideas considerably, and recent scholarly work in the psychology of adult development highlights what most middle-aged people learn for themselves: adulthood has its own evolving momentum.

The problems and the tragedies of adult life offer opportunities for learning and development, although few of us can use all of them to advantage. Some crises suit a need—even though they hurt: in meeting a challenge, we move forward. Others hit us too hard: we retreat, temporarily paralyzed, and become less, not more, than we were before.

I have written about the ways in which the discovery of disability causes parents to shrink back: they withdraw from other people and become isolated; they wither inside, losing their nerve and self-confidence for a while. When I asked one father how a parent might buttress and rebuild a sense of self-esteem, he replied by recalling the (erroneous) nineteenth-century American political slogan: "Grow or die." After the blow of handicap, many parents retreat from experience. Any step that involves moving out into life again, taking risks, trying the waters, putting out new sprouts, probably buttresses self-confidence—if it works. But success is vital. Failure only confirms the fear that has caused a parent to withdraw in the first place.

Many mothers choose to "move out" in one of two ways: they have another baby, or they join other exceptional parents in some sort of political or organizational activity. I suspect, from my limited experience with mothers of severely disabled children, that few mothers undertake both simultaneously. Of the seven women in our first mothers' group, one worked politically on behalf of disabled children. At the time of my writing, five of the others have children born after the disabled sibling.* All the mothers said that the new involvements had helped them.

I did not recognize Catherine Lederman when I saw her for the first time after her second child's birth. She was glowing with pride and pleasure, showing off the baby to a circle of admiring friends. Her face looked softer, more comfortable and relaxed—perhaps more ordinary. When the mothers' meeting started, Sara asked her how it felt to have Joshua. As she explained her pleasure and relief, she reflected, "When you have a retarded child, and you don't know the reason, you feel like there is something the matter with you. You wonder whether you *can* have a normal baby. The normal baby makes you feel so much better about yourself." She said she liked Ellie better, too. "We're so thrilled at all she's doing. She's rolling around and getting into everything. And she doesn't go 'unh—unh' any more. If she really needs me, she cries. But she plays by herself, she doesn't need me every minute. Because I can't be there every minute, with the baby." Joshua reaffirmed Catherine's biological normality; he also helped her and Ellie to put some useful limits on their relationship.

Having a new baby carries some risks. Despite the old adage, lightning can strike twice, even where the defect has no hereditary component. Ninety percent of all pregnancies terminate with the birth cry of a healthy infant; 10 percent run into some sort of difficulty—miscarriage, stillbirth, or congenital defect. Frightening odds, when one has joined the less fortunate minority. Parents of a disabled child worry a lot during any subsequent pregnancy—and often they worry in silence. Charles Hannam, whose oldest child has Down's syndrome, found himself composing the comforting speeches he would make to his wife in case of a second tragedy. He also planned ways to kill the baby if it, too, turned out to be abnormal. His wife rehearsed privately for the same disaster, but neither admitted these fears until much later (Hannam 1975, pp. 17–18). Patricia O'Conner told the mothers' group that her anxiety subsided only after the new baby sat unsupported and began to crawl. That was nearly eighteen months after conception, a long time to endure additional worry—especially since

* Ray Barsch's data (1968, p. 201) suggest that both the age of the parents and the severity of the handicap influence decisions about future children. In Barsch's large sample, most mothers under thirty had babies born subsequent to the handicapped child; older mothers, by contrast, tended to limit their families, especially in cases of severe disability. My own observation coincides with Barsch's; only today the cut-off age for "older" would be closer to forty.

an older child's disability creates tensions of its own. When I was pregnant with Cait, Jay had anxiety attacks so severe that he could neither move his arms nor make a fist.

In addition to anxiety, the decision to have another baby may inspire new guilt. Realistically, babies and pregnancies consume energy that might otherwise go to the disabled child. In addition, a normal baby usually brings his or her parents a special pleasure. Tasting this new happiness, sensing the magnitude of their investment in this child, parents may feel disloyal. Is their enjoyment of the normal baby a rejection of the older disabled child? In our mothers' group we discussed these feelings. Nonetheless, all the mothers with new babies rejoiced in their decision: they were growing, not dying.

Because of the risks, because the decision to add another member to a family is intensely personal, parents avoid crusading for new babies. They do, however, urge other parents to join a parent organization. I have spoken earlier of the ways in which these associations can help break down a parent's isolation: they may buttress confidence as well. Even the step of moving into something new can boost morale. But a parent group has further potential. First of all, it offers one the chance to use a painful experience to help others. Work with disabled children can be discouragingly slow at times. Sometimes the work itself and a child's subsequent achievement build confidence; often they do not. Talking to other parents can produce gratifyingly immediate results. Parents tell one another about a good special school or unadvertised public health services. Valuable information grows on the parental grapevine. Mothers also exchange small bits of practical lore: constipation plagues many children with orthopedic handicaps; their mothers share hints on helpful foods and effective patent medicines. Blind children need special help in learning skills that sighted children pick up through imitation: a mother explains that her child mastered finger feeding by searching for M&M's on his highchair tray. The list of problems is endless; but by listening and being together, parents support each other.

Encounters with other parents also reassure a parent about himself. The mother of an autistic child points out that her group helps partly by showing parents how ordinary other mothers and fathers are: "They need to find out that other people are not peculiar—just because they have an emotionally disturbed child doesn't mean the parent is an emotionally disturbed parent" (Klebanoff 1971). The families of emotionally disturbed children benefit most from this sort of reassurance. Guilt, unhappiness, and atypical interaction with one's child can distort a parent's self-perceptions to a point where one may see oneself in Leo Kanner's unflattering portraits of "cold, humorless, perfectionists." Checking out other parents can balance the picture.

Dealing with a child's disability and a family's reaction to it usually stimulates growth and change. Even when the adjustment is not ideal, parents move beyond the initial phase of almost paralyzing grief. They learn to cope and to help their children and themselves. Often, because so much remains to be done, they forget how far they have come. Encounters with parents whose children are younger or more recently disabled can highlight the progress. Perhaps for this reason, I remember warmly all my early conversations with other mothers and fathers.

When Jody was eighteen months old, a doctor from the hospital asked me if Jay and I would talk to a couple whose baby had just been diagnosed as blind and retarded. We agreed eagerly, and they arrived later that afternoon. As soon as they sat down, I was overcome by the similarity of our situations. They also had an older child, had planned a family of two, and were delighted when the second baby was born, apparently healthy and of the desired sex. Then, in less than two weeks, their world had caved in. They learned first that the baby was blind, and then that she had all sorts of other problems. Unlike us, they were struggling with the question of whether to bring the child home from the hospital or to place her directly in an institution. In many other ways, listening to them—particularly to the husband—was like going back eighteen months or a year. We talked about the issue of placement, about special problems of living with Jody, about this young husband's wish to "protect the family I already have," and about his wife's terrible grief and fear. Jay and I saw their overwhelming loneliness: both were grief-stricken; each wished to spare and protect the other; yet they seemed to disagree fundamentally about what ought to be done. I remember thinking, those poor kids, they have so much to go through. At the same time I felt an enormous sense of accomplishment because I knew that, eighteen months before, we had stood where they were now, at the absolute bottom; now we were coping and looking quite happily on the world and ourselves. That couple taught me how far we had come. And in doing so, they helped me to help them, for I told them what I believed: they would make it through. The experience would not destroy them.

Chapter 5

Marital Stress

A CHILD'S HANDICAP attacks the fabric of a marriage in four ways. It excites powerful emotions in both parents. It acts as a dispiriting symbol of shared failure. It reshapes the organization of the family. It creates fertile ground for conflict.

In earlier chapters I touched on the sources of certain feelings—fear, loneliness, guilt, anger—in life with a disabled child. In the first section of this chapter I carry this emotional portrait a step farther and look at the strains that fear, fatigue, and anger impose on a marriage. My emphasis is on the ways that individual unhappiness can drive two people apart, even when they share many of the same sorrows.

We integrate important events into our lives by investing them with meaning. In the second section I focus on ways in which a child's disability may subtly shift each parent's perception of the marriage. At the magical and metaphorical level where so much of the emotional life is lived, a child's disability calls the union into question. Practical reality reinforces the tendency to confuse the health of the children and the health of the marriage, for the disability touches most of what parents do together: it influences the circumstances of sleep, work, mealtimes, outings, and so forth. If a handicap constricts a couple's life at every point, the marriage becomes a prison.

Even under more favorable conditions, a disability usually changes what I think of as the family organization—the systematic way a family functions as a group. In the third section of this chapter I explore some of the ways that such alterations may occur. Two issues stand out: first, the increased vulnerability of the family to meddling on the part of outsiders—experts, relatives, and nonprofessional helpers; and second, the difficulty, even within the family, of guarding some private space for the mother and father, so that they can solve private disputes and reinforce the ties that bind them to one another. Families adapt to a disability by changing the ways they do things— say, at meals or bedtimes. Most of the adjustments make good sense, but they can strain family relationships in unexpected ways.

These pressures operate subtly. The distance between parents grows imperceptibly as each battles fear, guilt, anger, or fatigue, as the child's disability colors how each sees the marriage, as they reorganize family rituals to accommodate unusual needs. Far more obvious, and perhaps more troubling, are the almost inevitable disagreements about the child and his or her treatment. The fourth section focuses on the differences in values, belief, and personal style which drive parents to various sorts of combat. A child's disability can magnify differences that cut close to the heart.

Marriage is something like a seesaw. In order to make this toy work, two children balance at either end, one going up as the other comes down. Many marriages operate on a similar model: parents adjust to one another in a complex way that enables them, generally, to maintain some sort of equilibrium. Thus, couples deal with problems ranging from uncertainty about the disability to homework and discipline. The seesaw capitalizes on difference, using it to maintain stability.

Despite all the problems, most marriages survive. In section five I describe some of the adjustments that help mothers and fathers to maintain the vital ties between them. Parents learn to search out sources of support both inside and outside the family. They learn to recognize their own ambivalence and to notice the ways in which it feeds conflict. And they learn to listen to feelings that anger sometimes obscures.

A child's disability strikes his parents at a point of peculiar vulnerability, but the problems it creates for a marriage arise, in other ways and for other reasons, in many families whose children are healthy and normal.* I have talked to different audiences about the material in this chapter; people usually nod in recognition—yes, this is what shared trouble is like in any marriage. "Happy families are all alike; every unhappy family is unhappy in its own way," writes Tolstoy in the famous opening line of *Anna Karenina*. I disagree: all happy families are not alike; nor are unhappy families always different.

To observe that particular problems are not unique to parents of the disabled is not to minimize the suffering they cause. Even problems that exist in one form or another in many marriages strike exceptional parents with peculiar force and intensity. Partly because exceptional parents need support even more than other people do. Partly because few couples expect a child's troubles to divide them.

From *Romeo and Juliet* to *Love Story* our culture has encouraged the notion that when a man and a woman really love each other, adversity firms their commitment. Many people believe that a child's disability will strengthen a "good" marriage, rather than weaken it. Even Josh Greenfeld, surely one of the most ironic and skeptical parents on record, observes that "at first I thought it [having a disturbed kid] would draw us closer together, necessarily cement our relationship" (1972, p. 78). Parents who write about experiences with a family disability rarely attempt to dispel this notion. Few mention substantial disagreements with a wife or a husband. (Those who do include gripes and problems often write anonymously.) Most emphasize their partner's sterling qualities and stalwart support.†

I doubt that these parents consciously mislead their readers. They may gloss over unpleasant memories in order to protect their family's privacy and to avoid disturbing sleeping ghosts. In undertaking to

---

* Readers who want to think more about the strains ordinary parenthood imposes might dip into *Ourselves and Our Children*, by the Boston Women's Health Book Collective (New York: Random House, 1978).¹

† The professional literature builds on quite different assumptions. Social scientists have studied the dynamics of "exceptional" marriages exhaustively (see, for example, Farber 1959; Farber 1960; Boles 1959; Fotheringham, Skelton, and Hoddinott 1971; Farber, Jenne, and Toigo 1960) and most have concluded that disability does create various sorts of strain. However, these analyses depend heavily on idiosyncratic measures of marital "integration," and few make sense to the general reader. Even if their findings were not buried in dusty monographs, professional writers too often adopt a style that submerges individual feelings and problems beneath a deluge of aggregated statistics. Perhaps their conclusions inform the vision of social psychologists; they rarely touch the lives of ordinary people struggling to understand their own marriages.

describe their child's progress they have not necessarily committed themselves to revelations that would tear their marriage apart. Airing old resentments in print can break a hard-won peace.*

A mothers' or a fathers' group offers greater privacy, but even here there are constraints. Most people see problems in their marriage as a sign of personal failure. A combination of pride and personal loyalty may prevent one from sharing concerns about a deteriorating relationship, and from analyzing points of friction. A good group elicits this sort of discussion eventually, but participants tread warily for months or even years.

The general silence only increases the misery of parents who see their own marriages falling apart.

Sadness Divides People

In marriage, as in other realms, the rich get richer, and the poor get poorer. When you are happy, problems look smaller, the shortcomings of children and spouse seem funnier, or at least easier to bear; giving is easier, getting less necessary. Unhappiness erodes the margin in any relationship. Fear threatens communication. Fatigue shortens nerves, reduces joy and tolerance, drains life of its natural color. Anger may miss its proper target and attack the relationship between husband and wife. Fortunately, not all these problems occur at the same time or in every family.

Fear

Fear divides parents even before they know what is wrong. Both the mother and the father notice worrisome developments. Sometimes each one agonizes quietly, not daring to speak the words aloud, afraid to hear fears confirmed, reluctant to aggravate the worries of the other.

Normally one parent breaks this troubled silence eventually. But when you are frightened yourself it can be particularly upsetting to

* Divorce may free a parent to speak of these matters. A few single parents report that the problems of raising a disabled child strained their troubled marriages to the breaking point (Rhodes 1972; Kovacs 1972; Brown 1976).

hear your fears articulated. Frightened people sometimes seek reassurance, and guard against confirmation of their fears, by exaggerating. I understand this strange stratagem because I used to practice it myself. I would passionately confront my husband with the specters of my imagination. I hoped he would contradict me; yet when he did so, I grew irrationally angry. His reassurance only intensified my anxieties. Escalating my exaggerations, I cut myself off from real dialogue. At the end of such an exchange, both of us felt puzzled, hurt, and lonely.

In the absence of definitive, credible diagnosis, each parent's imagination follows its own path. Each may react with startled horror to the novel fear the other voices. Louise Wilson had worried about her son Tony for years. He had been difficult, demanding, and unhappy almost from birth. No one labeled the boy, but teachers shared his parents' concern and suggested various home remedies. Mrs. Wilson argued that Tony needed psychiatric help; her husband worried less and advocated stricter discipline. At ten Tony went to camp. After visiting him there, Jack Wilson saw his son's problem in a new and serious light.

There was a long lane out to the main road. I looked back for as long as I could, and saw him standing there, a lonely figure with an upraised arm, very small. We rode for a mile or so without speaking until I could hold back no longer.

"Jack, how do you think he is, really?"

"How?" Jack's voice roughened. "I'll tell you how. Tony is psychotic. Tony has schizophrenia."

I thought it was my husband who had lost his mind. "Jack, for God's sake, what are you saying? You can't know what you're saying?"

"Did you see him, lying there on the grass? Cut off from everyone. I saw it and I see the figure as plainly as I have ever seen anything in my life."

My strength drained away. "Jack," I pleaded, "are you really making any sense at all? He's shy—granted. He's a poor athlete and he's afraid to play because other boys are always so contemptuous of a poor athlete. That's not at all unusual."

"This is different. The flat manner. The abnormal appetite. I'm aware I'm not qualified to diagnose, but it's something that, as a doctor, I *know*. God help me, I wish I didn't."

"Jack, with all respect to you, you're not a psychiatrist."

"Please," he said. "I know what I see."

He turned on the radio and began to drive very fast, which was not like him at all. I saw he did not want to talk. He looked strange, unfamiliar to me. I put my head back and thought: *No, he's wrong, he's got a tendency to be pessimistic anyhow. He admits he has. I will not listen to these graveyard thoughts.*

We did not mention the word "schizophrenia" again. I dismissed the whole thing as an emotional outburst, a father's hurt pride. (Wilson 1968, pp. 66–67)

Mrs. Wilson drew back from her husband's "graveyard thoughts." Frightened by his terrors, she snapped the communicative doors shut. Tony entered psychiatric treatment, but seven more agonizing years passed before the professionals reached a diagnosis: Tony was schizophrenic.

On the one hand, a parent wants to know the worst, to end the period of anxious waiting—to exchange butterflies in the stomach, if need be, for a lead weight on the heart. On the other hand, each of us clings to hope. As long as the truth remains in doubt, a mother and father may unconsciously balance one another—the one expressing hope while the other voices anxiety. They may switch roles periodically without ever really sharing the burden of their misery.

For most families the period of uncertainty ends in some sort of diagnosis. After a few false starts family and professionals arrive at a consensus about what ails the child. This can take a very, very long time—seventeen years in the case of Tony Wilson. In the meantime doubt and disagreement may have ravaged both the marriage and the children.

Marie Killelea illustrates the process by which a diagnosis can draw a couple closer together. At first, having nothing definite to go on, she and her husband tried to hide their concerns from one another. Finally the uncertainty became unbearable. Mr. Killelea demanded more information from the doctor, who told the couple that Karen had cerebral palsy. Shocked by the grim diagnosis, the Killeleas began at last to talk. Marie bitterly observed that although their prayers for Karen's survival had been granted, "She has existence—but no life." At first her husband drew back, but Marie forged ahead:

"I have been looking forward to Karen being as beautiful as Mother, as intellectual as you; I was sure she would be sweet, and popular with girls and boys alike. I knew she'd dance well, be a fine tennis player."

He moved over beside me, with Karen in his arms but I didn't look at either of them.

"Besides," I confessed bitterly, "when I pinned her first diaper in place, I was thinking of her first 'long' dress. It would, of course, be white and diaphanous."

"I know," Jimmy said. "I'd even thought ahead to the day when she'd be a lovely wife and mother." (Killelea 1952, p. 28)

In general, the more severe the disability, the earlier the diagnosis. Hence, a mildly handicapped child may divide his parents—and confuse his siblings—longer than one with more serious problems. Nancy Ramos, then president of the California Association for Neurologically Handicapped Children, told journalists Peter Schrag and Diane Divoky that many children with learning disabilities come from single parent homes; "But it's not the broken marriages that cause LD, it's that the learning disabled child broke up the marriage in the first place" (Schrag and Divoky 1975, p. 62). Schrag and Divoky raise skeptical eyebrows. Mrs. Ramos, however, may have been right. Picture the repeated arguments about what ails—and what will help—a child who is always just a *little* different from what family, teachers, and peers expect. Neither parent convinces the other. The child does not "grow out of it" as hoped. Both the mother and the father invest more heavily in their different positions as their concern grows. Over the years an issue of this sort can entangle everyone in the family.

Ambiguity separates people because each battles private fantasies alone. The terror that an outsider sees—even when that outsider is husband or wife—is the tip of the iceberg. The larger part lies submerged in each mind, too fearful to discuss, too personal to share.

Anger

Parents of handicapped children have, as I emphasized in chapter 2, many reasons for feeling angry and few arenas for expressing that anger. Inwardly they may rail at God or fate, at the doctors who failed to inform or help them, or at the child himself. Various sorts of consideration can prevent an open confrontation with any of these adversaries—particularly with the child.

When caution or inhibition shields the true target of frustration, feelings usually bounce off in another direction. One of my friends tells me that when she has had a bad experience at the hospital, she comes home and tells her husband about it. She cannot yell at the doctor: she needs his services; anyway, she is instinctively polite to strangers. When her voice rises an octave, her husband feels she is blaming him. She knows he is not at fault, but in fact he does take the brunt of her outrage.

Similarly, some parents find that the natural irritation they feel with their disabled child—and often they have successfully disguised it from themselves as well as their families—contaminates their relationship with one another.* This can happen insidiously, since blame usually raises questions. Suppose a boy knocks his cup off the table, spilling cocoa and broken shards over the floor, the newspaper, and an older sister's science project. His mother snaps at her husband for using a china cup and for setting it too close to the edge of the table. Is she misdirecting her anger? It is hard to tell.

When a little girl's shrieks ruin the evening meal, does her tired father feel angry? Does he blame the child herself, the mother who fails to quiet her, or the malign fate that linked his destiny with both of them? When a ten-year-old ruins expensive prostheses, does his mother blame the boy's carelessness or the father who took him boating? Or does she shrug philosophically, observing that boys will be boys? The answers depend on many imponderables, including just how angry and ill-used each person already feels.

Few people admit to displacing anger, and yet we probably all do it unconsciously on occasion. As Jay and I struggle to understand the anger we felt toward one another in the second year of Jody's life, it seems to us that our inability to focus our frustration on Jody himself might have contributed. When our dreams lay in fragments at our feet, when a crying baby interrupted every activity, fury and frustration were inevitable. But how could we blame Jody, who suffered, through no fault of his own, more than anyone else? Longing for solutions that no one could provide, we turned on one another.

Fatigue

Like fear and anger, fatigue brings its own train of problems. Although not all handicapped children exhaust their parents, weariness is a common fact of life.† Louise Wilson's son Tony visited his insomnia on his parents, refusing to leave their bedroom when he was unable to sleep himself. Karin Junker (1964) remembers that for the six years that her autistic daughter Boel lived at home, she never slept more than two hours at a stretch—or four hours in the course of the

---

* These ideas grew out of a conversation with Ruth Shir.
† Charles Hannam interviewed fifteen parents of moderately retarded children and reports that every parent spoke of tiredness as a problem (1975, p. 44). This is probably not entirely a matter of sleep patterns, since a more rigorous study of Down's syndrome preschoolers reported somewhat fewer nighttime awakenings than among normal children of the same age (Carr 1975, p. 125). However, all these children required much more physical care than did their normal peers.

night. Most parents of severely disabled young children face similar problems, at least for a while. Their feelings probably parallel those of any new mother who finds her sleep continually interrupted by an unpredictable infant—except that most babies sleep through the night sooner or later.

Fatigue frays nerves, and most exhausted parents growl at one another (or at their children). Over the years of Noah's life, Josh Greenfeld's journal bears witness to the difficulty of tolerating the intolerable without a decent night's rest.

Last night was a bad night. The cares of the day had piled in on Foumi: Karl sliding in sand piles, dirtying his clothes constantly. Noah his usual untoilet-trained self. People dropping in unexpectedly in the early evening. And then the avalanche excitement of Halloween tumbling in with the noisy parade of kids at the door trick-or-treating. By bedtime she was done in, sobbing tiredly, uncontrollably, not even quite knowing why. Finally the snivelling stopped and she slept.

And then I got up at midnight and decided to check Noah. He was dry. I took him to the bathroom. He began to yell and howl. So the night wore on, with Foumi up and sobbing again.

And this morning, red-eyed, she was arguing that we would have to put Noah in an institution soon. She pointed out that our cat, Brodsky, operates on a much higher level than our son; that at least he knows not only how to communicate his vital needs but also how to attend to them; that for the sake of our own survival we have to get a respite from the problems of Noah; that Noah is simply becoming too much and that we must remember that three is a bigger number than one. (Greenfeld 1972, p. 117)

Fatigue exacerbates existing tensions as effectively as it creates new ones. One father observes that he and his wife snap at each other from time to time. "It's what we would do normally, but we have got a little accelerator in the house that causes provocations" (Hannam 1975, p. 44). It is not simply broken nights that tire a family. Strained relationships, disagreeable routines, a sense that life takes out more than it puts back—all these drain parents' energy and leave them weary right through to the bone marrow. Ordinary parents feel the same frustrations: a constant drizzle of problems and tasks, a play without intermissions.

Although physical exhaustion curdles most dispositions, it can be a fairly straightforward sort of enemy. Josh Greenfeld identifies it readily enough; he knows when weariness rather than basic incompatibility causes an argument. Such perceptions enable parents to avoid bitter post-mortems and to keep fights transitory.

Sometimes, however, fatigue becomes so pervasive that it is hard to locate and difficult to combat. Life loses its color; a gray film settles over the emotional landscape. Even if babysitters are available, parents feel too tired to go out. Old recreations give less pleasure than before. After a while the family abandons them. Nothing new seems possible or worth doing.

Tired people come to take exhaustion for granted. I remember the first months of my oldest child's life. She was an altogether normal baby, and I went through the routines of child care and household management but was surprised to find that I accomplished little else. A trip to the supermarket seemed to exhaust my energy stores for the day. Remembering the heavily scheduled weeks preceding Liza's birth, I concluded that I must have pushed myself harder in the past. I never guessed that I was now quite tired from pregnancy, delivery, and nursing. Then, when Liza was five months old (it seems early now), I weaned her to a bottle. Within a few days I noticed an astonishing change: shopping no longer depleted me; I was inventing unnecessary errands for the simple pleasure of walking outside with the baby. I started to write while the baby napped, instead of collapsing with a detective story. I felt altogether different. Yet until my energy came flooding back, I did not know I had been tired.

Even people who understand their decreased vitality may do little about it. Fatigue perpetuates itself by preventing people from energetically seeking—or even imagining—a different way of life. Solving problems normally involves change, and change requires effort. To a truly tired person, most "solutions" look like new problems.

I know from my own experience that an exhausted mother can resist change with paradoxical vigor. When Jody was fourteen months old, he was still taking two bottles during the night. I rarely slept four hours at a stretch. Jay wanted us to get some sort of help—someone who could live in and manage some of the nighttime feedings. Much as I like the idea, I doubted its feasibility. I invented endless objections: I would feel guilty; I would hear Jody and wake up anyway; besides, we were managing okay, weren't we? Then, without our ever raising a finger, the solution presented itself. A young Japanese woman, visiting the United States for several months, was living temporarily with friends of ours while looking for an apartment. Because I did not really imagine it would come to anything, I suggested that she stay with us—and feed Jody his nightly bottles. As soon as she showed an interest, I got cold feet. Another person would intrude on our family's privacy. Weren't things going okay actually? I didn't really feel tired. Jay pressed me. Yes, he said, there would be problems, but things were not okay. We did need help. Well, I said, okay, but just for a week.

Without Jay's insistence, I would never have found the courage to take this major step (I capitulated because resistance required more courage than changing did). Yet the benefits were incalculable. Of course, Reiko's presence reduced our privacy—but it improved our lives in countless ways.

A husband who is not himself exhausted, and drawn into a web of pessimistic assumptions that preclude any change, may be able to find a solution. He knows his wife well enough to gauge her real needs; he can temper determination with insight. Outsiders can help, too, by thinking for the weary couple. Sometimes when a solution finally appears, parents wonder why they endured the problem unnecessarily for so long. John Murray writes:

> Peggy wakes for a bottle at 3:00 A.M., as she does every night, and is hard to put down after. Little John wakes, cross and hungry, at six. I'm near tears when Rosalie arrives for the day, having had him fussing and whining for two hours. Perhaps there was some rational alternative—he must be tired, waking so early: put him back in bed for a while? But neither Emily nor I thought of it. The trouble is we become so tired—are so deeply, heavily exhausted—that we don't *think* of the rational alternatives. Debilitated. (Murray and Murray 1975, p. 88)

Solutions to the problem of exhaustion are as various as imagination can make them. Most parents find that school helps immensely. It gives regular relief from the child's demands. By providing a round of activities, supervised play in the open air, and the necessity for early rising, schools regularize sleep patterns. Increased time for friends, work, and other interests helps mothers fight world-weariness.

Some tired parents will read these pages with a deepening sense of gloom. They will object that they have neither the space to accommodate a student helper nor the money to pay a housekeeper, that their child is too young for school and too dependent for respite care. They may be right. Each family needs to invent solutions that match their own values, resources, and problems. At a certain point they may need courage and action more than they need new ideas. Taking a step—any step—can help people to feel somewhat more in control of lives that are out of control.

"Faith in the Union"

Somehow the rhythm of our lives, the good fortune of our marriage, seems to have dissipated. It is hard for Foumi to believe in me and for me to believe in Foumi anymore. Successful monogamy, of course, must be based on a faith in the union if nothing else. And how can we have faith in a marriage that has biologically backfired? (Greenfeld 1972, p. 56)

All of us think magically as well as logically. Each of us analyzes the advantages and the drawbacks of a new house or a new job, but each also responds to intuition—to the feeling that a place is somehow right or wrong—lucky or unlucky—for us.

It is the same with marriage. We look to a husband or wife for love, and comfort, and certain sorts of affinity. We also hope for good fortune and promise. Blind faith in the union itself can carry a couple over rough periods of rage, misunderstanding, and want. Symbols fortify—or undermine—that faith.

The vitality of healthy children reassures parents about their marriage as well as about themselves. Children are tangible, lovable symbols of their joint undertaking. In thriving they bless a parent's choices —the choice of spouse, the decision to have children, the style of parenting. When a child's development goes seriously awry, it calls the whole enterprise into question.

In earlier chapters on guilt and anger I described some results of parental efforts to make sense out of the handicap. Some people shake a defiant fist at the cosmos. Others guiltily assume the blame themselves, concluding that their own mistakes have caused their child's disability. (Both groups—my husband calls them "externalizers" and "internalizers," respectively—see a sort of order in the universe which disinterested observation might not confirm.) The same impulse that leads some parents to blame the calamity on themselves, on God, or on the fates can point an accusing finger at the marriage itself.

In the mothers' group Rosalyn Gibson described the frenzied dance of her imagination in the weeks following the discovery of Nancy's blindness. Guilt and uncertainty tortured her. Searching for some sort of explanation, she went back over her life. She remembered the determination with which her parents—and Howard's—had fought her marriage. She began to wonder whether she and Howard had not done wrong to oppose their families' wishes.

She had not questioned her decision during the long years in which she and Howard had made a home and raised three healthy children. But now that the marriage had "biologically backfired," as Josh Greenfeld puts it, she saw it in a new light. At such moments few parents can help noting, at least unconsciously, that if they hadn't gotten married, they would not be facing this heartbreaking problem.

Because Rosalyn was, as she told us, "driving everyone crazy," Howard suggested that she visit a psychiatrist. She told the doctor her story; he listened with terrifying solemnity and responded with a single question, "Do you think you did wrong?" She stopped cold. "Of course not. We loved each other and were right to get married. We considered their feelings and tried to make it easy for them. But they wouldn't meet us halfway. We didn't have any choice." "Well," the psychiatrist looked severe, "if you didn't do anything wrong, then it doesn't make sense to feel guilty about it." He rose to terminate the interview. His unbending solemnity gave his pronouncement authority; Rosalyn stopped feeling guilty. She had defeated her own magical thinking with the newer magic of psychiatry.

Any child complicates his or her parents' relationship in practical as well as symbolic ways. From the moment of conception, parents' ties to one another tangle with duties to their offspring. Someone must perform basic household and child-care routines—usually either the father or the mother. If I fix the children's box lunches, Jay can savor a second cup of breakfast coffee. When he washes the breakfast dishes and reminds Caitlin to wear her boots, he allows me time for a leisurely shower. Thus, much of what parents do for their children they also, indirectly, do for each other. Josh and Foumi Greenfeld experienced the strains of this triangular connection. They juggled responsibilities, searching for an arrangement that would allow both of them to keep their sanity.

Noah had one of his classic days—frequent toilet accidents, constant shrieks, and then a beaut of a night. I don't think he ever closed his eyes—or allowed us to. So this morning found Foumi going to the closet, packing a suitcase: "I can't go on. My hair is turning white, my eyes can't focus. I'm losing my voice. I'm not painting. I feel I'm simply throwing my life away because of this crazy kid." All I could do was agree. There is no solving the problem, there is only the deferring of it. Meanwhile, I guess I have to share more of the unpleasant labors. (Greenfeld 1972, p. 168)

The physical and emotional costs of living with Noah escalated. Sometimes Foumi felt that she must leave her husband and sons in order to survive. Josh considered abandoning the family, too, though perhaps for somewhat different reasons (Greenfeld 1972, p. 71).* For a while Noah engulfed his parents. They searched out medical and educational services and finally started a day care center of their own. They planned and planned again, laundered, replaced and repaired in Noah's wake. Days passed, with neither time nor energy left over for Josh's writing or Foumi's art. Years went by. Life-sustaining hopes withered as Josh and Foumi taught and taught again, and Noah learned only to forget.

In the absence of acceptable residential placement, Foumi had to leave Josh if she wanted to escape from Noah. Her threat, however histrionic, carries a note of quiet realism: our society accepts—even expects—termination of marriages; it recoils from a mother who abandons her own child. Culture and experience teach us to see the tie between parents and child (or at least mother and child) as virtually indestructible. This assumption has implications for a marriage even when practical difficulties of day-to-day care have been met through residential placement. Consider the reflections of Karin Junker when she discovered that she had accidentally driven her car off the road, on her way to Jarna. She was returning Anders, the younger of her two handicapped children, to school at the end of the summer holidays.

I stepped out of the car to see how close we were to the ditch. The white-gray fog closed in on me, and I could see neither heaven nor earth. Only the small voice was coming through the car, muffled as it were. Yet I was alone—the decision would be mine, not his.

"Annis and Mummy drive to heaven now . . . to heaven, Mummy! Annis and Mummy together. Not to Jarna, Mummy! Drive to heaven!"

It was dangerously close, that stumbling abyss enticing. It would be sentimental if it weren't true, if it hadn't happened. But what actually happens is seldom sentimental. It can only be reported in various degrees of sentimentality, and I can report now that the temptation has never been greater than it was at that moment, the tiny voice persisting:

"Mummy and Annis drive to heaven now!"

* Such thoughts (and threats) occur in "normal" families, too. Jane Lazarre (1976) describes a similar scene between herself and her husband in the early months of her first child's life. The fatiguing necessities of a difficult child's care eroded her strength and perhaps her reason. After a certain point only extreme measures seemed to offer any hope. Like Foumi, she began to pack her bag amid tears and recriminations. Like Foumi, she relinquished the impulse, unpacked, and tried again.

It would have been so easy in the fog. So much easier to explain than "sleeping pills," or any other means. The fog was actually as impenetrable as described in English novels. And the sea below, so close, so accessible. There was no sentimentality in this case.

This was the tempter.

Then I remembered a poem I had recently heard: "The greatest sin— to take the life that God you gave. . . ." I could hear it so clearly. I recognized all the arguments. I knew how all—or many of us with this fate—might have played with the thought, listened to it in secret moments, perhaps enjoyed it as one might enjoy the sweetness of forbidden fruit. But we always have to face this double consideration, three-double: our defective child, ourselves, and the others—our immediate dependents who perhaps need our aid, whom we must not fail. Perhaps they even love us. Anyway, it would hurt them. Have we then the right?

I shook myself in the fog and walked quickly to the edge of the road. Now I could hear the waves break below. How far below or how close I do not know. Nor how deep the water. It no longer attracted me. It had lost its interest. (Junker 1964, pp. 249–50)

Mrs. Junker could break free of her painful responsibilities only through suicide—the final severing of *all* family ties. Elsewhere she describes her marriage as good, yet her husband's love did not hold her back from the precipice. Like Foumi Greenfeld she momentarily forgot that bond in a sudden intense longing to escape the pain her children brought her.

At certain points in their lives, many mothers and fathers find family life constricting. We give up a great deal of freedom to become parents. Any reasonable person regrets this loss occasionally. Some people long for a vacation from emotional responsibility, from the worry about children's happiness and well-being. Others remember with nostalgia a period of greater flexibility: a child places new restrictions on work, play, sleep, and sex. A third group misses economic independence—the freedom to quit a disagreeable job, to try a new career, or to defy a stupid rule.

With luck, the pleasures of parenthood outweigh the loss of liberty. A child's disability can shift this balance. Concerns for the future weigh heavily on both parents. Practical responsibilities nibble away at the slim margins for recreation and leisure. Dreams of lost promise return—unreachable, but deceptively fresh and green.

Despite genuine affection between husband and wife, the family may come to seem like a prison. Two unacceptable alternatives seem to confront the depressed parent—let us say the father. He can flee, saving himself and abandoning his wife and children. Or he can stay, learning to hate his family, perpetually mourning his own lost possibilities.

Few parents abandon their families. Many dream occasionally about freedom and flight. Emily Murray writes:

John and I have been quarreling each weekend and finally reached a terrible state. Dying for him to come home, happy when he arrives, then, perhaps resentful of his freedom, I start something. But each time, when we try to discover what we are quarreling about and can't find any definable cause, we realize it is our grief for Little John, our sense of our lives not going forward but stopped, self-devouring. We stand over him, fearful of every change because it will cut down his future. During one quarrel I found myself thinking: If only I could fall in love with someone else and run away and start over. Not so much a formulated thought as a gut longing. As if I could ever leave either John. (Murray and Murray 1975, p. 78)

Some people threaten to leave in an effort to communicate the depth of their despair or to short-circuit their own fears of being abandoned. Most keep their fantasies private.

Not every one confuses the difficulties of child care with those of maintaining a marriage. Some parents never imagine that they might escape exhaustion and despair by leaving their family behind. For others, fantasies of this sort prove self-limiting. The open road loses its charm as life improves at home. Still, many mothers and fathers need help in learning to disentangle their feelings about the marriage from the child and his or her disabilities. Like so much of the rest of life, a part of the trick is in separating problems into manageable pieces instead of fusing all issues into one giant wax ball of misery.

An exchange between Rosalyn and Howard Gibson suggests the difficulty, both practical and emotional, of disentangling family relationships from one another. At our second couples' meeting, Howard spoke of the future. He said that when the children were grown, he intended to buy a van and tour the country. "And," he added, with a significant glance at his wife, "I want *her* with me." Rosalyn looked away from Howard and caught the eye of a friend. Her voice, though barely audible, carried a note of determination: "Well, there'll just have to be three of us."

As he insisted on his dream, Howard seemed to force Rosalyn into an unpleasant choice between her obligations as wife and as mother. Actually, he was probably seeking some sort of reassurance, some indication of her commitment to him. He had accepted responsibility for this difficult child. Perhaps he wanted to tell Rosalyn that he envisioned a future for the two of them, a future that he would postpone but not deny. He needed to look forward to a return of joy and spontaneity, to an escape from the prison of Nancy's needs and limitations. He asked his wife to affirm her loyalty to him, to separate it from her duty to Nancy. This was hard for Rosalyn, who has had to cope with her own divided feelings. On this occasion she balked. A year later she told us they had bought a new van. She was nervous about the expense but excited, too. The van simplified some of her problems with Nancy. Perhaps it also allowed her to share a dream with Howard.

Another of our mothers, Lucy Forrest, saw very quickly that her retarded son Christopher was straining her relationship with Kevin. As she struggled to meet her obligations and balance her life, she discovered that small steps could make an immense difference. The decision to find a babysitter was an example.

It was hard to do. She had the babysitters' numbers on her refrigerator for weeks before she dared to call. Finally she dialed nervously, explained Christopher's problems to the woman who answered the phone, and said that she had heard that her daughter sometimes babysat for handicapped children. The mother rebuffed her brusquely: "Oh, she doesn't do that any more."

Lucy retreated for a few weeks, licking her wounds. Then she called the next number, and the next, and the next. Eventually she found the right person—a nurse who warmed immediately to her children and could obviously handle any contingency.

Lucy and Kevin went out to dinner. At the restaurant nervousness gripped Lucy. She asked Kevin whether they should call home. He reassured her: the children were in capable hands. It was time for the two of them to enjoy an evening together. And they did. Lucy was radiant—almost evangelical—as she told the group her story. She said that now she could put up with anything during the week, knowing she would be going out Saturday. She noticed that she enjoyed the kids more. She looked forward to seeing them on Sunday morning.

By forcing herself to call a babysitter, by continuing her search in the face of rejection, by setting aside time and money for shared pleasures away from the children, Lucy proved to herself that Christopher's limitations need not wholly define life. Her efforts spoke of her commitment to Kevin, and of her eagerness to affirm their relationship as husband and wife and to protect it from the encroachments of children.

The Organization of the Family

A child's disability can cause problems which one may loosely term "structural," problems rooted in the organization of the family and in the ways in which family members connect to one another.

Salvadore Minuchin, in an excellent theoretical book on family therapy (1974), speaks of the necessity for boundaries within and around a family, boundaries that are firm enough to endure over time but flexible enough to permit other relationships. His analysis illuminates some of the troubles that can arise in exceptional families.

Minuchin sees the creation of boundaries as the first task of a married couple. The man and the woman must free themselves from their family of origin (as the psychiatrists call it) and set up a separate space for the two of them. They must persuade their parents to see them in a new way—as a husband and a wife, rather than as a son and a daughter. They need physical and psychological space that belongs only to the two of them—space to work out the terms of their partnership. They must create boundaries that protect their autonomy as a couple without cutting them off from the rest of the world. Normal adults in fact have great difficulties achieving this complex balance. The first years of marriage are often hard.

If children come, the structure changes: the couple must mark boundaries within the family as well as around it. Thus in all families Minuchin sees two basic systems. There is the parents' system and the children's system—mother and father in one, brothers and sisters in another.

Family members gain a lot from participating in these smaller systems as well as from belonging to the larger family unit. From their brothers and sisters children learn about dealing with equals; they find support for impulses toward independence, and confidence in coping with the wider world of children. In order for the children's system to teach and support, however, it needs a measure of independence. The mother and father must acknowledge some boundaries around the sibling system—to give the children room.

Parents, for parallel though different reasons, need to demarcate space of their own where children do not intrude. For one thing, most couples require privacy in order to negotiate conflict. Without room to fight, they submerge their differences or perhaps detour anger and frustration through one of the children. Even in the absence of friction, they need to protect their connection to one another from the encroachments of other people. Time alone together allows parents to get the understanding that an adult gives better than a child.

To say that there are boundaries around these two systems is not, of course, to imply that the bonds between children and parents do not matter. Indeed, these relationships shape the lives of every family member. Both systems operate in the context of the wider family setting. The boundaries are highly permeable. Nonetheless, unless they exist, neither children nor adults will get what they need from people their own size.

Minuchin does not specifically speak of the effect of a child's disability on the organization of a family. I believe, however, that a severely disabled child threatens important boundaries at two points. The first is within the family. The second is at its edge.

Within the family, a severely disabled child—let us suppose she is a girl—may not fit comfortably within the other children's system. She may require so much physical care from her parents, and occupy their thoughts so completely, that she seriously encroaches on their time together. The connection between such a child and her parents may nearly replace relationships with her brothers and sisters.

Even parents of a mildly handicapped child can imagine how such a restructuring of family life might occur. The more challenging question is how to avert or to reverse it. The exact strategy depends in part upon the child. Some parents can strengthen the children's system simply by disciplining themselves to back off a bit—to let children fight and settle their differences without parental interference. This course will inevitably involve some pain and risk. I remember several years ago, when Jay and I were encouraging Liza, then seven, to express anger more freely, she complained that although we allowed her to yell at us, we did not let her tell off her little sister. I was surprised—I was sure I had not told her not to yell at Caitlin. "No," said Liza, "you don't say anything, but whenever I get mad at her, you come running in and say something like 'Caitie, would you like to help me set the table?'" I realized she was right. Even while congratulating myself on not taking sides, I was interfering between them. Their angry voices *did* make me uncomfortable, and I was afraid being yelled at would hurt the baby. When Liza described my behavior, I saw that I was intruding as effectively as if I had forbidden them to argue.

So I tried to hold back. It was not easy. The next time I heard Liza yelling at Cait for snatching her toys, I wanted to swoop in—to reassure the baby and protect Liza from her own angry feelings. I checked myself. I learned that they could settle many, if not all, of these disputes on their own. Caitlin learned quickly to stand up for herself—and to make fewer bratty demands. Soon there seemed to be less yelling in general, and they spent long hours together absorbed in play. I have learned, over the years, how much they have to give one another, and how generally good they are at negotiation and diplomacy.

In our family this comes up much less often with Jody. Sometimes, however, the girls do yell at their brother. Once when Liza was seven or eight, she was describing some frustrating problem to me and Jody began to laugh. She turned on him in fury, shouting that he should not laugh at other people's misery. At first I tried to "explain": Jody was not really laughing at her; he probably did not understand how she felt. But Liza objected that he always laughed when other people cried. Realizing that she was right, I tried to give her feelings a little more space. After all, how do I know what Jody understands? And as the years have gone by, although I have often wanted to interfere and explain, to replace rage with rationality, serenity, and forgiveness, I have come to feel that when Liza or Caitlin yells at Jody they take him more seriously, in a way, than I do when I "explain."

Often parents interfere in order to protect a child physically rather than emotionally. The Massies prohibited physical fighting between their children in order to protect Bobby from bleeding episodes. A reasonable rule—which Susie remembers breaking stealthily. Since she sometimes hit her older brother, she blamed herself for his illnesses. She longed for reassurance, but no one knew about her worries. When Bobby got well, the battles began again. "Rages would come over me and I'd go pull his hair . . . he was so bossy and know-it-all that I wanted to take his crutches away . . . something really mean like that" (Massie 1975, pp. 163–64). The rules of the household and the realities of Bobby's disability prevented the two children from working out the terms of their relationship, and interfered with Susie's getting the support she needed. Circumstances tied the Massies's hands: they could hardly encourage their children to fight it out. Such occasions force parents to choose the lesser evil. Not all problems have solutions.

Hemophilia creates a hideous trap for families, because the children's apparent normality conceals a terrible fragility. Marie Killelea, by contrast, could grit her teeth and watch Karen take a few knocks because she knew that her daughter was actually in no more danger than a normal child. Karen's obvious vulnerability found protectors as well as tormenters among her equals.

Karen had laboriously worked her way over some three inches of ground to pick up a clothespin I had deliberately placed beyond her reach. As I watched, one of the children, from the house next door, just as deliberately snatched the clothespin from Karen and moved it away beyond her reach. She cried in chagrin and disappointment and then started after it all over again, laboriously inching her way across the ground. The new boy had been standing, watching. He turned, and came up to the kitchen window and knocked. I leaned out and said, "Hello, my name is Marie. What's yours?"

"Dale." He was curt. "What's the matter with her?"—and he pointed to Karen.

"Well, Dale," I answered. "God didn't make her arms and legs as strong as yours and mine. We have to teach her to walk and use her hands. She's learning, but it's very hard work and she needs a lot of help."

As I spoke Dale's eyes grew wider and wider and his bright cheeks lost a bit of their color.

Scratching the calf of his left leg with his right foot, he pondered my remark, looking hard at Karen and the unattainable clothespin.

"Didja see what they done?" he said stiffly.

"Yes," I answered, "but it doesn't happen often and if I butt in, it wouldn't be good for Karen. Besides, it would make the children resent her."

He jerked back to me and spoke savagely, "I'll kill the next brat that teases her," and swung away.

At the offender he yelled, "Yah oughta be ashamed, you stinker. I'll bust you one if ya do that again."

His language wasn't choice but it was effective.

I closed the window and went back to my ironing, while he remained standing over Karen, his fists rolled at his side.

She acquired a champion that day, acceptable to the youngsters because he was one of them. For the six years that Dale lived in our neighborhood she was never teased when he was around. (Killelea 1952, pp. 63–64)

Some parents consciously control their own protective impulses in order to strengthen a child's relationships with people his own age. Of course, this will not by itself prevent him from intruding into his parents' relationship. It may help, though: as brothers, sisters, and peers include the disabled child in more of their play, parents' duties decrease. Children take over some of the tasks of entertainment and teaching, allowing a mother and father more time for themselves and perhaps a chance to rebuild their own alliance.

This approach does not always work, however. If a child has few play skills, if his disability interferes with communication, if his understanding lags far behind that of his brothers and sisters, even the most skillful efforts may fail to integrate him into the world of normal children. My own daughters share a surprising number of interests, friends, and activities, despite the five-year difference in their ages. Although they sometimes include Jody in their play, he contributes rather passively. Because he cannot share his own ideas or insist on a place among his sisters, he remains somewhat outside this particular children's system. They feel this lack, and express it in different ways as they grow older. I, of course, feel obliged to provide Jody with the companionship and entertainment he cannot arrange for himself. There seems little likelihood that he will be part of a strong brother-sister system. Our theories cannot change those facts, but they can help us as parents to anticipate other difficulties.

Jay and I have not solved this problem. We try to find opportunities for Jody to join in with his sisters, and they do the same. They are more likely than we to succeed, and have over the years found imaginative things to do with him. More successfully, we also work to protect some space for the two of us—time when we know we will be alone together. This means firm bedtimes for the children, and times to play tennis, run, or go to the movies over the weekends. We do not always succeed. Sometimes work demands escalate, babysitters become busy and unavailable, and children proscrastinate away their bedtimes. In the midst of other pressures we may not even notice that we are spending less time together as a couple. Soon we feel it in other ways. These are general problems, of course. "Exceptional" parents probably need *more* time alone together than other parents need; they often get less.

In addition to altering the alignments *within* the family, a disabled child can weaken boundaries *around* it. A child's disability usually puts a family in touch with a variety of professionals and other experts. The nature and the extent of these contacts varies widely from family to family. Poor families often fail to get good medical care. Some children get limited technical assistance in hospital, clinic, or classroom. For families who can afford it, the influence of experts extends into the home as well. Physical therapists design programs for parents to carry out. Occupational therapists suggest better ways to feed, dress, and bathe the child. Doctors perform corrective surgery. Nurses describe a regimen of postoperative care which parents implement. Teachers try out educational strategies in the classroom and explain the importance of consistent home follow-up.

These efforts help the child grow and may lessen the family's isolation. They speak of society's dawning commitment to the handicapped and encourage our hopes for the growth of a tolerant, concerned community. They can also reduce a family's independence and autonomy. Recently, the historian Christopher Lasch published an impassioned polemic *Haven in a Heartless World* (1976) denouncing the increasing power of professionals and experts and deploring the effects of this power on families. I do not myself agree with Lasch's argument: most families need more help, not less. Nonetheless, I think some of Lasch's concerns are well founded—particularly for families with a disabled child. All the advice, the dependence on expert opinion and approval, the vulnerability of people in trouble—all this can infantilize parents and restrict their freedom to solve problems and make choices in their own way. Medicine has done a great deal for the disabled, but a medical model—any model based on hierarchies of clients and expert professionals—has serious limitations. These limitations matter most at the points where problems become human, not technical.

Nor do the intrusions stop with professionals. Friends, relatives, and even casual passers-by offer tips and information. The man collecting quarters at the turnpike tollbooth urged me to consult a doctor about my son. "He's sleeping with his eyes open. Believe me, that's not normal." Everyone gets this sort of advice. But if the difficulties resulting from a child's disability have leached away a parent's self-confidence, even friendly suggestions can seem overwhelming.

Intrusions can go well beyond advice. A family may change the entire composition of its household in order to meet the handicapped child's needs. Reiko came to live with us when Jody was fourteen months old, and stayed six years, helping with Jody's care, going to college, and experimenting with several new careers. Marilyn Segal

(1966), Clara Park (1967), and Sharon Ulrich (1972) mention a variety of domestic helpers. Other families move in order to accommodate a grandparent or another relative within the household.

These additions to the family often lighten the workload and, in doing so, improve parents' dispositions. They also create new pressures, even under the best of circumstances. Linda Davidson's parents are a good example. Linda told the mothers' group that her mother really got her through the first year of Marianne's life, helping to nurse and feed a baby who seemed almost lifeless for a long time. When Linda and George bought a new house, they made sure it included an apartment for her parents, Mr. and Mrs. Lewis.

Linda still describes her mother as her "ace." She depends on her for routine babysitting, reassurance, and emergency back-up. Mrs. Lewis helps out cheerfully. Nevertheless, there are some problems. Mrs. Lewis and George shared extremely cautious, protective attitudes toward Marianne. Together they make it hard for Linda to try anything new. For example, after several years of driving Marianne to school herself, Linda began to think of letting her go on the bus with the other children. George left the decision in her hands, "because I'm the one who takes care of her all day." But he restated his position on schools and other outside agencies: "They're only doing a job. You can't expect them to care the way you do." Mrs. Lewis objected vigorously to the change, saying she would rather stay home from work herself than see Marianne ride to school in the cab. Their combined opposition killed Linda's tentative impulse: "I'd have to take the whole responsibility. If anything happened, it would be my fault."

Adding new people to the household, either as guests or as family members, upsets an existing balance. Old treaties and boundaries get redrawn. Sometimes one person begins to feel left out, hemmed in, or just uncared for. Even when alliances do not shift, any reduction of privacy can seriously strain family relationships. During the first months of Christopher's life, Lucy and Kevin Forrest took him to Philadelphia for an evaluation at the Institutes for the Achievement of Human Potential. The program of patterning and stimulation that the staff developed for Chris required the help of many people outside the family. It occupied the better part of each day, seven days a week. While Chris remained in the program, volunteers trooped through the house constantly, helping with the patterning. Lucy found the strain tremendous. Kevin hated the lack of privacy. They argued over whether to continue the program. Looking back at the experience, Lucy told the mothers' group, "I can't tell you how many times during that first year I thought we would get a divorce."

In our family Liza once complained that the presence of a third adult deprived her of the privileges of the oldest daughter. Although her analysis seemed farfetched at first, I began to understand it as I watched our family. When Reiko was away, Liza took a great deal of responsibility for her younger sister; when Reiko was at home and we were out, Caitlin sought Reiko's help with problems, not Liza's. When there were more adults to share the work, we asked less of her —and gave her fewer responsibilities. I noticed a difference in our dinners, too. With three grown-ups at the table, conversation tended to center around adult interests. When Reiko was away, both girls, but especially Liza, got a larger share of the floor. Liza had a point.

The traditional nuclear family—Mom, Pop, Sis, and Bub—can seem banal and isolated. Changes that increase the flexibility of its bound-aries enliven the family unit. Nonetheless, a nuclear family is the norm in most American minds, and children care a lot about norms. A boy who already feels somewhat different because of a disabled sister may see a grandmother's constant presence as a further mark of family deviance.

I want to stress here that I am *not* advising against these additions to the family. On the contrary, I think such changes can save parents' health and sanity. Aside from physical relief, a concerned grown-up can provide much-needed psychological support. My own experience has been that a third adult can improve family living in any number of ways. I know, though, that change touches every family member. Some people—adult and/or child—may feel that they are paying the costs while others collect the benefits. They may be right. When this happens, they need at least the satisfaction of having their views heard.

Only a minority of families attempt to reallocate the burdens of care by adding a new person to the household. Most distribute the necessary chores among family members, with the mother covering more bases than anyone else. Some families work out different pat-terns: experimenting with roles is a phenomenon of the time, in both "normal" families and those with disabled members. Whatever the arrangements, a disability can complicate parents' feelings about the domestic division of labor.

The balance of gains and losses in choosing to work at home, raising children and maintaining a household, rather than working outside, obviously depends on many things. One of these is the quality of family life—the particular pleasures and pains involved in being with children most of the day. If a child taxes a mother's physical and psychological resources too heavily, she feels that she is giving more and getting less than she needs. Even if she sees her husband assuming certain responsibilities, she may resent his freedom and the regular breaks from "exceptional parenthood" that his job provides.

This is not simply a matter of who works full-time and who stays home. Children's problems preoccupy many women even after they rejoin the paid labor force. Fathers seem better able to set domestic concerns aside and to focus on other pursuits. My friend Jill Flanner, who recently returned to graduate school, describes the division of emotional labor in her marriage, and the resulting tensions between her and her husband, Roger. Their daughter Frances has a number of physical and educational problems. School has been hard for her, and she vents her frustrations on her family. Although Jill and Roger have worked hard to share the work and to support one another, the path has been rocky.

Jill says that Roger has always been extraordinarily helpful, but that his work schedule limits his involvement to weekends and evenings. She cannot help resenting the vast amount of extra work involved in raising Frances, and she wishes that Roger could share more of the burdens. It is not just the teacher conferences, the trips to doctors and clinics, or the ongoing search for psychological help, she says. It is the worry as well. Roger just does not seem to get as upset as she does.

When Frances was eleven, her parents and teachers decided she needed more help than she could get in an ordinary classroom. Jill looked at several special schools and talked to all the experts. With misgivings she finally agreed to place Frances in a small special class in another public school. The night before the move she lay awake for hours, worrying. Would Frances be happy in her new school? Had they been right to send her into a separate classroom? Roger listened sympathetically—as usual—when she described her concerns, but obviously the impending transition troubled him far less. His calmness bothered Jill. She wondered whether she was neurotic or overanxious. Because this happened so predictably she avoided sharing many worries with her husband.

Men, too, notice the difference in family life. Peter Lederman worried guiltily about Catherine, who lost hours of sleep every night tending to Ellie. And Charles Hannam wondered how his wife survived the anxiety of her second pregnancy, without the distraction provided by an outside job (Hannam 1975, p. 19). An impression that he can do little to help either the child or his wife may compound any guilt the husband feels about the origin of the disability. This feeling does neither parent much good—particularly if the wife shares it.

The presence of a child with a disability can, then, change the structure of the family in a number of ways. It may weaken the boundaries that protect the autonomy of different systems within the family. It makes the family more vulnerable to the intrusions of outsiders, particularly doctors and other professionals. And it can make difficult or unpalatable the traditional division of roles.

Difference and Disagreements

There are a lot of good ways of raising children. Most of the time we choose between the various alternatives by instinct, with our values, childhood memories, and personal hang-ups playing into decisions that are not wholly rational. Few couples agree at each fork in the road, even when the children are normal and the choices ordinary. Disability raises the stakes of conflict.

Parents disagree, quite fundamentally, on the nature of their obligations to the disabled child. They assess his or her future options differently and favor different plans of treatment. They will probably cope somewhat differently with the emotional stress of parenthood. They may view professionals in a very different light. Because the issues are momentous, they negotiate many conflicts in an atmosphere charged with the profoundest emotion.

When a child is so severely handicapped that professionals suggest institutional placement, parents often disagree about the relative merits of home and residential care. There are no right and wrong answers, and sensible people realize that, in human terms, each option carries a large price tag. Naturally parents often compute the costs and benefits differently. In one family, for instance (see chapter 4), the father wished to institutionalize his severely handicapped baby, in order "to protect the family I already have." His wife wanted to care for her at home. Both strove to safeguard the welfare of those they loved; each weighed conflicting longings and obligations on a private scale.

Every family has to decide how much they owe the handicapped child. Some mothers and fathers can resolve this question without much ill-feeling—using one another as sounding boards, but standing more or less together. Other families (probably the majority) have to negotiate at least a few important disagreements. Lucy Forrest observed to the mothers' group that before Michelle's birth, Christopher was her whole life. She spent most of each day playing with him. When Kevin came home from work, she needed a break and expected him to take over. Kevin sat down with Christopher willingly enough, but after a while he wandered off to do something else. Feeling let down, Lucy complained to her husband, "But you only played with him for half an hour."

To me, half an hour seems a long time. Few people in our household can concentrate on entertaining Jody for that long, and Jody is in fact more responsive than Christopher. To Lucy, who worked with and worried about Christopher for most of every day, half an hour seemed very little.

As Christopher grew older, Lucy's ideas changed. She discovered how much she cared about other relationships, and decided to let those people make demands on her time and energy. If she was going to give them more, she must sometimes give Christopher less. Looking to the future, she imagined the difficulties of caring for an adult-sized Christopher. She said that it would kill her to place him, but she knew she would do so if the price of keeping him at home rose too high. "You have to think of yourself. You have your own life to live. You've gotta think, Is it worth it? Is it worth getting a divorce over? Is it worth having your children hate you?"

She knew an older woman who was still caring for her forty-year-old son at home. Like Christopher, he lacked the self-help skills of a healthy toddler; his mother changed his diapers, fed, dressed, and bathed him. At sixty her strength was failing; she could no longer get him out of bed. The result of her life's work: her other children hated her for sacrificing the family to their disabled brother. Lucy saw this woman as an awful warning against a one-sided existence.

Even when a mother and father agree about the level of their commitment, they may disagree about treatment and handling. Each parent decides what matters most; each evaluates the likely result of training and effort. Families of children with impaired hearing must choose between a number of competing and antagonistic approaches to deaf education. As I have mentioned, parents of the "brain-injured" —which includes most autistic, retarded, and cerebral-palsied youngsters—face a decision about the merits and the relevance of a controversial treatment called "patterning," promoted by Philadelphia's Institutes for the Achievement of Human Potential and widely criticized by conventional medicine. Even when no orthodoxies war over the child, sensible people disagree about the efficacy or the practicality of a particular treatment. The whole field of learning disabilities is a minefield of theories, treatments, prescriptions, and dogmas, many of which cannot be tested satisfactorily. At the deepest level these are not professional or technical questions: they are human, and the buck stops with the parents.

Sometimes mothers and fathers of exceptional children face peculiar difficulties because they are divided internally as well as between themselves. Each partner feels deeply ambivalent—about the child, the future, the advice of experts, and many other problems. Ambivalence is, however, confusing and upsetting. Sometimes mixed feelings get swept under the rug, to be expressed in a conflict between husband and wife. This occurred with us. When Jody was around eighteen months old, Jay (and several other people) felt strongly that we should begin to make inquiries about residential placement. I felt equally strongly that we should wait. Although I expected that Jody might eventually live elsewhere, I wanted to care for him at home while he was still small. Without being unpleasant, I refused to budge from my position. Yet my feelings were, of course, profoundly divided. Jody exhausted both of us; his care consumed all my energy and most of my time. Residential placement would have offered unimaginable freedom. I am sure that a part of me yearned for a simple long-term solution to the problem. But another part—a part that I liked better, and therefore gave license to speak—wanted to give Jody everything I could. Jay's feelings were probably equally mixed, but after weighing the issues, he came down on the other side for a while. We survived what amounted to an undeclared war.

The marital seesaw sometimes provides a welcome relief from painfully mixed feelings.

There are times when Little John is crying and crying and we can't seem to find the right way to help him stop, that John says with terrible intensity, "Sometimes I think this will kill us all." As soon as he says it, all *my* helpless despair ceases, and I become calm and certain, feeling that of course we can go on. I told him tonight, "We just can't *think* like that." (Murray and Murray 1975, p. 97)

Hearing her husband state his despair so passionately freed Mrs. Murray from her own doubts for a while. In this case the seesaw is functional: it allows each parent to reassure the other, even as it magnifies the distance between them.

In other cases, however, seesawing of this sort jeopardizes communication. A person who speaks to one side of our ambivalence—to feelings and urges that we have renounced or subdued—can upset a precarious internal balance. In the most basic arguments in a marriage —over money, sex, relatives, or children—partners often argue with themselves as well as with one another.

One mother, writing a private memoir about another sort of family tragedy—the loss of an adolescent daughter to a religious cult—described the way in which she and her husband fell into opposing roles:

I came to see myself as the pivotal one in the family, the glue that keeps things together. I knew that if anything happened to me there was no one who cared enough or would be patient enough to try to reach Betty. Contact for a couple of years was very tenuous but we did keep in touch with her as she travelled around. My husband considered her as good as dead—irretrievably lost. His pessimism wore very heavily on me. In the morning when I am rested I am usually optimistic but he couldn't allow me even that; his gloom started in the morning and hung over the household. I would angrily tell him, to assure myself as well, that as long as a person is alive anything is possible.

Judith Green resents her husband's despair, in part because it mirrors her own. David undermines her hard-won optimism with his gloom. His refusal to reach out to Betty probably speaks to her own recurring doubts about the girl and the strength of the bond. Naturally she feels bitter.

Either partner's ambivalence raises the emotional stakes of marital conflict. Mixed feelings prevent both husband and wife from listening to one another's ideas, and from hearing the loneliness and the desperation that each is really feeling. Shared, but unexpressed, ambivalence can also—and equally tragically—limit emotional options, prolonging or intensifying a miserable stand-off. Perhaps Mrs. Green's tireless efforts to reach Betty allowed Mr. Green the freedom to act out his despair. He did not have to do *anything*, because his wife was doing everything. If something *had* happened to her, David might have changed; if he could no longer count on Judith to search for Betty, he might have done it himself. Similarly, her optimism may have reinforced his pessimism and vice versa. Each person counterbalances the other; each unconsciously adjusts his or her position to preserve a certain equilibrium.

Seesaws of this sort can help a family. They can also freeze people into roles that allow them to express only one side of their feelings. Catherine Lederman sometimes saw this happening to her and Peter. On many occasions she described to the mothers' group the angry desperation she felt when Ellie fussed. It was always the same sound —not a full-fledged cry, but the discontented "unh-unh-unh" that could continue for hours, even days, on end. Sometimes Catherine exploded, shouting at Peter, at Ellie, and at herself that she hated her daughter and felt like killing her.

Peter never echoed these sentiments. Instead he talked about Ellie's infant charm. Responding to her golden curls and pink-and-white beauty, he described her as "a little ray of sunshine."

Then one day Catherine told us an interesting story. The previous weekend Peter had been tired, anxious, and depressed. He was worried about his work. Ellie fussed for hours, as usual. Finally Peter had erupted: "It's driving me crazy. I feel like killing her."

His outburst horrified Catherine. "Don't say that," she shot back. "It scares me."

"Well," replied Peter more calmly, "how do you think *I* feel when you say it all the time?"

Suddenly she realized how frightening her outbursts must have sounded.

The unwritten rules of the Lederman household allowed Catherine to express extremes of anger, frustration, and even hatred. Catherine's account suggests that both she and Peter paid a price for her freedom. Peter was normally too scared by his wife's rage to examine his own. He could acknowledge only love. Catherine probably failed to realize how much she actually loved her little girl. Peter's explosion expanded their picture of themselves a little. Catherine saw herself protecting Ellie, expressing concern undiluted by irritation. Peter felt some of his wife's anger and frustration. By "being" Peter for a few minutes, Catherine learned something that helped her to change.

A division of emotional labor can make husband and wife feel farther apart than they really are. This happened to the Ledermans and it has happened to our family. The division of domestic labor can magnify difference in somewhat the same way, by offering a mother and a father quite divergent means for coping with a shared tragedy.

The traditional family set-up, in which a man works full-time while his wife assumes primary responsibility for their children, offers a man the opportunity to spend many of his waking hours in a world untouched by private tragedy, however good or bad that world may be in other respects. The diagnosis of a child's disability may reshape his vision of the world, but it rarely changes the way the world sees him; his on-the-job responsibilities continue as before. A job allows both an escape from the child's problems and a setting that helps to establish continuity in life. Outside work helps people to avoid defining themselves exclusively in terms of a child's disability.

Women who stay at home full-time often find that a hurt child fills their lives and dominates their thoughts. ("I got bingo the other night," Barbara Sullivan announced to the mothers' group, "and I didn't even know it. I was worrying about Luke.") There's another side to this, however, and here the women seem to do better. Immersion in a child's immediate needs provides important opportunities for coming to terms with loss. The mother learns routines for caring for her child, finds help, locates services. Daily exposure forces her to confront her own doubts and to re-examine painful feelings. Frequent consultations with doctors and other professionals teach her whatever is known about the child's problems. Under favorable conditions these routines of caring build confidence and help a mother to "work through" her feelings. She becomes the expert on her child.

Almost equally important, ordinary life usually offers a woman more support for child-rearing worries. Some of this support is personal: in many families women cultivate ties with family and friends. They are the connectors and builders and maintainers of networks; they talk to their mothers, sisters, friends, and neighbors about the problems of child care. Cultural norms and stereotypes may also help, by emphasizing the central role that parenting plays in their lives. Problems of child rearing, after all, are the stock-in-trade of mothers' conversation. Magazines that discuss child development and parenting are "women's magazines." A woman who worries constantly about her disabled child is following a cultural script in important ways. If the major crisis in a man's life concerns a child, he may feel far more isolated. Jody's father recalls the way it worked in our family:

My feeling in the first couple of years was that often you were the focus of concern in your family (of course) but also in mine. The assumption was that Jody was in a sense more "your" problem. And so you got the concern and the sympathy.

These role differences can set the stage for certain sorts of conflict. Men who concentrate their energies on a career and do not discuss domestic difficulties with friends or colleagues, receive little preparation for exploring painful feelings at home. More limited exposure to children—to their own and other people's—may permit them to ignore developmental differences that disturb their wives. A woman who sleeps and eats at the pleasure of a handicapped baby may not be able to fit the disability into a larger perspective or to forgive her husband for worrying less than she does.

In describing their husbands' responses to a child's disability many women in the mothers' group use the once psychiatric and now popular term "denial." They see their husbands avoiding two related realities: first, the extent of the actual handicap; and second, their personal feelings—particularly their profound sorrow.

Elizabeth Black is a nurse and knows more than most parents about her daughter's medical problems. "Kimberley had mioclonic seizures. Ninety percent of kids with this type of seizure problem are severely retarded. And then she had the blindness and the cerebral palsy on top of that. So that meant the kid had zilch." She felt that even after the diagnosis her husband, Gary, clung to unrealistic expectations. Early on he had written his parents about Kim's difficulties and concluded optimistically, "We hope that she will learn to read and write." Elizabeth sat down and wrote her own, far blunter, letter. "We know that she will never read or write. We hope that she may learn to walk and say a few words." The debate continued for years. When Kimberley was three Elizabeth observed, "He wants to treat her as though she is normal. But she isn't."

Barbara Sullivan's experience parallels Elizabeth Black's. Barbara says that her husband thinks the doctors are crazy. Patrick still expects Luke to walk. He exercises him every day. He calls to me, 'Hey Barbara, look, he's trying to stand.' And I say, 'Yeah, Patrick, that's great. He's doin' good.' "

Barbara worries about whether Patrick is strong enough to face the truth. She sees the doctors alone, because his angry outbursts embarrass her. She hates passing on bad news. After the doctor told her that Luke was retarded, she postponed telling Patrick for six weeks. She lay awake night after night, running the scene through her head. She was not sure he could take it.

Many women feel that, even after finally acknowledging the extent of a disability, their husbands cannot—or will not—talk about their feelings. Elizabeth Black's experience is not atypical. She described taking Kimberley in for an evaluation because she worried about the little girl's slow development. Gary went with her. The news was shattering. But Gary went off to work, straight from the appointment, leaving her to cope alone with the crying baby and her feelings. "No support," she remarked concisely. He returned home at 10 P.M., after work and overtime.

"How are you?" Elizabeth asked.

"Oh, I'm fine."

"No, I mean how *are* you really?"

"Oh. Well, I guess I'm not feeling so great, after what they said this morning."

She waited, but that was all.

Some women find stoicism reassuring. A husband's stalwart endurance permits such a woman to explore her own suffering, to weep and wonder whether she will make it. One mother says confidently: "He's the strong one. I cry and he holds me." Other women see silent fortitude as an alarming indication of denial or indifference. They long to share their fears and doubts with someone who cares for the child as much as they do. As they struggle alone with agonizing doubt and difficult decisions, their resentment grows. Here for example, Helene Brown recalls her efforts to decide the future of multiply-handicapped eight-year-old Karen:

I had never felt so alone. No one had any advice to offer. My husband and I were faced with another monumental decision, and he had nothing to say. My mother suffered with me, but she was working to support herself; the problem I faced was beyond the scope of her imagining. She was a loving grandmother, but she wasn't a decision-maker. Nor were my uncles, my inlaws.

Daily I turned over and over in my mind my choices, my guilty reasons, and my fears. I was a quitter to want to send her [Karen] away. I was a monster to hate her for what she was doing to my life. I was selfish to want to keep her by me when she would be better off in a place where she could have training and therapy, where she would be like the other children. When I lay in bed, crying night after night beside my sleeping husband, I was harming four lives, not just my own. . . .

In my grief and frustration I grew to hate my silent husband, never realizing that he was suffering too. His dreams were broken. It was his child too—and his unhappy marriage. (Brown 1976, pp. 60–61)

Differences in role and temperament also play into conflicts about expert advice. To begin with, the division of labor in many families puts mothers and fathers in different roles vis-à-vis professionals. In our household, for example, I am the one who generally accompanies Jody to the doctor, the physical therapist, and other appointments. I bring home the latest suggestions. Usually their implementation requires more work and a change of habits. Because few of these suggestions have actually helped Jody much in the past, because most of us resist breaking old habits unless they cause obvious pain either to ourselves or to others, these changes do not occur readily. I find myself in the position of the household nag: "Remember to put Jody's hands on the bottle," "Remember he needs some chin support." Fortunately I am not always the one pushing for change, not always the one who remembers what others forget. Jay pioneered a change from warm milk to cold. He insisted that Jody would drink cold milk if we offered it persistently. He pressed everyone to stop warming bottles and not to give up prematurely. He was right. After a few days Jody had accepted the change, although for some reason we are back to warming bottles these days.

Usually there are practical reasons for one parent—often the mother—to handle the child's appointments alone. In most cases the second adult would need to take time off from work in order to come; that costs time and perhaps money as well. If it means taking a vacation day, the family misses out on a relaxed time together. But this reasonable division of labor often leaves the doctor-going parent "owning" advice and diagnoses that other family members refuse to buy.

Even parents who devise ways to share responsibility for experts and therapies may look at their professional helpers with different eyes. I, for example, tend to respond to authority like a good little schoolgirl. I want to complete the assignment and get a gold star. If someone believes that something might help Jody, I usually jump to provide it. Jay is both more skeptical and more practical. He evaluates each suggestion before deciding to try it; he opposes proposals that involve a lot of work for a small or unlikely payoff. He does not seem to worry much about gold stars.

Conflict over professional advice may have cultural roots. Some women (not all, of course) seek and accept help more readily than men do. Having learned to speak of their feelings, to admit unhappiness, and to accept sympathy and encouragement, they may form a strong, if temporary, bond with a doctor or therapist. A man who fights a losing battle with confusion and despair longs, at some level, for care and comfort. He may envy his wife's ability to solicit support. He may also feel somewhat jealous of the person on whom she depends.

Even if a father asks for support, doctors may not respond comfortably. Despite recent changes in medical school admissions, most physicians are male. Many have learned some ways of offering a woman sympathy, understanding, and perhaps even a limited sort of admiration. They may hesitate to comfort another man (perhaps they need comfort themselves). One father, reflecting on his own encounters with professionals, observed that a kind of locker-room competition seemed to color most all-male relationships. This insight illuminates otherwise puzzling scenes. Take the Wilsons' first encounter with "helping professionals," which occurred when Tony was eight years old. In a few short moments the psychiatrist managed to blame this couple for their son's as yet undefined problems and to disparage, quite irrelevantly, Dr. Wilson's medical specialty.

He began abruptly: "There is nothing really wrong with your boy." Of course! "I have reports here and we have just had a conference about him. He does have some internalized conflicts; for example, his drawings indicate that he is extremely unsure of his own masculinity. But a few months of concentrated work with him will straighten that out with no problem at all."

I saw Jack's mouth forming a question, but the doctor went on. "The problem, as always, is not the child. It is the parents. But you must have known that," he said to Jack. "Primarily the problem is the mother, although the father is by no means without responsibility. For that reason, I always suggest psychotherapy for both parents, with two different therapists, of course."

My hands began to sweat—from guilt, shame, fear? I do not know. But I sat there, cold, with the inner trembling that was to be a part of me for many years.

"If either one of you wishes to come to this office, I will be glad to accept you in treatment and to recommend a colleague for the other. If you wish to make your own choice of two other men, you may certainly do that."

"I don't understand," Jack said. "Could you possibly give us any idea of what has led you to this conclusion, some clue as to what you see is wrong with us?"

Now at last, there was a smile, very small, very tolerant. "Well, doctor, that's not something you can unearth in a few minutes. That is why we are going to need a great deal of time to find out. This isn't like surgery, with a predictable timetable for recovery," he concluded, rather patronizingly. (Wilson 1968, pp. 47–49)

Perhaps the psychiatrist mounted a pre-emptive attack, knowing that many surgeons (this was the late 1940s) looked down on psychiatry.

Competition need not create hostility. Often a doctor and a father take one another's measure and like what they see. But any camaraderie that develops gives the father little emotional support and does not form the basis for a close relationship.

When a husband sees his wife beginning to emerge from her cocoon of despair, ready to join a world beyond the family, he may have mixed feelings. He is glad that she is trying to heal herself and help their child, but he may feel somewhat left out and left behind. Loneliness and jealousy may impel him to attack his wife's support system in one way or another.

One way to bring a husband and wife closer together is to equalize some of their opportunities. In many traditionally organized families this means providing men with more support—from friends, family members, and professionals—and with more chances for constructive involvement with the child, while allowing mothers an arena for achievement outside the family. Changes of this sort bring the paths of husband and wife somewhat closer together and help them to cope in more complementary ways.

Some women report that the support of strangers changed their husbands' attitudes. Elizabeth Pieper saw a change in her husband Carl after their son Jeff had been patterned for a few months. An army of volunteers trooped through the house every day, working with Jeff on structured tasks. Some couples mourn the privacy sacrificed to such a program, but for the Piepers community involvement paved a road out of isolation. "With a modicum of hope, some specific responsibilities, and other people modeling an investment in Jeff, Carl began to show more interest" (Pieper n.d., p. 38).

Sometimes help comes through the support of a group. Mary Olafson writes that when their adopted daughter's development went awry, her husband abandoned all hope. When his wife reported small signs of real understanding, he assured her that she was kidding herself; he believed that Sigrette had no idea what she was doing. Several years later the little girl entered a therapeutic nursery school, and her parents joined a couples' group. The first meetings disappointed them: anxious silences were broken only by pointless bitching. But in time the atmosphere changed. So did Mr. Olafson. He began to listen patiently to Sigrette, to help her find the words she was groping for, and to invent light-hearted games to enjoy with his youngest child (Olafson 1978).

For a man who finds it difficult to face the full extent of the tragedy, an encounter with other men facing similar problems can bring real help. Elizabeth Black described her husband's response to the first couples' group. Gary had come alone—she had thought the meeting was only for husbands. He returned home excited, saying, "When's the next one? I want to go back and cry with that guy." He had listened silently as Andrew Gordon talked about Laurie—about the anger that engulfed him when he contemplated his daughter's problems, about his sense that the disability had changed his own life irrevocably, about the distressing questions surrounding her upcoming operation. Andrew's honesty moved Gary profoundly, although he said nothing during the meeting.

Elizabeth observed that Gary had never really wept for Kimberley and had tried to deny the extent of his daughter's problems. She felt that crying with Andrew would help him to mourn his own loss. Unfortunately, Gary and Andrew never found the opportunity to cry together, because they never managed to be at the same meeting again. Still, Gary gained something important just from listening to Andrew, although he did not get the long-term support that his wife found in the mothers' group.

Fewer men find help of the sort they want in a group. Fathers' groups face several major obstacles to success. First of all, most men work long hours outside their homes. In an effort to accommodate the most common family styles, social workers schedule meetings after dinner. At the end of an eight-to-ten-hour work day, an evening meeting may offer an uninviting prospect: a hurried supper, a cold car trip, an hour and a half with unhappy strangers, dark thoughts, and a delayed bedtime. A substantial minority of men work the evening shift. For them attendance is impossible rather than difficult.

The problems of a fathers' group go beyond the practical difficulty of finding a good time to meet or adding a new activity to crowded lives. Linda Davidson comes to the couples' meetings alone. She says that her husband never talks about his feelings, and she feels that the meetings could help him. He disagrees, asking, "What good will it do to talk about it?" Rosalyn says that Howard shares this view, asserting that "talking won't change anything." A young social worker once described to me the brief career of a group he ran: "The fathers came once, or twice at the most. They said the child had ruined their life, and they left." Noting the lack of real dialogue, he wondered whether social class differences might not bother men more than women. His school draws children from all walks of life: some fathers are executives; others depend on welfare payments and seasonal jobs. He felt that men had trouble seeing beyond these differences in dress, language, occupation, income, and status to the problem they all shared. The women discovered common ground more quickly, perhaps because they defined themselves as mothers first.

When a fathers' group dies for lack of interest or when certain fathers refuse to participate, it is time to look around for other ways to support the men and put them in contact with one another. Sometimes physical labor creates a promising setting. When a school needs new equipment, redecoration, or even storage space, the staff might mobilize a parent labor force. Painting and sawing side by side, fathers may begin to talk about their children. At the very least they learn that other fathers exist, and that they are ordinary, often likable human beings. At best they share feelings and experiences and leave somewhat less isolated than before. Physical work blurs class distinctions. A group, with its emphasis on talk, highlights the differences between the verbally skilled and the less articulate, between the educated and the uneducated. Jobs like painting and building draw on other experiences. The accomplished do-it-yourselfer may be a maintenance man, an ambulance driver, or a lawyer. A setting that requires real physical work creates, if not equality, a more neutral sort of inequality. And those who feel that "talking doesn't change anything" may prefer the more tangible goal of newly painted walls or a king-sized sandbox. Physical labor of this sort can put parents in contact with one another. It also allows men who feel excluded from their children's schooling and care to participate in another way.

The effect of a woman's job on a marriage may be more complex.

In our case I think it has been helpful, although I often feel guilty about not being home full-time and about not spending more time working with Jody, trying to help him to grow. Still, paid part-time work has allowed me successes that I have not achieved with Jody, and has helped me to regain some sense of control over my life. I think that it has helped Jay in some ways, too. For one thing, my latent capacity to earn a living eases a sometimes-deadening responsibility. The necessity of providing for five people, one of whom requires constant care and expensive medical treatment, circumscribes his work options radically—as fatherhood constricts those of many men. The knowledge that I could support the family if necessary lightens this burden a little. On the other hand, Jay has assumed many household reponsibilities to allow me to write and teach; this work, on top of a demanding full-time job, sometimes exhausts him. Every husband and wife pay a price for their choices in this area; they have to decide which costs best fit their emotional budget.

Whatever arrangements parents make to bring their styles of coping closer together, differences will remain. These notes from my diary remind me that our attitudes toward ourselves often shape our response to inevitable differences of temperament, style, and values:

When Liza was a baby I fed and bathed and changed and held her when she cried and took her temperature, and took her to the doctor. Jay whistled tunes to her and made her smile. If she smiled recognition for me, she smiled delight for him. Jay was the recreation director. When I saw him playing with her, both of them caught up in mutual delight, I felt guilty. I remembered that this was a part of parenting, but it seemed that there wasn't much of me left over for play. I was a conscientious mother, and I did enjoy the role. I didn't seem to build these times of play and delight into our time together.

Now, when I see Jay tickling Jody, and making funny noises for his amusement, I feel good—not guilty, not jealous. I still get overly caught up in mechanics and duty—have we remembered the bottle, have we included the green vegetables, have we done the range-of-motion exercises, has Liza practiced the clarinet? Nowadays, though, I arrange for pleasure sometimes, too. And now I'm *glad* that Jay fills a gap, that we complement one another.

I think I've learned to forgive myself for not being everything. I'm glad I don't have to be.

Coping

A child's disability may reveal fault lines in a marriage that no amount of effort and understanding can pave over. Some marriages collapse—and this need not be a bad thing. If a husband and wife's values differ fundamentally, if every act from folding laundry to choosing a therapy program requires an agonizing compromise, if anger washes over even the most sincere efforts at mutual support, it may be time to end things. Even a painful divorce can look good compared to inner death or a life of armed conflict.

Most people do not face such irresolvable conflicts, though. Most marriages survive. I have talked to some parents who feel that a child's disability has deepened their commitment to one another. The bond of shared sorrow and trouble and of happiness wrung from ultimate pain can enhance a relationship. Raising a handicapped child —raising any child—entails a great deal of learning, and learning helps keep a marriage vital.

The problem is to survive present pain and to find ways of alleviating the major stresses confronting a family. At certain points I have called attention to strategies that help people with particular dilemmas. I wish I could contribute more specific techniques for dealing with these difficult problems, and more examples of successful coping. The difficulty is not that few parents cope, but rather, as I have said earlier, that few talk freely about the strains on their marriage, or the ways in which they have learned to meet them. In consequence, I have to rely rather heavily on my own instincts and experience.

Most marital problems are stubbornly complex; even when approached with energy, insight, and humility, fixed patterns resist change. Nevertheless, a few ideas are implicit in what I have said. I want to explore them a little more fully.

First, and perhaps most important, both parents—and perhaps the children as well—need support from outside the family. A major disability strains a family's emotional budget. Each person needs extra sympathy and care, at least during the period of initial adjustment. The two parents find themselves listening to the anguish of older children while seeking special therapy, medical care, and education for the disabled one. They must cope with their own feelings—fear, exhaustion, guilt, sadness, helplessness, inadequacy. Often neither can spare resources for comforting the other. Yet each unhappy parent needs extra love.

No one should expect him- or herself to meet all these needs unaided. This advice, however obvious, is hard to follow. Most women, once they have perceived a need for nurturance, must either meet it or feel guilty. To recognize a limit to love is a further defeat. Rather than accept the fact that her husband needs care that she is too tired and sad to give him, a woman may simply ignore his pain. Rather than expose her own wretchedness to friends, parents, doctors, or social workers, she may ask her husband for more help than he can give.

I do not want to suggest that husband and wife should turn away from each other in seeking other sources of comfort. The sense that they are allies in a common sruggle sustains both of them in the battle against loneliness and despair. But when parents are *getting* support from friends, parents, siblings, and professionals, they feel more able to *give* support in their turn. Like many of the hardest-won insights, this seems banal and obvious.

I have said that outside support can help a man engage with his wife and family. Sometimes outsiders can also assist in the struggle to disentangle painfully mixed feelings. In doing so they may defuse conflicts.

In the spring, shortly after her third birthday, Ellie Lederman died. Probably no one is prepared for the death of any child, but Ellie's shocked those who knew her in a special way: her pink cheeks and baby roundness seemed to promise eternal good health.

No longer an exceptional parent, Catherine stopped coming to the group. Eight months after the wake I called to arrange a visit. I asked how things had gone since the spring.

"Last summer was very hard, but when fall came, things started to get good."

"You missed Ellie a lot?"

"Well, no. I felt tremendous relief and then tremendous guilt about the relief."

Catherine went on to say that Peter had been miserable, too, because he really did miss Ellie very much. His grief intensified her self-reproach. Imagining how I might feel in Catherine's place, I concluded, "That must have made real trouble between you."

"Yes," Catherine said. Things had gotten so bad she and Peter went to see a therapist who had run a couples' group they had belonged to for several years before Ellie's birth. This woman listened to their problem, nodding in recognition: "But that's the way the two of you are. You always polarize things." The realization that they were dealing with Ellie's death as they had dealt with other issues in their lives seemed to break a log jam. "Then," said Catherine, "Peter began to be able to feel some of the relief, and I was able to start missing her some." It helped to trace the outlines of their particular version of the seesaw.

The Ledermans found help because they had the courage to look for it and had built this sort of outside support into their marriage even before Ellie was born. Other couples face their problems alone. Like Catherine and Peter they learn that hurt and misery wear thin the fabric of love. Here Mrs. Wilson describes the volcanic aftermath of the family's first interview with a psychiatrist (see pp. 126–27):

Finally, alone in our room we confronted each other. "Well," Jack demanded, "do you still want to go to a psychiatrist?"

"Not that one. I loathed him."

"Why? Because he put the blame on you?" That was one of Jack's strong qualities; he could be incisively fair and objective even when his emotions were painfully involved. Tonight it was infuriating.

"No. Yes. I don't know. He was so sure about us! But he doesn't know anything about us! He spent only half an hour with us. How could he be so sure?"

"It's a theory," Jack said. "The current theory. It doesn't make sense to me, but then who am I to refute it? I admit I don't know anything."

"It's stupid!" My frustration sprang out in fury. "To think that I pinned my hopes on this! He didn't help us at all. I thought surely he'd have some definite advice about handling the child!"

"Would you be willing to undergo treatment yourself?"

"Yes, if you thought it made sense. But——"

"I've told you that I honestly don't think so. I don't see anything peculiar about us. Not more than most people, anyway," he said with a wry laugh. "But then, I may well be wrong. Certainly I'm not insulted by the idea."

"And you mean that I am insulted?"

"You act that way. If there's anything I despise, Louise, it's false pride. You aren't above criticism, you know."

"I never said I was! This isn't a quesiton of pride! I went to that man for advice. I was honest enough to admit that I needed direction, that Tony is a problem to me; I asked for help. I didn't ask to be told I was crazy."

"He didn't say you were 'crazy.'"

"Now you're sounding like him. You, who had to be forced to go! Remember, I know your opinion of psychiatrists. You've expressed it often enough!"

"I won't deny that I've said harsh things about psychiatrists, that I don't think they are scientists, and a lot of them are fakes. But at least I'll admit they can see some things I can't, if only because they come in contact with these problems by the hundreds and I don't. As a matter of fact, maybe there is something wrong with you, you certainly do mollycoddle the boy. Every time I come home, I find you reading to Tony, placating him, *buying* the peace of the household! Why, are you afraid of him?"

"What do you want me to do, cane him if he doesn't stand at attention. He's eight years old, for heaven's sake! Why don't you stay home, and see whether you can do any better?"

I glared at him, hating him at that moment, hating him for not helping me, even for having fathered this child who was wearing me out. (Wilson, pp. 51–52)

This dialogue suggests the cumulative effect of many strains I have discussed in these pages: fear and fatigue, a baffled and misdirected anger, struggles with a child whose difficult temperament darkens all the lives around him, the intrusions of credentialed experts into family life, unresolved disagreements over etiology and treatment, helplessness and despair.

But just at this moment the Wilsons surprise us. Rather than remaining victims of the blind impulse to lash out in pain, they stop and listen:

Then suddenly as it had come, my anger was gone and there were only fear and a desperate need for comfort. We were like two strangers, blaming each other because we were so frustrated and afraid. "We have such a long way to go," I said at last. "We mustn't let this turn us against each other."

For a long minute he looked at me, his eyes troubled and sad. Then he put his arms around me. "Louise, I'm sorry. But this thing has grown until it's larger than life. Yet truly, I don't believe there is anything in what that man said. If I did I would go back willingly. I do believe there's nothing wrong with Tony except he's tense and high-strung. And we are too, because we take everything too seriously. So he comes by it naturally. Let's just settle down and cultivate a sense of humor and live through his growing pains. I'll try and do my share and we'll work this out together."

Relief poured over me. This strong, good man was not only my husband but a doctor of great skill. Surely he was more to be depended upon than the arrogant, chilly little man we had seen that morning! Hope, which had been high earlier in the day and had been dashed brutally to pieces, came surging back. (Wilson 1968, pp. 52–53)

Insight can not solve every problem, but it is a weapon in the fight to keep unhappiness from corroding love.

The problems of disability crowd in most insistently during the initial period of adjustment—sometimes months, sometimes years. After a while the situation improves. The child grows older. Wounds heal. The family arranges for physical therapy, education, and medical treatment. The child enters school.

During the initial period, parents sense each other's vulnerability and avoid inflicting additional pain. If they blame one another for the disability, common decency usually prevents either from saying so. They skirt around important disagreements and brush the ordinary irritations of daily life under any convenient rug. However serviceable this strategy is in the short run, few couples can avoid conflict forever. Paradoxically, as the family situation improves, one or both partners may begin to speak more freely, and open conflict emerges. When the restraints are lifted, both may be appalled by the contents of Pandora's box.

I speak from my own experience. During the summer Jody was two, Jay and I had two major fights. I remember both of them well. The first occurred when Jane, my college roommate, was visiting us. As the three of us sat in front of the fire, discussing the time that had elapsed since we were last together, he told her how angry he had felt at my response to Liza's painful adjustment to nursery school. His voice trembled with rage. I was embarrassed. I was not accustomed to discussing marital problems with anyone else. I was also surprised: I thought we had talked these issues through long ago, and I was distressed to see that Jay was still angry. The next night we discussed what had happened. Jay apologized for bringing the issue up with someone else present, rather than alone.

I thought the incident was over, but a few weeks later, while other friends were visiting, I found myself teeming with anger and hurt. I asked him to walk to the beach with me; as we sat on the rocks, I voiced all my accumulated resentment and frustration. I was getting no work done. I was the only one who played with Jody, talked to him, or took responsibility for his physical therapy or development. I felt that I was bogged down in family life and constricted by school deadlines, while Jay remained comparatively free. Like Mt. Vesuvius, I erupted with astonishing destructive force. In the aftermath of this explosion I apologized, listened to his hurt, and tried to put what I had said into some sort of perspective. But I had said a lot, and the air cleared slowly. Jay's recollection of these two fights points to issues that surely disturb other couples as well:

I was mad at you for being the person who got all the support—a real father's gripe, I suspect, and something I guess many fathers of normal babies also feel—a mixture of left out and uncared for by a circle of people who think only mothers raise babies. Sexism runs two ways, at least. Jane triggered it off because she's a shared friend, although, irritatingly, more yours. Then, maybe I was mad at you for "winning" over Jody. Okay, I was going to accept him as one of the family, although it was hard for me to do. *Then* imagine how doubly infuriating it was to have you blow up over being constricted and call me "free" when I felt chained to a family with a disabled child—and hadn't wanted the child at home in the first place! A tangled knot.

No one enjoys learning that kindness and concern have masked a good deal of anger and even hatred. Parents weather these storms better if they can see them as a step in the process of recovery, a move toward strength and self-confidence. Resentments are an inevitable part of the adjustment to serious disability, and they are probably an inevitable feature of any shared life.

In this chapter I have explored complex reverberations of one sort of misery in the relationship between two people. Many of these thoughts can be generalized or restated in such a way as to apply to other problems and losses. I want to repeat something I said at the outset: that hearing about the troubles of "exceptional" mothers and fathers often transmits a shock of recognition to many people whose children have suffered nothing worse than a broken leg. "Normal" crises like childbirth, the trials of a new infant, sickness, hospitalization, moving, loss of a job, the death of friends and relatives, all these can strain a marriage in directly parallel ways. The pressure that ordinary trouble puts on people differs only in degree from the strain that comes with the bigger trouble called disability. Our response to adversity is profoundly relative. We make meanings out of what life gives us, and even the most outwardly serene family has its sadness and its wars.

Chapter 6

Brothers and Sisters

GRANTED PERMISSION to play with a cassette tape recorder, two small children decide to create a radio play. The younger speaks as a little girl while her older sister adopts the voice of a stern old witch. Their brother is severely disabled—he cannot walk, talk, or see.

CHILD: I'm gonna pretend that I'm three.
WITCH: A three-year-old. [*Menacingly*] I suppose you can't walk, can you?
CHILD: No.
WITCH: I suppose you can't see?
CHILD: No, but I can talk.
WITCH: Of course you can talk. Everyone can talk. What a foolish thing to say. And if anyone can't talk they should be expelled from this world and dropped into outer space.
CHILD: But my brother can't talk.
WITCH: What! Send him off to outer space.
CHILD: He's in a special school.
WITCH: Send him off to outer space.
CHILD: [*Hesitation and confusion*] I can't do that, because my sister will be angry if we send him out of the house.

WITCH: Well, instead of sending him out of the house you can kill him while you are in the house.

CHILD: Well, then my sister will be sad, and I will be sad too, and my mother will too and my father will too.

WITCH: What does it matter if you are sad? Tell your grandfather to do it. How's that?

CHILD: I don't have a grandfather.

WITCH: What! You don't *have* a grandfather? Everyone has to have a grandfather, foolish child.

CHILD: No. 'Cause my grandfather got shot.

WITCH: He got shot? [*Thoughtful pause*] Shooting, shooting. Yes, shooting. Then ask your grandmother. She can take the gun that was used to kill her husband and use it to shoot your brother. [*Pause*] Go get her this minute. Tell her to kill your brother.

GRANDMOTHER: [*From far away*] What, kill your brother? No succeed.

CHILD: She says "no succeed."

WITCH: She does? *I* shall kill him then. [*Pause*] Bring your brother here.

CHILD: He's in a wheelchair.

WITCH: A wheelchair? [*Voice softening*] Poor child. Bring him here. I shall give him a cup of tea. [*Pause—a wheelchair enters*] Well, hello there. So you can't talk, sir. Well, we'll soon take care of that.

CHILD: But he can sit.

WITCH: And now, I can't blame you. [*Pause*] But perhaps I *do* blame you. Why didn't you use signs, the communication system that would indicate that you wanted to be taught to speak?

CHILD: He goes to a special school.

WITCH: [*Ignoring her*] Now, use the signs, deaf boy. [*To Child*] Since your brother cannot hear. . . .

CHILD: Yes.

WITCH: Deaf children *can* be taught to speak. He is blind *and* deaf so let him put his hands on your lips.

CHILD: Okay.

WITCH: And, so he can learn to speak, I will not think of murdering him. But if he cannot learn to speak in ten years I shall kill him. Okay? In ten years you will be thirteen and he will be fifteen. Bring him to me in ten years. Teach him. Work on it every day except when you are in school.

CHILD: I also go to play group every day.

WITCH: Except when you are in play group and he is in school, work on it. Teach him to speak.

CHILD: But his teachers learn him to speak.

WITCH: Help them. Stop going to play group. Go to school with him and help his teachers to teach him to speak.

CHILD: Well, then my sister and my mother will be mad at me.

WITCH: I don't care. If you do not do it, your brother will be killed.

CHILD: I know, but the teachers don't need any help.

WITCH: Help them. Do as I say or your brother and *you* will be killed. Do it. Go. See you in ten years.

[*Singing*]
Oh, the people who in this world cannot talk
They should be out there.
They are so outrageous.
It's hard to tell whether or not they're mad
 or sad or happy or angry.
They may cry
They may yell
But what is that to me if he cannot talk?
So what if they cannot yell.
Well, he should be killed and he should be
 thrown into outer space.

CHILD: He's gonna grow up.

WITCH: [*Still singing*] And they cannot grow up if they do not speak. . . .

CHILD: He does speak now. He does speak now.

WITCH: [*Still singing*] And I shall be in very bad shape if he does not learn to speak. And so. . . .

CHILD: He can learn to speak now. He was too shy to speak before. He didn't want to speak because he was too shy before.

WITCH: [*As though coming out of a trance*] That was a long time, me singing. Ahh [*Strange, choked noises, suddenly—croaking, gasping voice*] I can't speak any more, I got laryngitis. Well, now, I was seventy when you met me and now I happen to be eighty. Well, I suppose I would have lost my speech anyway. So, you say your brother has learned to speak. Well now, have a big party at your house, and I hope the singing and dancing will know no bounds. I shall come to it. And I hope you are doing well in high school. Ahh. [*More gasps, choking*]

The feelings and ideas that these two sisters play out in their fantasy are not readily visible in their lives. They express occasional concern or curiosity about their real brother's difference. They answer their friends' inevitable questions with matter-of-fact accuracy, seeking adult help if the inquiries go deeper than their own information. They mention feelings of anger and confusion, protectiveness and embarrassment from time to time. They take note of his needs, and occasionally include him in their games. For the most part their behavior suggests that their main interests lie elsewhere, with their schools, their friends, their play and learning, their parents and one another.

Yet plainly their brother's handicap evokes powerful fantasies. Momentous feelings are at work. The older girl, assuming the role of a malevolent old woman, sings of sorrow, frustration, and a rage which sometimes bubbles up with murderous intensity. The younger child counters these alarming emotions with protective concern and appeals to authority. Confronted with the reality of the brother himself, the older child substitutes dreams of rehabilitation for fantasies of violent destruction. Terrifying questions about responsibility shadow this vision. The two children struggle with these together: How much do they owe their brother? How much can they leave to others? A guilty determination to sacrifice themselves on his behalf wars with an insistence that parents and teachers assume ultimate responsibility.

At the eleventh hour, as the younger girl engineers a happy ending, each child introduces a new "explanation" of the disability—one that relates it all the more closely to their own lives. Actually, announces the smaller, my brother is not so different from me as he seems. He fails to speak not because of some mysterious organic handicap, but simply because, like so many other children, he is shy. Concern and protectiveness slide over into identification; seen from a different angle, the major difference between brother and sister becomes a similarity.

The older child astonishes us with a different sort of "theory." As soon as the mute boy learns to speak, she, as the witch and villain, begins to lose her own voice. She chokes and gasps, her words barely audible. She reassures herself weakly: "Well, I suppose I would have lost my speech anyway." Her quavering voice tells another story: as the boy regains his powers, she loses hers. Is she perhaps wondering whether her own good health has been bought at her brother's expense.*

Parents care deeply about the ways in which a disability has touched the lives of able-bodied sisters and brothers. As a parent myself, I know that much as mothers and fathers wish to understand their children's viewpoint, we shrink from the less pleasant side of the truth. We want to believe that our normal children have grown wiser and more compassionate through the family's trials. If we must acknowledge that they have suffered too, we would like to believe that this suffering is not our fault.

---

* Other siblings of disabled children speak of parallel fantasies. Karl Greenfeld tells his father, Josh, about a recurring dream:

> You [Josh] die. And then Noah suddenly becomes normal. So Foumi [his mother] goes and kills the fathers of the other kids in our day-care center. But those kids stay brain-damaged. And Foumi gets caught and has to go to jail. (Greenfeld 1978, p. 365)

Brothers and sisters worry less about the question of parental culpability. Most long to hear their own feelings described and affirmed. A boy whose brother is retarded hungrily devours Victoria Hayden's reminiscences about life with her deaf sister. Ms. Hayden's loneliness and anger comfort him, because they mirror his own. A graduate student whose teenage sister has Downs syndrome recoils in shock from the wistful resentment siblings express in another book. Distressed, she challenges the teacher who recommended this study: "I've always loved my sister. Am I weird, or is there something wrong with them?" The message that reassures some people disconcerts others.

My primary goal in this chapter is to describe the pain and difficulty of growing up in a family with a severely disabled brother or sister. Like the two little girls I have just quoted, most children grapple with more dark feelings and troubling fantasies than they show. A disability chafes at sensitive points—points that change as time passes. Sadly, acknowledging children's pain often causes parents new anxieties of their own, particularly if it forces them to re-examine their own part in the on-going family drama. Again, I speak autobiographically.

In the first section of this chapter I explore some of the ways boys and girls respond to a sibling's disability. As I pointed out in earlier chapters, children's feelings parallel those of adults in many ways—they endure their own fear, anger, guilt, and loneliness. But children stand in a different relationship to the family and the disability. In consequence some problems loom larger for them than for their parents. Out of many stories I see a few common themes: embarrassment, identification, confusion.

Parents are extraordinarily vulnerable to their children's distress. I note in the second section of this chapter some of the obstacles confronting a parent who wants to help his children flourish in the face of their brother's or sister's disability. A child's perspective on the family difficulties can threaten the beliefs that enable parents to survive from day to day. His unhappiness can sharpen their guilt. Beyond this, parents often share with other adults in the child's life—teachers, neighbors, and grandparents—a mistaken sentimentality about the possibilities for shielding children from unpleasant feelings.

A disability usually shifts the organization and alignments of a family, as well as the feelings and expectations of parents and children. I talked about this mainly from the parent's point of view in chapter 5. In the third section of this chapter I describe the ways those changes in family structure affect able-bodied children. Often the disability sets children apart from one another, leaving the normal child yearning for a brother more like himself. As with other kinds of serious trouble—death, divorce, sickness—it also casts children in the role of pint-sized parents long before they would ordinarily assume this sort of responsibility for another person.

Despite all the problems of growing up with a disability, most families function adequately: normal children usually develop into normal adults. In the fourth section of this chapter I look at some of the experiences that seem to help children thrive in the face of difference in the family.

Responses to the Disability

Brothers and sisters of handicapped children feel the tug of what almost amounts to two different cultures. They stand with one foot in the world of normal classmates and the other in their exceptional family. They live among ordinary children; they long for simple fellowship with others their own age. Yet playmates sometimes treat a handicapped child cruelly. Forced to mediate, to explain, and sometimes to choose between conflicting loyalties, brothers and sisters can end up angry at the normal world, the disabled child, and themselves. Richard, a college student whose younger brother suffers from severe hearing loss and deformities of both arms, describes a recent crisis:

This past summer I worked at a playground. One day a bunch of kids and I were playing. Everybody stands in a circle and throws a ball to one another. And all of a sudden these little kids started dropping away from the circle. I was playing with them, so I did not really pay much attention to why some kids were dropping out. It was just slowly getting more and more quiet and I turned around: my brother was standing there. Of course, this is summertime, he has short sleeves on and these kids, even now I am tempted to say these little creeps, it really upset me—they made a circle around my brother, just made a circle around him and started looking at him and I just did not know what to do. On the one hand I felt like saying, and it upsets me now to think that I would say what I wanted to say, "Jim, hurry up and get out of here." Even now that I say it, it is totally disgusting and at the same time I wanted to say to all those little kids, "If you don't move now I am going to throw you all over the fence." Even now I have not resolved it—more than anything else, it shows me that I have not really come to terms with the whole thing. Furthermore, it gives me some appreciation for what my brother has to go through. He has to go every place. (Klein 1972)

At such a moment, emotions do not fit tidy categories. Loneliness, anger, guilt, embarrassment, identification, and confusion merge and battle with one another. Surrounded by people, Richard felt alone: his brother's presence set him apart from the normal children he supervised. The children's astonished horror widened the distance between him and his brother. Inwardly he raged against everybody who had put him in this uncomfortable position. At the same time, he reproached himself for disloyalty. Sharing his brother's stigma for a moment, he saw Jim's life through more understanding eyes. Even as the incident enhanced his feeling of identification, it shamed and confused him.

I have talked in earlier chapters about some of children's feelings— about their fears, their anger, their loneliness, and their guilt. Just as parents fear for the health of their normal children in the wake of a disability, very young children may worry about "catching" the impairment—particularly if they learn that it was caused by a disease like rubella or meningitis. Everyone, big and little, has a magical sector of the mind. Knowing how much they share with their family, children feel at risk themselves. Older children develop more adult-sized worries. If their sibling needs lifelong care or supervision, they may look nervously ahead to their parents' old age, wondering whether the responsibility will eventually fall to them. Even a mild disability, which poses little threat to ultimate independence, may shadow their vision of parenthood and make them afraid to have children of their own.

Children feel angry: at parents, at the disabled child, at the wider world, at God or fate, perhaps at all four. Some blame their mother and father for the disability itself (just as they blame them for any new baby). A handicap creates unusual needs; many children envy their brother or sister this special attention. And older children may rage secretly about the sometimes colossal sums of money spent on diagnosis and therapy—resources that might otherwise finance family comforts and college tuition.

Anger and jealousy can generate guilt. The disability seems at one level to excuse provoking behavior and to explain special privileges and expenditures. When feelings fail to follow this generous logic, when a child finds himself yelling and teasing instead of helping, self-reproach seems nearly inevitable.

A child's disability can isolate brothers and sisters in several ways. Inside the home, the disability sometimes inhibits communication. A mild or ambiguous handicap may go unlabeled or even unacknowledged. The sense that an important subject is taboo—and the anger that comes with such a realization—cuts children off from their parents, creating embarrassment and reserve. Even in households where candor reigns, children hesitate to reveal ugly feelings. The able-bodied children in very small families sometimes endure a particularly poignant sort of loneliness, a longing for a "real" brother or sister with whom they might share more, one who could reflect their own feelings and experiences.

In dealing with the wider world of friends, classmates, and teachers, able-bodied children at times feel painfully different. Their family diverges from the white picket fence ideal of *Fun with Dick and Jane*. Friends ask questions about an older retarded sister who cannot read and plays with toddler toys. Strangers in a restaurant stare at the wheelchair. Children complain that a difference in the family compromises their own normality, making it harder to be a regular kid leading a regular life.

Children and grown-ups play variations on some of the same themes. Like their parents, sisters and brothers have good reasons to feel afraid, angry, guilty, and isolated. Age and family position shapes experience, however; some issues loom larger for children than for parents. Specifically, brothers and sisters talk about embarrassment, identification, and confusion much more than adults do.

Even boys and girls who love and enjoy their handicapped siblings sometimes feel embarrassed by obvious differences. Elizabeth Black told the mothers' group that her daughters—fifteen and sixteen—take Kimberley's handicaps in stride and include her in their teenage antics. Their friends play with Kim too, responding to her as they might to any other baby. But Elizabeth remembered an occasion when they were all out shopping. The drug that controlled Kim's seizures had left her limp and floppy. She slumped over in the stroller, looking odd. One of the girls kept asking her mother to straighten her up until Elizabeth had to reply, "Let her go. She's okay. I can't always be straightening her up." She knew the curious glances of passers-by upset her daughter.

In a paper written for a special education course, the older brother of a mildly retarded boy recalls that his embarrassment increased with the passage of the years:

When I was younger I knew he was different because my parents treated him in a slightly different way.

I was embarrassed and hurt when people said he was retarded. When they would ask, I would always say, and do say, no. We had a pretty good relationship at home, make-up and play silly games and such. Although I guess I could be cruel to him—I still loved him.

It was getting more difficult when I grew older, though. I grew more and more ashamed of him and our relationship dropped rapidly to the point where it is now. I guess he knows that he embarrasses me in a way, so he stays away. We call occasionally, but would never be together at any time unless it's in one of our parents' homes.

The long unresolved embarrassment which this young man describes derives in part from the ambiguity of his brother's handicap. Explanations were difficult because no one had ever diagnosed the problem, and neither his parents nor the professionals could agree on a label. Joan Hundley, describing her older son Roley's difficulties with autistic David, mentions a similar difficulty: lacking a diagnosis, Roley could not explain David's odd behavior to his friends (Hundley 1971, p. 21).

When strangers turn their heads to examine a wheelchair, hearing aid, or walker, the other children in the family often read criticism or distaste into their intercepted glances. Marge Helsel, now a professional in special education, remembers that at age eleven, "I was certain that everyone was looking at my brother with his obvious handicap and then wondering what was wrong with the rest of us" (Helsel 1978, p. 110).

Just learning that kindly concern underlies much of the curiosity can make a real difference. In the mothers' group Linda Davidson described a recent shopping trip, "Last Wednesday was a half day at school, so I took the girls to the Mall. I picked up Lauren at school, with Marianne already in the car. She took one look at the carriage [a wheelchair, recently acquired] and said 'Are you taking *that*?'" Linda knew that Lauren was concerned about looking different, but she pointed out that she could not very well carry Marianne around the Mall in her arms. Then Lauren asked whether Marianne had to wear her protective helmet. When Jennifer got into the car at the elementary school, the two girls exchanged significant looks, and the questions started all over again. "Do you have to take that?" "Does she have to wear this?" "Then when we were walking around the Mall an older couple came up and began to talk. (I find that older people are more compassionate than people our age.) They asked about the chair, and whether there were funds for things like that. They were really interested and concerned. I thought the girls would be embarrassed, but as we walked away they both exclaimed, 'Now weren't they *nice!*' "

Children sometimes handle embarrassment by putting a little distance between themselves and their brother or sister. Doreen Collins recalls a train trip in which retarded Kim misbehaved. Her younger brother quietly changed his seat, presumably hoping that strangers would connect him with a more ordinary family (Collins and Collins 1976, p. 163). Parents help their children by acknowledging these feelings and allowing the child some control over the situation. Betty Pendler (chapter 4) complied with her seven-year-old son's request that she leave retarded Lisa at home when she picked him up from Sunday School. She noted later, with pride and pleasure, that he voluntarily included her in some other activities.

Children conceal embarrassment, noticing their parents' efforts to include the handicapped child on outings. Hearing the grown-ups criticize strangers who stare at the family, children may wonder how their mother and father would judge *their* most private thoughts. This is too bad, because actually most parents can understand children's self-consciousness even if they do not share it. Memories of our own childhood help us to imagine their agony. At least, I have found this to be true for me. Sometimes in restaurants, for example, I ask the waitress to warm Jody's bottle. Once Liza told me that this made her uncomfortable. I did not then understand why, but I remembered small things that had embarrassed me as a child, and felt a bond with her—one that was strangely heightened by her failure to understand my particular childish agonies when I described them.

A couple of weeks after this conversation I was unloading the wheelchair from the car at the swimming pool. Since I could not push Jody and carry all the gear, I handed Liza his bottle. Then I remembered the restaurant incident and asked if she would rather carry the towels and suits. She nodded, and we smiled at one another. I felt happy about having made things a little easier for her.

Remembering the developmental basis for such feelings helps parents to accept their children's embarrassment. Nearly all children go through stages of raging conformity. They want regular clothes, regular language, regular skills, and, yes, a regular family. They feel embarrassed by a mother who works—or by one who stays home—by a father who drives a truck, or by one who flies a private plane. Neighborhood norms assume disproportionate importance in their lives. If parents observe a new reluctance to include the handicapped child in play with friends or trips to the store, they need not conclude that they have failed, or that these attitudes will endure forever.

Frances Grossman's (1972, p. 105) study of eighty-three college students with retarded brothers or sisters suggests that there is a strong element of identification in these feelings of embarrassment. In her sample, young people with a retarded sibling of the same sex reported more embarrassment than those whose sibling was of the opposite sex. This makes sense, and it reminds us that children resemble the handicapped child more than parents do—and identify with him in a special way. Diane, a college student recalls:

I can remember being embarrassed about Cathy because she is really, I guess, quite upsetting to see for the first time. . . . I can remember in a bus terminal we had to spread a blanket on the floor so Cathy could crawl around and get a bit of exercise. A crowd gathered and I hated the people so much. I was just terribly embarrassed and I wanted to hide Cathy and I wanted to protect her from these people who were glaring, although she certainly did not know what was going on. (Klein 1972)

Diane longed to shield Cathy from the staring crowd, although she saw that Cathy's handicap provided her with all the protection she needed: Cathy did not recognize the problem. This was no comfort to Diane; her desire to hide Cathy merged with a wish to hide herself. Staring at Cathy, the passers-by assaulted Diane as well.

The curiosity of onlookers probably embarrassed Cathy's parents far less. They had, after all, chosen to spread the blanket on the floor; they could end the scene at will by gathering up the child and returning her to chair, bench, or lap. They had power that Diane lacked. Beyond that, grown-ups have a certain distance from such a scene. Children define themselves through their families. They see the resemblances between themselves and their brothers and sisters—similarities in physique, temperament, taste, aptitude. A handicap may lead them to question their own health and capability. One young man told Frances Grossman about the way his mildly retarded older brother imperiled his vision of himself: "When he does something which reminds me of what I did, it just makes me feel worse about what I am" (Grossman 1972, p. 111).

Children discover resemblances between themselves and their handicapped family. The larger community reinforces an inevitable tendency to identify with their brothers and sisters by seeing the family as a social unit, generalizing about family members, and expressing surprise when children differ markedly from one another. Carol Michaelis bitterly recalls the woman who refused to believe that her son the Little League star could have a retarded brother (Michaelis 1974). Catherine Lederman encountered the same prejudice. Her neighbors, the O'Haras, have three children: the eldest is retarded; the second is deaf, but of normal intelligence; the third is an ordinary kindergartner. Recently a new acquaintance told her that *all* the O'Hara children were retarded. Knowing this statement to be false, she began to wonder about the expectations awaiting her own son.

Victoria Hayden introduces her autobiographical analysis of the impact of handicap on "the other children" with these words: "All the members of my family are disabled. But most people recognize only the disability of my deaf sister" (Hayden 1974). Robert Meyers notes more than once that his brother's retardation, and the family's response to it, "retarded my development" as well (Meyers 1978, p. 36). Their strong language shocks us into recognition of their pain. It also reveals a powerful identification.

Identification with a handicapped person creates a particular sort of vulnerability. It also can impel children to assist and comfort their brother or sister, and to work toward understanding a different perspective. One young woman spoke of an intense interest in her college's special education courses, and a hunger for insight into her brother's experience. She wishes *she* could have a seizure, "just to understand what it's like." She says he whimpers during the seizures and she worries that he may be in pain (Grossman 1972, p. 134). This young woman's impulse to step into her brother's shoes speaks of a wonderful kind of fellow feeling. It also suggests exceptional confidence in her own strength. She and her brother share a name, a heritage, and a family; she would like to share his experience if she could.

Identification can help children to see events from the point of view of a handicapped brother or sister, as Jay and I have learned from our daughters. I remember once Caitlin asked about the times before she was born, when she was "inside Mummy's tummy." Jay told her that he had been worried that she might be blind or brain-damaged like Jody, that he was so relieved and happy when she was born and he could tell she was okay. Liza stopped him and said that he should not talk that way in front of Jody, that she thought it would hurt his feelings. We did not know, she said, how much Jody understood. If he did sense our meaning she did not think he would feel very good about hearing his father talk that way.

Like adults, children puzzle over questions raised by the disability. No one fully "understands" the handicap at first. Each of us wonders why it had to happen to our family and what it will mean for our lives. Parents ask some questions no doctor can answer. Nonetheless, in coming to grips with confusion, parents have two advantages children lack.

First, and probably most important, parents are fully grown adults. Their understanding, although perhaps temporarily impaired by shock, sorrow, fear, and anger, is mature. They *know* far more than their children—about the workings of the body, about growth and development, about disability, about death and responsibility, about getting help. Age and experience help them to understand what they are told, to recognize confusion, and to ask questions. Their children may be very young at the time the doctor makes a diagnosis or when they themselves notice a difference in the family. Terms like "brain-damage" mean very little to them. Some have never heard of the brain before; they cannot grasp its central function. A three-year-old, hearing that disease caused her brother's blindness, worried about her own frequent head colds. A two-year-old, learning that his sister did not walk "because her brain was hurt before she was born," imagined a continuing pain inside his sister's head. A college student told Frances Grossman that because both her aunt and her sister were retarded, "I always wondered when I was younger if there was some relationship in our family—was someone meant to be retarded in each generation or something; this used to bother me, I think" (Grossman 1972, p. 134).

In addition to the important gaps in their understanding and information, children lack a first-hand source of information. Parents take their handicapped children to doctors, teachers, and therapists. These experts form opinions and answer some questions. Able-bodied children, even if they accompany them on such visits, rarely ask questions of their own. They make what sense they can of overheard conversations and rely on their mothers and fathers for basic information.* If parents cannot answer their questions, few have a better resource.

Parents are often their children's best informants. They know them intimately and can guess at the limits of their understanding. Nonetheless, children, like parents, occasionally need more objective, distant sources of information. Clare Potter told the group, for example, that Grant has never asked her directly about Melissa's problems "although we've always been very open with him." One day he visited a friend while she went shopping. Their baby, although younger than Melissa, was toddling around. Grant considered the matter and asked his mother's friend, "Why Lisa walk and Melissa not walk?"

For reasons best known to themselves, children sometimes hesitate to ask the basic questions—and many scowl uncomfortably when parents themselves start an open-ended discussion. Some parents interpret this silence as indifference or "acceptance," but to me it parallels the teenager's reluctance to talk about sex. The subject is plenty interesting, but some feelings retreat from parental inspection.

Confusion and misinformation come to light more frequently as statements than as questions. Elizabeth Pieper, whose son Jeff cannot walk, remembers three incidents from his sister's early childhood.

One day when Julie was four she threw herself at my legs, clasped them tight, and declared that she would put me in jail forever. I had broken her brother so that he could not walk!

Later, at five, she refused to say her prayer one night and lay glaring at the wall.

"I hate him," she announced with deep anger.

"Who?" I asked.

"I hate him. I can't help it." Finally she flipped onto her back and fastened a fierce glare on the ceiling. Pain bound her body tight. "I can't help it. I hate God. He made my brother crippled."

* Many conversations between parents and doctors could confuse and frighten a child. For example, Gil Joel, who has cerebral palsy, recalls some of what he heard doctors tell his parents before he was able to speak: "His brain is being crushed." "All he needs is a few electric shock treatments applied to the soles of his feet." "He'll outgrow it by his seventh birthday." "Don't feed him. Don't bathe him. Put him in a dark room and forget about him" (Joel 1975, p. 12). Fortunately, this was a long time ago. But it is still true that adults who are themselves upset may fail to consider what a child is hearing as they talk.

Even in her pain I could not comfort her. The authority of my own religious belief was too heavy upon me. One does not defy one's Maker. As I fumbled to clarify our theology, I fervently regretted having sent her to Sunday School where she learned that human sin caused imperfection, and that imperfection is a symbol of sin.

Later the same year, she came home from kindergarten and announced that she knew what had happened to Jeff. Her teacher had told her. I did not eat good food for my baby and that is why he turned out bad. It was an open, forgiving statement. Six years later she may still believe it. The college texts I have seen on birth defects are barely more accurate or less simplistic. Neither are the public-service announcements on television. I still do not know what to say to her, and she might not believe me anyway, in the face of the prevailing public education. And so for now I let it go. (Pieper n.d., p. 85)

In this case a mother's own puzzlement prevents her from disputing a child's faulty theories. On other occasions, a parent can clear up a misunderstanding once she has discovered it. I remember that when Cait was two she insisted that her friend Brendan was a girl, despite all I could say to the contrary. I attributed this confusion to the ambiguities of modern dress and hair style: both children wore overalls and short straight hair. I suggested she accompany Brendan to the bathroom, hoping to settle his gender once and for all. A thorough examination failed to alter her opinion. Then she said, "Brendan can walk. Boys don't walk." Of course! Jody could not walk, and Jody was the only other little boy in her small world. Her cousins, our next door neighbors, Liza's friends, and all the visiting preschoolers except Brendan, happened to be girls. *They* walked, but Jody did not. So Caitlin had concluded, logically enough, that only girls walked.

Once I understood her ideas, we discussed other boys who walked —all the ones she knew were older, unfortunately. I explained that Daddy, like Jody, was male. That he had once been a little boy, and that he had walked. We looked at boys walking in stores and on the street. She finally agreed: Many boys did walk. Then, of course, she raised the next question: Why didn't Jody?

Parents deal with children's confusions one at a time, as they come up. Lengthy prophylactic explanations, which seek to answer every question before anyone asks it, work no better for disability than for sex. Children are almost bound to incubate a few alarming fantasies before their developing understanding brings the truth within reach or a helpful adult clarifies the matter.

Parents

Like the turn of a kaleidoscope, diagnosis of a disability alters the composition of a parent's world. Everything, and most especially the able-bodied children, looks different. Parents may hover over their normal offspring, afraid that the same malign fate that has felled one child will take aim at another. Or they may focus intensively on the hurt child, taking everyone else's welfare for granted. They may argue and negotiate with one another, or they may find their attitudes reasonably well matched. In all events, they usually count heavily on their other children's "wellness." On a purely practical level, the disabled child absorbs a great deal of time, energy, and money; a crisis with another child drains over-spent resources. Perhaps equally important, the disability gobbles up the emotional savings allotted for "family problems." The mother who is asked to face further difficulties may simply freeze in disbelief—or begin to see herself as a modern day Job. Marilyn Segal, whose daughter Debby has cerebral palsy, writes that when the doctors decided her older son might have a spinal cord tumor, "I refused to let myself comprehend what they were saying. Nothing serious could be wrong with Ricky. Our family had already received its portion of heartache." Her husband's mind worked differently. Perhaps Debby's problems had worn him down to the point where he almost expected further disasters. For the first time in their life together, his wife saw him cry (Segal 1966, pp. 57–58).

Parents depend on the other children to shore up their sagging morale. Clara Claiborne Park writes:

It would be hard indeed, in today's climate of opinion, for parents of a seriously deviant first-born child not to feel they were in some way responsible.

But we were lucky; we had Sara, Becky, and Matt. Responsive as well as intelligent, they functioned well in school, in the neighborhood, and at home. If it is fair to lay failure at the parents' door, as much should be done for success. It was of course possible that our success, like Mrs. I.'s, could be dismissed as a facade, its hollowness shown up at last by this small, atypical baby. Occasionally, in nightmare descents into compulsive objectivity (after all, objectivity was part of our syndrome) we might see it that way. But these nightmares could not stand the light of day. A look at our children would dispel them. We were proud of them. We had done a good job with them. We knew it, and knew that others knew it. This knowledge and this pride sustained us as we read the formulations of the Bettelheims of this world—this, and a certain natural skepticism which had been with us even before Elly made us need it. (Park 1967, pp. 130–131)

Like Clara Park, Tony Wilson's mother defended herself against psychiatrists' accusations by pointing to her younger children. Their achievements and vigorous health sustained her. They encouraged her to resist the psychiatrists' formulation, to believe that she had not, after all, driven her son crazy.

These women endured more brutal assaults than most parents—criticisms that were no less devastating for being incorrect in the light of subsequent research. Even when all the accusations sound inside our own heads, we need reassurance about our parenting. Better than anyone else, our healthy children encourage us to see ourselves as normal human beings. We invest heavily in their well-being.

Our children's loving, protective feelings warm our hearts, but we resist the other side of their reaction: anger, jealousy, loneliness, or embarrassment. However much we long to accept these emotions and the stark need with which we hear them expressed, however much we want to comfort and reassure, to say that there are no "bad" feelings, but only bad acts, still our children strike our Achilles heel. Rosalyn Gibson speaks in the mothers' group of the hurt she feels as she watches her older children with Nancy. On nights when she waitresses, the rest of the family divides up the evening chores. The children pitch in willingly enough—except that no one wants to feed Nancy. They are not eager to be with her at other times either, to mind her or to play. Sadly Rosalyn notes, "And they've gotten to tiptoeing past her—and so do I. Now that's awful, tiptoeing past a child who is blind." When Nancy hears a footstep, she fastens herself onto the passerby, "just as though she has suction cups on her hands." If they disengage themselves, no matter how gently, she screams for forty minutes or more. Rosalyn understands her children's eagerness to avoid such scenes (she sees herself following their example), but she also wants some evidence that they enjoy their little sister.

Rosalyn Gibson saw her children's feelings and felt sad. Many other families avoid open confrontations. When no one disturbs the surface calm, parents may wrongly conclude that all is well. Devin

Thornburg, who interviewed families with disabled children in order to learn about the feelings of able-bodied brothers and sisters, describes a case in point:

At one point, Ms. T. was remarking that she "didn't feel that the children had any trouble dealing with Lucas," and I noticed Cindy quietly shaking her head on the other side of the room. I decided to pursue her silent dissension when the parents had left. . . .

I thought that I might help Cindy out by asking about her quiet disapproval, when her mother had been speaking. She was silent for a few moments, then said in a low voice:

"I think Mama's wrong. I mean, I can remember a lot of times when I couldn't do the things I wanted or have them see that I could do things like. . . . Well, there was this one time when I got all A's on my report card! All A's! That's something for me. Anyway, I came running through the front door and Mama was all excited so that I thought that she already knew. Well, it turned out that Lucas had said his first word, and Mama was so happy. So, I said, "Mama, I got all A's, I got all A's," and she said, "Oh, that's nice. Guess what? Your brother said so-and-so today." And went on and on about it. But I didn't say nothin'. But that really hurt me, you know." (Thornburg 1978, pp. 24–25)

Cindy allowed her mother to believe that none of the children "had any trouble dealing with Lucas," although she told the interviewer a different story. Perhaps she realized her parents' vulnerability.

A student whom Jay and I taught in our special education course helped me to see silences of this sort from the child's point of view. This young man—I will call him David—had grown up in the shadow of another sort of tragedy: his sister had died when she was seven years old. David felt that his parents expected him to redeem their devastating loss, to agree, even to prove, that his sister's death had meant something. "As a sibling who has lived through that experience, there was a good ten years that people didn't talk about certain aspects. There is a whole mythology that siblings are put under pressure to live up to, as far as how it strengthened the family. Well, that's part of it, but there is an awful lot more there."

After listening to this story in class, Jay summed up the message that David got from his parents:

JAY: You mean "By God this experience will have redeeming merit for you?"

DAVID: Yeah. "By God, I better find some meaning in this." You don't want to deny that altogether, either. You don't want to say that there was no value in the experience whatsoever. But I think more often than not there is a *real pressure* to live up to the parents' expectation in that area.

JAY: Well, all of us are making meanings out of these things. And the parents are struggling to make meanings which are very painful and sometimes real triumphs, but they sometimes forget that the meanings they've made are not the meanings that the children are making. So that one could see both things. It was perhaps not at all bullshit from their point of view, but the confusion was to suppose that that would be the meaning for you.

Our children's views sometimes threaten the beliefs that enable us to cope with our situation. Even after we become more comfortable with ourselves, our children's unhappiness touches us deeply. We love them, and we feel responsible for their pain. Sometimes our guilt defies reason. Karin Junker, for example, feels that she has short-changed her son Sten. She remembers the afternoon long ago when he showed off his brand-new sister to a friend. Touched by Sten's enthusiastic interest in the baby, Mrs. Junker choked up. No one knew then that Boel was autistic.

Later I was to remember this too, how I was forced to fail him in his pride. I don't believe he himself has ever thought about it. But I have never been able to forget the eager eyes of the seven-year-old, the proud gestures outside my window that snowy afternoon. (Junker 1964, p. 31)

It is as though she has cheated him of the sister who might have responded to his love.

Joan Hundley blames herself for her son Roley's difficult childhood.

My first marriage, years earlier, had been a wartime one, and I had never been happy. Roley was born at the end of the Second World War and the first five years of his life had been most disturbed. My unhappy marriage had left its mark on him.

Having little David made it impossible for me to devote the necessary time to either of my other children. Ellen got by well enough, but Roley could never take little David's presence with ease. Many times when I should have talked with Roley I was either not available or just too tired. Some of Roley's friends, however, took to little David without worry. One of them said he had the greatest admiration for any kid who could get away with urinating where he pleased, paid no attention to authority, could blow like a trumpet, and hop as if on a pogo stick.

Not long after he joined the Air Force Roley bought a car on hire-purchase. One Friday, while trying to drive overnight from Adelaide to Melbourne on week-end leave, he smashed the car up. He was in the hospital for two weeks in South Australia and didn't let me know because he didn't want to worry me. He knew that no one else could feed little David. When I heard about this I felt awful. I knew Roley needed me. (Hundley 1971, pp. 45–46)

Unblinkingly honest analyses of the problems that a disability visits on normal siblings may leave parents feeling angry, depressed, or guilty. Glowing accounts of warmth, joy, and cooperation in other exceptional families deepen their gloom, convincing them that they don't measure up. The notion that parents' attitudes shape children's response to disability inflicts special pain on the parent who allows himself to hear the seamy side of his children's feelings.

All sorts of factors, then, may raise barriers to talk within the family. There is the parents' own vulnerability—their need to protect themselves from the darker side of their own feelings, and their reliance on comforting myths about the disability. There is the sense of responsibility parents feel for their children's experience—their desire to provide their children with a happy family and to avoid burdening them with sadness and loss. Finally, there is the cultural myth—perpetuated by parents and professionals alike—that holds parents responsible for their children's attitudes. All these factors help to convert children's normal reactions into a threat to their parents' happiness and create misunderstanding between the generations.

Such a situation can leave children alone with their feelings. Even outside the family they encounter subtle—and not so subtle—pressures to love their handicapped brother or sister unreservedly. Children's books about handicap, when they touch on anger, jealousy, fear, or guilt at all, tend to emphasize the transitory nature of such emotions and to end on a determined and upbeat note of acceptance and warmth. Adults approach children's darker feelings with tremendous caution, fearing to raise issues they won't be able to handle.

Fortunately many children tell their parents and teachers how they feel anyway. Sara Blaine described to our group a candid exchange with her teenage daughter. Rebecca was preparing for a friend's visit, while Kenneth, who is deaf and multiply handicapped, misbehaved. Sensing Rebecca's growing fury and embarrassment, Sara asked how she might help. When Rebecca remained silent, Sara guessed her thoughts: "I bet right now you'd like me to kill him." Rebecca agreed that she would.

At other times, Sara reports, her children have asked their parents why they had such a child and why they allow him to remain at home.

Remembering the concept of the seesaw I would guess that these children trust their parents' strength. They can wish aloud for their brother's death or disappearance because they know the limits of their own power. Their mother and father can protect their brother; they can endure anger; they can enforce a boundary between thought and action.

Family Life

Children grow up in a family whose organization reflects the impact of a disability. In the previous chapter, I suggested ways in which this different family structure might place stress on a marriage. I will now consider the pressures it exerts on normal children.

Most parents want to see their handicapped child participate in the activities of brothers and sisters on some sort of equal footing. Hence we often hear about sisters and brothers who treat their handicapped sibling as one of the gang, or show signs of special love and affection. For example, Maureen Thompson often describes to the mothers' group the ways in which her older boys include Kevin, who has cerebral palsy, in their play. "You should see him in his stroller, flying down the hill at ninety miles an hour. . . . I'm kind of glad to have boys, because they really roughhouse with him. When my niece comes over she likes to baby him." Probably seeing the three brothers at play reassures Maureen of Kevin's essential normality, and his capacity to "make it" in the world beyond the family.

Clare Potter is pleased by the way her son Grant plays with Melissa and shows her off. She proudly told the group about a recent incident. Melissa began to coo as Grant sat watching a favorite show in the other room. "I said to him, 'Grant, I think your sister's calling you.' He got down off the chair, switched off the TV, went in the other room and picked her up."

These scenes hearten parents. They love their normal children all the better when they see them offering love to a vulnerable brother or sister. They like themselves a little more for their own part in creating such a family. It is natural to savor such pleasures—and perhaps to brag some too.

It is important, however, not to turn a blind eye to the other side of the situation. The handicapped child is different, and many parents find that their normal children treat him or her somewhat differently. The mother of a blind child observes:

All the children treat Elizabeth differently than they do each other. They are never sharp or cross with her and if Elizabeth takes advantage of any one of them I have to be the one to step in. I've never made them feel that they must sacrifice themselves to Elizabeth or let her become a burden. (Ulrich 1972, p. 49)

Elizabeth is less "different" than many disabled children. She walks, talks, reads, and writes, and attends a regular school with children her own age. Her mother and a number of other people have helped her to circumvent the developmental hazards of blindness and learn the skills that will allow her to function in a seeing world. Nevertheless, her brothers and sisters have created a special set of guidelines for dealing with her—rules that set her somewhat apart from the rest of them and emphasize her vulnerability.

Every disability represents some sort of loss. At best this means only the absence of some physical capability—the use of one hand, the ability to see with normal acuity—but in many cases the loss is social as well as physical. The disability prevents a child from participating fully in the activities expected of children his age. Families provide more flexible settings than schools or playgrounds, but the loss is real even at home.

For example, a person with a severe communication disorder often creates a sort of emotional vacuum in the middle of the family. A child who cannot communicate is still very much a person. But he is a person whose ideas, experiences, and feelings remain largely out of sight, inaccessible to others. He fails to give us many of the rewards we expect from other people, whether they be friends or family. My own son, Jody, does not change in the same way his sisters do. He does not startle me with his idiosyncratic vision of the world—although his world, if I could look into it, would undoubtedly surprise me at least as much as theirs. He does not challenge my ideas, or point out my shortcomings, or comment on my friends and relations. Nearly everything I believe about his world I have projected from mine. Because he is unable to *tell* us about his world, each of us in the family constructs our own vision of it. We spin it, like spiders, from our own insides. And each of us, I think, feels the loss of a firmer, stronger, more two-sided relationship with Jody. Each of us sometimes makes the mistake of thinking that there are two children in the family, not three. We know that Jody shares our most basic needs—for love, for warmth, for good food, attention, a comfortable bed, and affirmation of his own importance. He is as fully human as any of the rest of us. He cries and laughs and is extraordinarily sensitive to the emotional ambience of the household. But because he cannot speak, because his capacity to communicate is limited, he presents a somewhat opaque surface. It is hard to "know" him. Another mother describes her frustration this way: "It's just that he can't do anything for himself. You see you've got everything to do— you think for him, you're practically *being* him, really" (Hewett 1970, p. 36).

Josh Greenfeld writes of his sons, aged two and a half and four:

My sons: Karl is truth. He looks like a boy, reacts without deviousness, his life never that far from the surface. Noah is beauty, sensitive rather than sensible, his life throbbing away in some subcellar. Karl laughs, audibly, openly. Noah smiles, silently, mysteriously. (Greenfeld 1972, p. 47)

The difficulty of "knowing" an autistic or profoundly retarded child, or the child with a severe communication disorder, can frustrate siblings as much as parents. They yearn for a relationship of equals, for someone with whom they can play and tell secrets, someone who shares their child-view of an adult world. Even when normal siblings perform some of these functions, they sometimes imagine the special relationship they might have with *this* brother if he were more accessible.

Even a milder disability can interfere with this sort of reflection, companionship, and learning.* The able-bodied member of a two-child family may feel very much alone. Michael O'Donnell's younger brother Peter finished high school with difficulty, but without any

---

* The developmental psychologist Selma Fraiberg reports that even after ten years of work with "normal" blind children—youngsters she describes in glowing terms as talkative, active, and mischievous—she and her staff felt "something vital missing in the social exchange" (Fraiberg 1977, p. 95). She believes that the blind child's failure to make eye contact and to give and respond to expected facial clues limits communication in important ways. Immersed as she is in the lives of blind babies, Fraiberg compares her encounters with sighted infants to meetings between fellow countrymen traveling in a foreign land: just as the compatriot endears himself by sharing our idiom and our "tribal signs," the sighted baby speaks our native language with his face and eyes. In subtle as well as obvious ways, a handicap can undercut efforts to "know" a child. Brothers and sisters feel this loss keenly.

official label. In a paper written for a course Michael reflects sadly on his family.

But I have to force my brother out of my mind. When he intrudes, it makes me feel bad. And I feel bad for all of us. I feel bad for him, naturally, as I cannot remember any really happy moments in his life. Not one coup, one success, one lucky or good thing. My parents lie awake night after night thinking of how Pete's going to "make it" after they're gone. And me.

I feel bad for me because I wish I had a brother that I could really relate to. I wish I had a brother I wasn't somewhat embarrassed by. I wish I wasn't in the approach-avoidance slot of being my brother's keeper.

As the family grows older, Michael sees his relationship to Peter changing. He is becoming more like a parent—a single parent. He finds his position solitary and frightening.

Am I my brother's keeper? The inner and my parents' implicating outer voices say yes.

OK, it is yes. But you know when I hear the record, "He Ain't Heavy, He's My Brother," I shut it off. Because the thought of having to carry my brother, at least for now, is very, very heavy. Maybe I resent having the responsibility for something that I may have problems carrying off.

This sense of responsibility seems to have entered Michael and Peter's relationship only since Michael reached maturity. Many able-bodied brothers and sisters feel it earlier. Some complain that they became parents long before they were ready—parents of their handicapped brother or sister.

From the time Roger began going to physicians and consultants, it seemed to me that I carried a five-hundred-pound lead weight around in the front of my brain. Never out of my mind was the idea that my brother was retarded, needed special attention, needed special care, and that I had to provide some of it. . . .

My role in those days was someone who was always around to help care for Roger. That was my mother's phrase. My father called me his "good right arm." Roger himself called me "Dad" before he corrected himself and called me "Bobby." . . .

I never felt I dressed like a kid, never felt comfortable with the clothes I wore, never felt I knew how to act as a boy or a teen-ager. I was a little man. (Meyers 1978, p. 36)

Victoria Hayden, whose younger sister was deaf, sounds a very similar theme.

When Daddy spent a year in Korea, I became Mother's sole helper. My role as second mother to Mindy held some prestige and much responsibility. It took away from play-time with children my own age. And, just as a mother serves as an example for her children, I was expected to be an exceptionally "good" little girl. The high standards my mother set for my behavior, though, had not only to do with my setting an example; her reasons were also practical. Mindy's impetuous behavior left her with little patience, energy, or time to put up with shenanigans from me. . . .

The responsibility I felt for Mindy was tremendous. One year, when my "babysitting" duties involved periodic checking on my sister, Mindy wandered away between checks. After a thorough but fruitless search of the neighborhood, my mother hysterically told me that if anything happened to Mindy I would be to blame. I felt terrified and guilty. I was seven. (Hayden 1974)

Both Victoria Hayden and Robert Meyers stand in a rather lonely position. They are, in some sense, closer to their parents than most children, by virtue of their status as honorary adults. But they are not *really* parents—and Robert Meyers suggests that the sense of responsibility he felt for Roger limited his relationship with his parents instead of enlarging it. Neither are they *really* a sister and a brother; their responsibilities remove an important element of give and take— of reciprocity—from the relationship.

Brothers and sisters are never—or rarely—equal in the way twins, classmates, or parents are. Children vary in age, size, strength, and aptitudes. Few parents expect the same behavior of all their offspring. Because inequality of this sort is inevitable, a disability disrupts a family in some ways less than it disrupts a classroom or other group that rests on an expectation of roughly equal capabilities. A fourteen-year-old can perform more chores than a five-year-old—and benefit from a later bed time. Nevertheless, these differences often rankle: the fourteen-year-old grumbles that *he* always carries out the garbage, while the five-year-old only sets the table. The five-year-old requests a pocket calculator for Christmas because her brother got one last year. Parents try to reconcile both to their lot, and to create equal expectations wherever possible. *Everyone* must refrain from fighting at the table. *All* children bring their dirty plates to the kitchen after dinner, straighten their own rooms, and participate in weekly house-cleaning. *Everyone* carries something on the picnic, even if it's only paper cups. Both parents and children know that not all rules apply to everyone; but if one person is exempt from nearly all customary expectations, everyone feels uncomfortable.

We were rearing two families. There was one set of rules for Tony, and another for Jane, Sarah, and Freddy. The three were required to wash their hands before dinner, to sit up straight at the table, to speak respectfully. Tony slouched and spilled and thrust his dirty hands into the mashed potatoes but no one said anything about it. We were thankful, we thought the evening a success if only he kept the peace and left everyone alone. This standard made sense for Tony; first things first, and the first thing was to put him at ease and never mind the dirt. But making that clear to the other children was difficult indeed. All they could see was the unfairness. (Wilson 1968, p. 108–109)

The Wilson children were quite right: the whole situation is profoundly unfair. It is unfair that one family must live with schizophrenia, autism, blindness, or retardation while others do not. It is unfair that some children must function as adjunct parents even before they go to school, while others successfully avoid responsibilities of all sorts well into their second decade. The brothers and sisters of the handicapped child learn to cope with this unfairness, and with their own response to it, the sorrow and the anger.

However when we consider the ways in which families accommodate to a child's handicap, fairness takes a back seat to other issues. The major problem with many changes in family structure is their potential for isolating family members. In the ideal—perhaps imaginary—family, each child receives two sorts of support, one from his parents and the other from his brothers and sisters. The differences I describe reduce children's access to at least some family members. Sometimes the handicapped child stands outside the circle, either because his handicap interferes with satisfactory communication or because family custom puts him in a separate category from his brothers and sisters. In other households, he remains a true child, but an able-bodied brother or sister assumes quite grown-up responsibilities. In either case the children do not share a world beyond adult reach, as many other siblings do; they lose the reciprocal support and companionship that peers can provide one another.*

* According to Grossman (1972, p. 103) the clinical literature indicates that retarded children disrupt small families more than large ones. Grossman's own research shows no strong statistical relationship between family size and sibling adaptation, probably because few students from small families volunteered to participate. Her anecdotal evidence suggests that students from two-child families found retardation more disruptive to their family than those with a number of normal siblings (p. 103–104).

Coping

I have focused, up until now, on the difficulties that the able-bodied child faces. These problems are real enough, and assume major importance in the lives of some children. Nonetheless, the sheer length of my discussion creates a misleadingly gloomy impression. It may suggest that for the brothers and sisters of the disabled the developmental path is strewn with frightful hazards, that all but the most skillful parents can expect to see their "normal" children bruised irreparably by the experience of family living. The truth is quite otherwise.

In fact, as I have said before, all happy families are not alike. There is good reason to believe that the differences between an exceptional family and an ordinary one are as often for the better as for the worse. Frances Kaplan Grossman, after thoughtful interviews with eighty-three college students with retarded brothers or sisters, concluded that the experience of growing up with a disabled family member had actually benefited about half of the young people. She felt that it had probably hurt the other half in one way or another.

Human complexity thwarts our impulse toward statistical precision, of course. Children severely disturbed by a sibling's disability would never have found their ways into this sample, since severe disturbance usually precludes college attendance. Grossman acknowledges problems in method and presents her figures with appropriate diffidence. Her general message sounds about right: a handicap inevitably changes the experience of each child in the family, but exceptional families offer normal children unusual opportunities as well as unusual problems.*

* It is very very difficult to get more precise estimates of the impact of one child's disability on his siblings. Although a number of studies have posed the question, sample selection and research methods limit the inferences we can draw about the wider population of siblings.

Several investigators have asked *parents* about the adjustment of the able-bodied siblings. Hewett (1970), Lonsdale (1978), Carr (1975), and Barsch (1968) offer evidence that children with a handicapped brother or sister manage as well as those with more ordinary families. Lonsdale finds the percentage of children with "behavioral disorders" to be about the same as that in the general population. Carr reports that 14 percent of the families with Down's Syndrome preschoolers had normal children who "gave some trouble at home"—as opposed to 31 percent of the control families. (In either case the "troubles" were rather routine: "cheekiness," "playing up," attempts at independence.) Barsch's sample

I have dealt with a range of the problems. It is hard to discuss the opportunities without sounding sentimental, but they are an important part of the truth about a difference in the family. Parents and children alike speak of such benefits as increased tolerance for human difference, a less casual acceptance of the blessing of good health, and a sense of specialness* concerning the familial bonds. (Grossman comes up with a very similar list; apparently when people try to explain their feeling that they have learned something, they use similar terms.)

What makes a difference? Why does the relationship with a handicapped brother or sister enhance some children's lives while diminishing those of others? Can concerned adults help children weather the problems and get something good out of the experience? Can brothers and sisters discover constructive ways to manage the inevitable difficulties?

The answers to these important questions are far from obvious. Brothers and sisters of handicapped children, though often articulate about the difficulties of growing up in an exceptional family (Hayden 1974; Klein 1972; Grossman 1972) seldom analyze the ingredients of their own success. Grossman explores the influence of religion, relative

---

is the most representative, including children with all sorts of physical and mental handicaps. After talking to several hundred mothers and fathers, Barsch concluded that "brothers and sisters of the cerebral palsied, mongoloid, organic, deaf, and blind seem to accept their handicapped sibling and present no significant continuing problems to their parents in this regard" (p. 197). McMichael is less sanguine. She writes that 21 percent (eight) of the siblings of the physically handicapped children she studied showed moderate or severe signs of failing to adjust to the disability. However, McMichael also judges more than half of the handicapped children to be in equally severe emotional difficulties and takes a gloomy view of parents as well. All her children were drawn from one special school in England; there is no reason to believe them to be typical.

Researchers who talk directly to sisters and brothers—as Grossman did—probably learn a lot more about the range of their responses. On the other hand, they are limited to volunteers, who may be a self-selected group of the more enthusiastic and articulate. Cleveland and Miller (1977) report on questionnaires completed by 90 older brothers and sisters of institutionalized retarded adults: "The majority of the siblings, in all the variables explored, reported a positive adaptation to the retarded sibling and the experiences surrounding having a retarded sibling." Unfortunately, we can only guess at the attitudes of the 231 siblings who failed to return the questionnaire.

Clinicians who have followed many families over a period of years probably can tell us as much about the outlook as any of these studies. It is therefore cheering to hear from Allen Crocker, who presides over the Developmental Evaluation Clinic at Boston's Children's Hospital, that "it is, in fact, the common observation of clinical workers that siblings of children with handicaps have a most reassuring record of salutory accommodation" (Crocker 1979).

age, sex, income, family size, degree of retardation, physical handicaps, and parental attitudes, and draws an extraordinarily complex picture of family adaptation—one that further decreases the reader's faith in simple explanations for children's adjustment. One important conclusion may be that families are too intricately complex to generalize about: it all depends.

Grossman's findings, frustrating though they are to those seeking answers, help set what brothers and sisters say in perspective. Grossman finds that her college-age informants describe a range of different problems with their retarded sisters and brothers, and that the family styles depend in part on social class. Retardation touched the lives of middle-class and working-class students in somewhat different ways. Children from wealthier families focused on emotional hazards: they worried about their own attitudes toward the retarded child and his or her impact on their parents. For many working-class community college students more practical problems took precedence: girls in particular often assumed heavy responsibilities for child care in order to relieve their mothers, and found their own lives constricted accordingly.

A particular handicap or complication elicited different responses in different families. For example, some retarded children suffered from physical handicaps as well. The presence and severity of these physical problems affected the community college women and the private college men in different ways. The upper middle-class men actually seemed to adapt *better* if their brother or sister had severe physical stigmata; the opposite held true for the working-class women (Grossman 1972, pp. 99–103). Grossman explains these findings plausibly enough by noting that physical handicaps added to the practical problems of care, thus increased the burdens on the working-class girls. Upper middle-class mothers, however, expected little practical help from their children—especially teenaged boys. Physical handicaps actually helped some of these siblings by speeding the process of diagnosis and clarifying the family's problem.

These specific findings form bits of two larger pictures. In the working class, where more children assume practical responsibility for child care, specific characteristics of the handicap directly influence the quality of able-bodied children's lives. In the better-off families, by contrast, parents' attitudes seem to matter more. Such quantitative findings illuminate the elaborate trade-offs inherent in each family style. Of course, no one should assume that the terms "middle-class" and "working-class" describe in any profound way the nature of a family; differences within each group surely matter just as much as differences between classes. Nonetheless, Grossman's findings are suggestive.

Individual brothers and sisters present an equally complex portrait of the mix of things that go into "successful" adaptation. When the children of two lawyers talked to Devin Thornburg about living with their multiply-handicapped sister Catherine (see p. 47), they emphasized feelings rather than practical problems. The older children agreed that Catherine's behavior sometimes infuriates them, but they find support of various sorts within the family. Kevin appreciates his father's matter-of-fact acceptance of his rage. Eighteen-year-old Judy concludes, "I think the most important thing is that we all share the burden, and it just hasn't been that tough, really" (Thornburg 1978, p. 21). For these children the primary agenda is emotional. Both parents work full time; a nurse cares for Catherine at home. The children themselves assume few parental responsibilities. They do sometimes need help with rage, frustration, jealousy, and embarrassment. They get it from one another, and from their parents.

Important as this sort of support seems, other children flourish in a different sort of atmosphere. A community college student describes his family's view of six-year-old Marty, who has Down's syndrome:

My father had that saying: "This child that we have is so innocent that he is not capable of sin, so he must be almost like an angel. And so because he is so holy and so special, and because he probably won't be with us long, we ought to be glad to do anything for him." This is exactly what my father used to say: "Whenever you do something for Marty, you ought to just think it is like putting in a word with God. When he dies and goes to heaven, he will put in a good word for you." (Grossman 1972, p. 107)

Having choked on some of these pieties myself, I would expect such an attitude to cramp free expression of feelings. Yet Marty's brother feels he has learned important lessons from him:

Yes, if I stop to think about it, it makes me appreciative of how much I really have when I see how, at the present, how limited he is. And I never thought of myself as being very smart, but compared to him I realize I have a lot of unused potential, where it seems he is using everything he's got. (Grossman 1972, p. 95)

His older brother finds Marty easy to love and perhaps this—rather than the vision of him as an angel—makes the difference.

One young woman, discussing the impact of her sister's retardation with a psychologist and three other college students, observes that she and her family have gained a lot:

> I think that speaking from my own life, it has been a tremendous experience insofar as my personal growth goes. It made our family extremely close. We have some sort of special bond between us that we share, and *will* share, for the rest of our lives. I cannot imagine life without Cathy. I feel that it has been marvelous for Cathy as well as for everyone involved. We have learned so very much, we have developed patience and understanding. (Klein 1972)

She contrasts her attitudes toward the disabled with those of her fiancé: he believes that people like Cathy would be better off if they had not been born. Because he has never spent time with anyone like Cathy he does not understand that although her pleasures are different, they are real. "He cannot see that her joy in life is playing with people, listening to music or being well. Her joys are simply not what our joys are." Cathy's even disposition and her evident pleasure in life reassure Diane:

> Her life is not hard as long as she has love and care and plenty to eat, she is very happy. She has a delightful disposition, she is always smiling; she is always laughing. I have sort of felt that I am glad she is this way, it sort of protects her, it shields her from the pains of the world. (Klein 1972)

Such a child, despite her tragic failure to develop normally, provides sisters and brothers with satisfactions and a sense that the family has met a challenge.

Neither the clinical literature nor the recollections of grown siblings provide guidelines for integrating a disability into family life. Aggregate statistics tend to blur the contradictory complexities of particular families. Individual reminiscences lack analytic sharpness and sometimes forge connections that exist only in retrospect. Contradictions abound. One college student blames his parents for a childhood shadowed by excessive responsibility; another welcomes the role of substitute parent, finding in it an escape from jealousy, and an affirmation of her own maturity.

We may reconcile some of these contradictory messages by invoking a rather obvious notion dear to the hearts of good teachers:

success helps people grow. Good teachers make sure that their students succeed as often as possible. They know that mastery fuels self-confidence and brings students—adults and children alike—back for more. Teachers usually concentrate on conveying skills and encouraging curiosity; the doctrine of success applies to other human relationships as well.

Families develop different agendas for themselves, individually and collectively. Some emphasize cleanliness and obedience, others concentrate on affection, mutual support, accomplishment, thoughtfulness, reliability, or emotional openness. Some exist more for grown-ups than children; others emphasize children and ignore the needs of adults. The list of values and virtues can undergo almost endless permutations. Families also have different goals in living with a handicapped person. Each child sees his own relationship with his brother or sister against the background of these family expectations. Thus, turning to the preceding examples, we gather that Catherine's family valued candor, emotional insight, and mutual support very highly. In relation to Catherine, Judy and Kevin feel successful: they have found ways in which she resembles other people, learned to recognize their own changing responses to her, to talk about their feelings, to give and receive support. No one asks them to babysit or sacrifice their plans to an ambitious therapy program.

Marty's parents make different demands. They ask their children to love Marty and to see him as an eternal innocent. Marty's older brother apparently achieves this goal without much difficulty. He likes Marty more than his other brothers and sisters anyway. He interprets Marty's character much as his father tells him he should. The religious motif "works" for him, as it might not for another child.

Diane's responsibilities are practical as well as emotional. She and her older sister help care for Cathy, curtailing their own activities when necessary. She guiltily remembers occasions when she vented her frustrations on Cathy by scaring her or spanking her when she cried. Her sense of the ultimate success of the family enterprise balances this guilt: Cathy remains "a really delightful child." The rest of the family has grown close, supported one another, and "developed patience and understanding." A conviction that the family enabled a handicapped child to learn and grow helps able-bodied brothers and sisters to feel good about their experience.

I remember a young woman who came up to me after I talked about families of handicapped children. She said that she knew from her own experience that a family's contribution could be vital. Doctors had diagnosed her youngest sister as retarded in the first year of her life. But it has not worked out that way—now she is finishing high school, is involved in theater, singing, and lots of other things, and is a "neat kid." "So I know that the family can make all the difference." Her parents, she remembered, concealed the diagnosis from everyone, and were upset when she learned about it from a neighbor. "I don't think my middle sister ever found out."

I wondered how she had felt about the whole situation as a child. "Well," she reflected, "my father impressed on us that we were to teach her everything we knew. I grew up thinking she was very special, and I loved her very much." Her sister had been slow all through school, but her parents and sisters provided intensive and continuing help. My informant concluded: "I think she came out of the womb with some kind of damage, but the family experience is so important. It can make all the difference."

This young woman believed that family efforts had helped to overcome her sister's organic handicap. By giving her extra opportunities to learn, she herself participated in her sister's ultimate success. From this experience she drew a solid confidence in the importance of families—and, I infer, in the strength and value of her own.

This story suggests the value of success; it reminds us how much children gain from real responsibility for helping a brother or sister overcome a disability. It also qualifies my emphasis on the values of openness and telling the truth. In order to maximize their youngest daughter's opportunities, these parents hid the diagnosis of retardation even from their other children. This practice, which sets off warning bells inside *my* head, seems to have worked out all right for them. Different families draw strength from different wells; they cope with stress in an impressive variety of ways. We ought not to dogmatize about other people's lives.

In writing about his brother Roger, Robert Meyers (1978) tells a more painful success story. The Meyers responded to Roger's mild retardation in a range of ways: with hard work, patient teaching, long searches for appropriate schools and professional help, financial sacrifice, protective concern, and unremitting worry; with secrecy and denial; perhaps with an overreliance on chemical solutions to constant stress—too much Miltown, Maalox, and alcohol.

In 1976 Roger got married. The wedding marked another step toward a more normal life than his parents ever expected him to lead.

He and his wife now live in their own apartment. Supplemental Security Income payments supplement Roger's salary as a part-time busboy. A social worker meets with them once a week and helps them with problems they cannot solve on their own. In matters of everyday living, they have achieved substantial independence.

Robert Meyers remembers the childhood he shared with Roger somewhat sadly. In early adulthood he withdrew from his parents entirely for a while in order to escape the continuing pressures to forswear real independence and to become Roger's third parent. From the perspective of his fourth decade, the balance sheet looks considerably more even. Robert has learned that his younger brother's retardation need not completely define their relationship, and that people change when there is room in their lives for growth. He has come to like Roger, as well as to love him protectively.

When Roger asked his older brother to serve as best man at his wedding, Robert decided—with Roger's blessing—to write a feature series on retardation for the *Washington Post*. He used his family's experience and Roger's marriage as illustrative material. Breaking the codes of family secrecy—codes that are an important and neglected aspect of family life—he speaks of feelings and experiences that were never discussed during his years of growing up. It is as though Roger, in successfully adapting to the larger world, absolved his family of their mistakes, and enabled them, finally, to speak their secrets aloud.

Robert Meyer's book should reassure families. His parents made many mistakes; they were ordinary people dealing with extraordinary trouble. Their normal son often felt constricted and ill-used; some of his early anger survives today. Nonetheless, as an adult he writes about his parents with perceptive compassion, and about his brother with surprised admiration as well as affection.

I have considered two sorts of success: an able-bodied child's success in achieving family goals and a handicapped child's success in overcoming (at least partly) the impact of the disability. I do not want to blur the distinction between the two. The success of the disabled child already occupies a prominent position in the parental consciousness. It would be cruel as well as wildly misleading to suggest that the future happiness of *all* children in the family depend on that success. My point is a little different: if a family has labored collectively on behalf of the handicapped child, then they share his or her victories. Their pride helps them cope with less pleasant things.

Clearly the success of the handicapped child, like that of his able-bodied siblings, is partly a matter of definition. Had the Meyers family hoped to see Roger apprenticed in a skilled trade, employment as a busboy would have disappointed them. Had Cathy's family expected greater developmental gains, they might have derived little pleasure from her radiant smile.

As a mother myself I know that parents cannot entirely control their expectations for their children. They can subject them to some sort of scrutiny and see how much room their hopes allow for real success in the present. Parents can try to help all family members—themselves included—share small-scale, everyday achievements.*

Brothers and sisters of handicapped children sometimes complain that they feel like miniature parents. Heavy responsibilities can drain the life out of anybody—big or little. Responsibility can weigh heavily on the thin shoulders of a child. Responsibility can also, under favorable circumstances, diffuse jealousy. A three-year-old feels less jealous of her new baby brother when she rocks his cradle than when she watches her mother feed him. In the same way, assisting in the care of a handicapped child may help a younger sister feel closer to her parents and less jealous of a sibling's specialness.

The issue with responsibility, as elsewhere, hinges on the outcome. The child who holds her brother for a moment before returning him to her mother's arms has achieved thrilling stature: she has stepped briefly into adult shoes; she has joined the ranks of the caring and the nurturing, and she feels good. When the new role becomes scary, oppressive, or simply dull, she sheds it and returns to other sorts of play, with the sturdy irresponsibility of favored childhoods. Compare her situation to that of seven-year-old Victoria Hayden (1974), who has "lost" her little sister. Victoria's problem is not the responsibilities themselves (although these seem hard for a seven-year-old), but the fact that she cannot fulfill them to either her satisfaction or

* The patterning program of the Institutes for the Achievement of Human Potential models such an approach by providing useful, highly structured work for many willing but untrained hands, thus allowing neighbors as well as parents and teachers to contribute to the child's success. And, perhaps more important, it works with a scale of development that is fine-grained enough to highlight even small gains. Such concentrated attention on one family member may generate jealousy and tension among siblings, but it does give them a chance to participate in a valued family venture. (I am not endorsing the Institutes' program. In the absence of controlled studies—and I do not know of any—it is impossible to estimate its effectiveness.)

her parents'. Her feelings of failure and resentment inevitably rub off on her relationship with Mindy.

Families are small places, whose values are partly formed even before children arrive. Most offer the young many opportunities they could never find anywhere else: a kind of unconditional love and a tolerance for—even celebration of—immaturity. Families become confining, though, and children need to venture beyond them. Confronted with different expectations, they see themselves through changed eyes. As they learn from the outside world, parents learn too.

In 1970 in London two educators and a small group of parents became concerned about the limited social opportunities open to disabled children. The six families began meeting every other Sunday, planning games and activities for all the children, normal and handicapped, and preparing a meal together. Over the years their activities expanded to include educational programs and collective vacations. Two enthusiastic parents wrote an account of this organization (Collins and Collins 1976). They describe ways in which they began to bridge the social isolation facing their children—the problem that brought them together in the first place. The group met other needs too.

Often for the first time, parents saw their handicapped children participating with other children in a situation where their difference required no explanation (Collins and Collins 1976, p. 19). Helping *other* handicapped children with cooking, crafts, and physical play, parents sometimes achieved a breakthrough: fewer fixed notions about a child's skills hampered their teaching efforts (pp. 21–22). Encounters with unfamiliar sorts of disability enabled a family to put its own tragedy into perspective (p. 23). Perhaps most significant for our present purposes, the group, which was called Kith and Kids, introduced children to disabled people outside their own families.

Doreen Collins notes with pride that, during a week of holidaying with Kith and Kids, her son Paul "had been incredibly good with Andrew, a Down's syndrome boy who followed him everywhere" (p. 163). Probably this observation helped her to see how much Paul had learned from his retarded sister and to accept his mixed feelings about her.

Maurice Collins recalls an incident of a different sort. He and another father had taken a group to see a soccer match. Richard, who was deaf, kept pushing the eye piece that Jamie, who was visually impaired, used to watch the game. One of the men signaled to Richard to stop these shenanigans, only to learn that he had missed the point. "He's only showing me where the ball is going to," Jamie explained. This evidence of sensitivity and concern delights Mr. Collins. He observes that few children would perceive Jamie's difficulty as quickly as Richard did (Collins and Collins 1976, p. 34).

The opportunity to see one's children performing well, whether at a violin recital, at a bake sale, or in a simple act of thoughtfulness, benefits all parents. Whether we like it or not, pride strengthens our energies and love. To watch our children playing gaily with a handicapped child, or offering imaginative but matter-of-fact assistance, can provide parents with special joy and reassurance. These experiences probably help the child who gives as well (although, since the story of Kith and Kids is told by parents, we cannot know how it looks to children). Brothers and sisters of the disabled speak of their own guilt for acts of omission and commission long past. The opportunity to protect, teach, and befriend another handicapped child may help relieve some of these painful feelings.

All parents and children communicate poorly on some subject. Some children prefer to investigate loaded topics like sex and disability in a more neutral setting than their family can provide. But friends, who happily relay a smorgasbord of fact and fiction relating to sex, usually know almost nothing about particular disabilities. It therefore makes good sense to provide children with better resources for exploring this touchy but vitally important subject. A group like Kith and Kids could make a good starting point.

As we try to help our able-bodied children cope with the reverberations of a family handicap in their lives, parents need to balance two counterpoised insights. First, our children's feelings mirror our own to some degree. And second, because they are children, their perspective diverges from ours in important ways. We are alike and not alike.

I do not mean to echo the mental health banality that if parents grieve, so will the brothers and sisters, while if they "accept" the handicap, their children will follow suit. My view is different. I think most parents feel, somewhere in their hearts, some anger, some loneliness, some guilt, some questions about their personal worth, some sadness, some fear. These feelings assume different shapes in different lives. Each of us can find traces of them, if we examine our souls. Our children navigate the same choppy waters, although their guilt and sadness look different from ours and find different sorts of expression.

It is sad to see our children suffer, when we want their young lives to remain unshadowed. Nonetheless, acknowledging the parallel between ourselves and our children brings some comfort. Looking at ourselves we notice that, despite some pain, we survive and even grow. Our child's disability has changed us; it has not warped us or left us worse people than we were before.

It might have, though. Without support, understanding, companionship, and some measure of freedom to step outside the situation once in a while—without luck—we might have shrunk as human beings, hunching over our anger and hurt, sealing ourselves off from life. So it is with children. Their needs resemble ours; their resilience mirrors our own. They need support and understanding for their feelings, freedom to work the family's difference into their lives in ways acceptable to them and their companions, and a chance to talk to other children who share some of the same problems. They need very much the same sort of support that we need, and they find it, with luck, in equally diverse ways.

We need to balance this insight by standing it on its head: our children differ from us in important ways. Their understanding is limited by their circumscribed experience and by their developmental needs. They stand in a different relationship to the disabled child, being brothers and sisters, not mothers and fathers. Their fears and feelings, though they parallel ours, are not the same. They may identify far more closely with their handicapped sibling than we do, because she or he resembles them more closely, because the wider world sees them through one lens. They vacillate more often between conflicting loyalties to friends and family. They suffer from greater and more basic confusion about the nature of the disability and its implications for their lives.

Fortunately, the confusions of a five-year-old often give way before a six-year-old's more persistent questioning. Adolescence may bring, along with a passion for being regular and an exaggerated sensitivity to family difference, a capacity to perform genuinely useful services. Perhaps it is this almost irrepressible capacity for change that enables the children in the family to cope as well as they do—and their parents to regain the hope and vitality that the original diagnosis threatened.

The process of change does not even end with adulthood, as the developmental psychologists are now beginning to realize. Equipped with a more mature understanding of the pressures shaping their parents' lives, able-bodied brothers and sisters may come to terms with some of the anger and jealousy that bothered them as children. Perhaps facing parenthood themselves, they look backward—and forward—with different eyes.

In his late twenties, Michael O'Donnell signed up for a course on special education that Jay and I were teaching. He was, he told us later, quite unconscious of his mixed motivations: in the introductory class he explained that the field interested him because of his professional experience in corrections; months later he realized he had also wanted to better understand his mildly retarded brother. He did not mention this brother until the end of the semester, but when the class discussed the impact of disability on a family he listened thoughtfully. He said he learned two important lessons. First, that "my position and feelings were not all that unique." And second, "that this was something that I could no longer make believe didn't exist."

As an adult Michael sought out a setting that could help him think about his brother's handicap and his own past. In doing this, he gained power. First of all, he learned that he was not alone—that other parents, brothers, and sisters shared many of the feelings that had secretly troubled him. This perception freed him from the bondage of secrecy and guilt, and helped him to think more objectively about his family. Second, and probably just as important, he glimpsed his own maturity: he *was* no longer a child, subject to his parents' decisions about the conduct of family business. He was a grown man, facing the likelihood of responsibility for his own brother. His learning occurred in a setting that took his adulthood for granted: a graduate seminar. Armed with adult knowledge, adult understanding, and adult status, he could begin to contemplate changing his family's way of dealing with his brother's disabilities.

Robert Meyers's decision to write a feature series on his retarded brother Roger laid the groundwork for other sorts of changes. In preparing his articles, Meyers interviewed people who had known his family at each stage of its development—adult friends, playmates, teachers—as well as public figures in the realms of policy making and mental retardation. He talked to his parents, his brother, his brother's employers. He looked at his brother's life and his growth through the eyes of a newspaper reporter. His image of his brother changed a little:

I have spent most of my life thinking of my brother as my "retarded" brother, not understanding his stubbornness, integrity, and ability to handle an independent (or almost independent) life, and not realizing how much we have in common. The thinking and research I undertook for the newspaper series began to open my mind.

One evening in Baltimore, someone who did not know my family asked what my brother did. I started to reply that he is retarded. Suddenly it struck me for the first time in the twenty-eight years of our lives together that mental slowness is not the sum of his existence. He is a man who is married, holds down a job, pays taxes, and writes poetry. I hope I will never forget that moment: I was in my car, driving down a dark street in Baltimore, and I'd been asked what my brother does.

I replied that he is in the restaurant business. (Meyers 1978, p. 156)

By ending a chapter this way, Meyers emphasizes the importance of this moment and the change it symbolizes for him. With such markers we chart our own growth and order the chaos of our experience. Meyers's story, moving though it is, reminds us (yet again) of the difficulties brothers and sisters face in striking the right balance in their dealings with their family and the world. Roger Meyers is not actually "in the restaurant business" as most people would understand the phrase. He is a busboy. Robert, in his sudden impulse to acknowledge his brother's equality, his complex identity, and his achievements, has slightly distorted the picture in a different way. But distortions of this sort do not remain immutable. Meyers is like a man trying to focus a camera, experimenting with many blurred images, seeking one that seems clearer than the rest. Next time some one asks him about his younger brother, he may answer more fully. The links between brothers, like the bonds between parents and children, never stop changing.

Chapter 7

Getting and Giving Help

Professionals play a big part in the lives of disabled people and their families. It often looks to parents as though outsiders hold the child's future in their hands. For their part, professionals often feel far less powerful than they appear to clients.

In this chapter I look at the parent-professional relationship from both sides. In the first section I describe parents' needs as they themselves see them, and I outline four ways that professionals can help. In the second I analyze some difficulties that doctors and teachers—the two groups that shape disabled children's lives most decisively—encounter in their work. In the third I suggest ways in which individual practitioners can do a better job.

No amount of restraint or empathy can banish all the problems that parents and professionals confront. Ours is a relentlessly psychological culture, one that sometimes assumes that changes in attitude will solve every problem. This is not always true, especially in the field of disability. Attitudes and insight do count, however, and I am confident that families and professionals could work together more successfully if each group understood the stresses in other lives more clearly.

How Professionals Can Help

Professionals help families in four ways. They identify and explain the child's problems. They can show respect for the child himself, the parent, and the relationship between them. They offer concrete assistance—services such as therapy, education, or corrective surgery. And they support parents emotionally.

Information

Parents need information about their child's problems. At the most basic level this means diagnosis: putting a label on the difficulty. Beyond that, parents want to know as much as possible about the origin of the disability and its implications for their child's life. Many questions cannot be answered immediately, and as long as uncertainties persist, they trouble family members.

In most cases, parents suspect a problem before anyone else.* But official diagnosis comes either through the medical community or the schools. Doctors preside at a child's birth. They see the child for immunizations and check-ups throughout the early years. Until the child enters school, parents discuss serious worries with a physician before consulting another professional. In the past, at least, many parents have complained that doctors failed to respond candidly to their concerns.

Many children present a confusing clinical picture, and the doctor shares the parents' uncertainties. Like them, he must "wait and see." However, some doctors postpone the job of confronting parents with an unpleasant truth even when the problem is glaringly apparent. Ethel Roskies, in her study of twenty children with thalidomide deformities, reports that the doctor in the delivery room assured more than half the mothers of their child's normality (Roskies 1972, p. 58). Considering the obvious nature of these children's differences we must suspect that some of the obstetricians consciously deceived their patients.

* Barsch reports, for example, that all the parents of blind, deaf, cerebral-palsied and Down's syndrome children interviewed for his study felt concerns before the child was six months old. Only a minority of the handicaps were diagnosed this early (1968, pp. 80, 83).

When the case is ambiguous—as it often is in instances of slow or atypical development—parents and physician sometimes unconsciously collaborate in minimizing the significance of the problems. Barbara Trace, whose daughter Joan still lacked the most rudimentary communication skills at age three, writes:

Thus, until this point, we had essentially denied to ourselves the existence of a problem serious enough to require seeking help for it. We had built up a fine rationale for explaining Joan to ourselves. Her prematurity, her individual rate of development, a probable immaturity of her nervous system, and frustration based on lack of language were some of the alibis that lulled us into inactivity.

In addition, another factor existed that carried great weight with us. Our pediatrician, who had known Joan from birth, was fully confident that Joan's development was normal. On routine visits to him, he always reassured us when we raised questions that we somehow could not reason away. When he observed Joan briefly in his office and in our home, he noted her bright eyes, her quick, searching movements, her dexterity, and her ready smiles. He appeared unconcerned about her lack of speech and her inability to relate to people. He felt that she had speech comprehension (a faulty observation on his part, we thought) and dismissed as exaggeration our accounts of her behavior. Since we considered him to be a competent physician, we trusted his opinion that Joan was actually bright and alert, and his conclusion that she was developing normally. His explanation for her delayed language responses was that she was merely proceeding at a different rate from that of her contemporaries. He felt that this was based on her marked prematurity. We welcomed his assurances. We wanted to believe him. I think that this was one of the most important reasons we did not become alarmed and did not seek further opinions.

At our request, our pediatrician prescribed tranquilizers once or twice to help reduce Joan's hyperactivity, but she did not respond to them.

We plodded on with the eager anticipation and fervent hope that each new day would release the words we hoped lay merely dormant within Joan. This expectation remained unfulfilled. The days continued to be long and miserable. They varied only in that some were more intolerable than others. None were good. (Kastein and Trace 1966, pp. 40–41)

Reassurance can immobilize parents, even when they seem to welcome it. Fortunately, in this case, another pediatrician (consulted when this doctor died) spotted the problem at once and steered the Traces toward a speech therapy program.

Parents of a Down's syndrome boy waited six months before hearing of their son's handicap. Later the mother suspected that the doctor had tried to test her own readiness for diagnostic information by remarking on the baby's brightness at the three month check-up. The effort backfired: instead of talking about her worries the mother clutched at the encouraging comment "as a drowning man would at a straw" (Hannam 1975, p. 33). When parents greedily devour little morsels of reassurances, doctors naturally hesitate to confront them with the bleak truth.

Even when the physician threads his way through the intricacies of a confusing clinical problem, overcomes his natural reluctance to inflict pain on another human being, and offers a diagnosis, he may not have entirely met the family's need for information. Many mothers and fathers do not fully understand the diagnosis after one consultation. For one thing, interviews are often quite brief.* In addition, the shock of hearing their child labeled (even if they themselves noted the problem and pressed for a diagnosis) may temporarily prevent parents from thinking clearly, listening, and asking pertinent questions. Every one of the couples who talked to Charles Hannam about experiences with their retarded child felt that they needed more than one interview with the person telling them about the handicap (Hannam 1975, p. 24).

Medical jargon also interferes with communication.† Many parents later admit to interviewers that they did not understand that their child would be retarded when the doctor used the word "Mongoloid" (Ehlers 1966; Hannam 1975). With problems like cerebral palsy, language delay, and learning disability, medical terms can create even more confusion. Doctors and nurses often avoid using lay language to protect their patients from unpleasant stereotypes. Sometimes the parents miss the point altogether. Catherine Lederman, for example,

* Among the 177 couples with handicapped children interviewed by Ray Barsch (1968), a clear majority complained that the doctor had spent too little time explaining the diagnosis to them and answering their questions. About two-thirds of the families were satisfied with the doctor's attitude toward them and their child. Sheila Hewett (1970) reports similar results with a large sample of English parents of cerebral-palsied children.

† Korsch and Negrete (1972) studied doctor-client communication in the pediatric outpatient department of a large hospital and found vocabulary posed a significant problem. They catalogue a number of misunderstandings of technical terms and observe that doctors "resorted to medical jargon" in more than half the 800 interviews they observed. Interestingly, college-educated mothers were not significantly more satisfied with communication than those with less formal education. Medical lingo baffles everyone, regardless of background.

told our mothers' group how encouraged she felt when the doctors summed up Ellie's problems with the phrase "delayed development." To her the word "delayed" suggested that Ellie was slow now, but would catch up later. She thought of a train that was delayed: it is late, but eventually it does arrive. Later she realized the bleak truth: "That's not what it means at all. It means she is a retarded child."

Lacking clear-cut evidence that early diagnosis benefits the child, some doctors believe that their silence gives families "a few more good years." Actually, however, parents usually sense that something is amiss, and incubate fantasies which undermine their happiness as effectively as the truth. A convincing diagnosis, however bleak, may actually reassure them.

Most parents want to explore causes as well as cures. Their burning curiosity upsets some professionals, who worry that further knowledge might provoke more self-reproach and observe that as long as the handicap is there, treatment matters much more than origins.

In fact, however, parents who do not know the cause of the disability torture themselves in all sorts of ways. Catherine Lederman confessed that Ellie's unexplained retardation made her feel inadequate in some basic biological way. She was afraid she was not capable of bearing normal children. In a desperate search for reassurance, she even consulted astrologers. One of them told her that she was being punished for sins she had committed in an earlier life. Centuries ago she had worked in a convent, helping the nuns to care for retarded boys and girls. Secretly, she had betrayed their trust and mistreated her charges. The astrologer predicted that all her children would be retarded.

Sadistic quacks like this are comparatively rare, but Catherine's experiences reminds us that when science and reason fail, we often turn to magic. Even an awful truth can rescue people from self-destructive fantasies. Take the case of the thalidomide babies. We might expect the mothers to reproach themselves for their part in the tragedy. Yet when Ethel Roskies (1972) asked twenty mothers how they felt when they learned that a drug they took had caused the deformities, seventeen replied that they were greatly relieved. Presumably they suspected something even worse.

Parents need information for many reasons: to understand puzzling behavior, to set reasonable limits and expectations, to restore communication—if not consensus—in a divided, uncertain household. They need to resolve the inner dialogue I have talked about before and to begin to regain some control over their lives.

Diagnosis often requires time. However, parents report that when professionals seem candid and explain their own reasoning in jargon-free English, uncertainties become easier to bear.

Respect

When doctors, psychologists, or teachers withhold information or evade questions they implicitly criticize parents' good sense. When they discuss a child's problems candidly with the family they convey respect for their hearers' intelligence and judgment. One mother observes: "In a sense we do become the experts on our children. And it really helps to know that somebody in the professional world thinks that you're intelligent and that you can handle the information whatever it happens to be" (Kelley et al. 1978).

A disability shakes parents' self-confidence, as I emphasized in chapter 4. Dead ends along the road to diagnosis and treatment can further erode their faith in themselves. Some professionals use their great psychological power to help mothers and fathers to rebuild. They listen and observe. They show parents how much they are helping their child. Luke Sullivan's doctor is a good example. He tells Barbara that she is the expert on Luke, that no doctor will ever know him as she does. He makes sure she knows that she and her husband Patrick are doing a good job. At one check-up an intern asked why Luke had not had an operation or a brace. The older doctor replied, "He doesn't need one. His mother exercises him every day, stretching the muscles. She's gotten them so good that he doesn't need an operation."

If the doctor delivered vague compliments indiscriminately at the end of each consultation, the effect would be patronizing rather than helpful. His remarks convey respect because they are specific and accurate: Barbara and Patrick work hard to keep Luke's muscles from tightening up; they observe him carefully and teach him imaginatively. The doctor notices this and pays welcome tribute.

A habit of serious respectful listening pays dividends for professionals as well as families. People who observe children in homes, schools, and doctors' offices often note that they act different in different settings (Osher 1978). The doctor, the teacher, or the psychologist who attends to what parents tell him learns more about a child than those who think of parents as usually unreliable sources.*

Parents appreciate it when outsiders respect their child, too. The often critical Elizabeth Pieper recalls with warmth a doctor who perceived the little boy as well as the medical difficulties.

> Dr. Biagi treated Jeff to a lollipop to gain his cooperation and called his nurse in to see a five-month-old baby relish the treat. It was one of the few times Jeff was treated like a valuable, real-life child. The doctor called him by his name, played with him, examined him carefully, and enjoyed Jeff for himself. (Pieper, n.d., p. 17)

When a doctor or teacher enjoys a child in this way, he offers parents a chance to savor the ordinary but delicious pleasure of parental pride and delight.

Evidence that professionals *like* the child softens the blows. When the staff at the Xavier Hospital evaluated Melissa Potter, for instance, they had bad news for her family. At age two the little girl was eighteen months behind in motor development and a year behind socially. Her mother, Clare, emphasized the positive when she talked to the mothers' group: "The social development is much more important to me. Her responsiveness is what has kept us going."

As Clare talked about the Xavier staff, two things stood out. First, her appreciation of the professionals' honesty. "I'm accepting it much better because they're completely open with us. They tell us everything." And second, their affection for Melissa. "The whole hospital staff adores her. They want to keep her six weeks just so they can play with her. I told them, 'No. We want her back.'" And, she noted, "We're finally getting some answers."

I find that my notes provide many examples of professional respect for children, but rather few instances of comparable respect for parents. A parallel finding† in a study of doctor-patient communica-

---

* For the most part the great breakthroughs in the education of the handicapped have come through intensive and prolonged work with one child. Samuel Gridley Howe, Jean Itard, and Edouard Seguin spring immediately to mind. If a professional wishes to follow their lead in making original contributions to the field, she or he will have to listen seriously to parents' observations, since children spend most of their time at home.

† Korsch and Negrete (1972) analyzed videotapes of 800 interviews involving a sick child, a doctor, and a parent. They report that while 46 percent of the doctors' remarks to the children carried good feelings—"positive affect"—only 6 percent of those addressed to the parents could be so construed. The parents' most common complaint was that "the doctor showed little interest in their great concern about their child."

tion in a large emergency room suggests that practitioners trained for work with the young may support children better than they do parents. This is common in the schools, where many teachers—often good ones—see themselves as rivals of parents (for a thoughtful discussion of this problem, see Lightfoot 1978).

Services

All children require appropriate schooling, and increasingly the law in the United States is insisting that they get it. A variety of other services can help the family to cope with specific consequences of the disability: physical therapy, advice about mobility equipment and architectural adaptations, occupational therapy, help from the visiting nurse, baby sitting, respite care, counseling for the child or another family member, home teaching, a network of other parents with parallel problems, financial help with medical bills, equipment, or medications. Some parents know exactly what they need, and a few even know where to get it. Others never hear of—or even imagine—services that might improve their lives immeasurably.

It is remarkably difficult for parents to locate the services that do exist. The state funds some programs, while counties and towns sponsor others. A third group owe their existence to private philanthropic organizations, to church groups, or to hospitals. No one seems to know exactly what is available for whom under what circumstances.

I was reminded of this gap last summer. Because Jody had turned seven I needed to find a new school for him. The head of his current program gave me two possible names and suggested I call the special education department in my town for further suggestions. The preschool coordinator there gave me two more names, while pointing out that I should actually be talking to another woman in an office across town. When I called this lady she offered two suggestions of her own. I noted with interest that my three lists did not overlap at any point.

I started my calls to the schools. Even though each person I talked to added his or her own suggestions, the list soon dwindled to two. The first program served young adults only; the second was residential; the third and fourth lacked ramps and elevators and could not accommodate wheelchair-bound children; the fifth taught academic subjects only. I marveled at each new problem. It seemed that no one really knew the available programs, or who they served, although everyone was receptive and eager to help.

Other parents locate schools and other services through an equally haphazard process. In consequence, agencies connect with only a fraction of their potential clientele. Many parents muddle through without much outside help.

In the early years, parents rely on doctors rather than educators for guidance. Doctors, although they readily refer puzzling children to neurologists, opthamologists, and other medical specialists, often hesitate to put families in touch with other kinds of services. Many just do not know what is available. But quite a few appear to distrust other professionals and their meddling. A study (now in progress) of the effects of PL 94–142, the federal law mandating education for the disabled, suggests that this distrust shapes the experience of many families. After interviewing ten couples whose preschool children needed special education services, researcher Mary Jane Yurchak of the Huron Institute reports with astonishment that most of the parents sought help *against* the advice of their pediatrician. Despite enormous differences among the families and children, six or seven case histories sound variations on the same theme. The doctor responds to the child's irregular development with reassurance or, perhaps, medical referrals. When the child reaches the age of three, the parents suggest contacting the school system. They hope that preschool special education services will help him overcome his difficulties. The doctor vetoes this move, speaking of the dangers of labeling, and encouraging the mother to continue to rely on her own imagination. These particular mothers overrode their physician's objections to outside help; presumably many others do not.*

Professionals also hesitate to put parents in touch with similarly situated mothers and fathers. Many believe that these people lack the training necessary to help (Katz 1961; Bassin and Drovella 1976) or that parents who organize parent associations have "bad" attitudes.† Some professionals distrust the idea of any sort of parent organization. The Rehabilitation Institute of Montreal, for example, discouraged the parents of children with thalidomide deformities from organizing a group. The staff described the father most interested in pursuing

* Yurchak, personal communication.
† Katz, in studying the evolution of various groups organized by parents of handicapped children in New York City, interviewed professionals about their attitudes toward the groups. A number expressed concerns about untrained people trying to help people. Others worried about the characters of the parents involved: "In the interviews social work professionals a number of times expressed belief that some leaders of the groups seemed to be disturbed individuals. They observed that emotionalism and negative attitudes made some parent leaders difficult to deal with." (Katz 1961, p. 127)

this idea as "acting out"; in such contexts psychiatric explanations become political weapons (Roskies 1972, p. 131). The antagonism between parent groups and professionals seems unfortunate, since many mothers and fathers derive reassurance from their contacts with other more experienced parents.

Emotional Support

Discovering a child's disability precipitates parents into a new sort of adulthood. The woman who endures childbirth, midnight feedings, and colic follows in the footsteps of her mother and grandmother, of Abigail Adams, Elizabeth Cady Stanton, Queen Victoria, and Betty Freidan. Like it or not, most women over thirty-five consider themselves experts on her dilemmas and anxieties. When the same mother discovers that her child is in some way disabled, she steps outside the mainstream. Routine advice becomes irrelevant; few friends and neighbors have faced this problem. So the mother turns to professionals for the support and guidance that is so hard to find elsewhere. I remember that in the first year of Jody's life I actually looked forward to doctors' appointments in spite of the pain they often brought. In these settings I felt taken care of, although it is hard to say why. Many people worried more about my well-being than the kind but rather remote physicians to whom we entrusted Jody's care: my parents, my husband, my brothers, my friends, all were eager to help. Yet with everyone else I felt desperately in charge.

Perhaps it was because the doctors *knew* more than I did; with them I could ask questions. For everyone else *I* was the authority. I had seen the doctors, and I knew all that they had told me. I could sometimes comfort Jody when others failed, although I was not very good at it. At home, I was always the court of last resort. In a doctor's office I gratefully surrendered a little responsibility.

Professionals support parents simply by helping their children. In offices and schools which deal with other exceptional children, disabilities seem a fact of life rather than an extraordinary visitation. Many parents also need more personal help: they need companionship, and reassurance in the face of loneliness, pain, fear, anger, guilt, and fatigue.

The family that abandons a stance of strength, self-sufficiency, and optimism to ask for help takes a long, frightening step into the unknown. Professionals can encourage them by acknowledging their own concerns and by listening carefully.

Difficulties Confronting Professionals

In previous chapters, the voices of parents have of course overshadowed those of professionals. This book is, after all, primarily about families. Mothers and fathers speak with eloquence and insight about the way it feels to bring up a disabled child. They know the tribulations of doctors and teachers far less intimately. Only the professionals themselves can talk about these with authority.

I have been a teacher of one sort or another for most of my adult life, and I am going to draw on my own experience and that of my students and colleagues in what follows. I am not a medical doctor. To find out about the doctor's point of view on families and disability, I interviewed six pediatricians. In undertaking these interviews, I wondered whether a child's disability upsets doctors in some of the same ways that it upsets parents, and whether the doctor's response to tragedy, and his own feeling of helplessness, may pose particular problems. I concentrated on pediatricians in general practice because I was curious about the doctors' feelings during the period of uncertainty which usually precedes definitive diagnosis. I also wanted to hear about changes the doctor sees occurring over time, both in the parent's perspective and in his own. Doctors spoke to me about dilemmas they faced in dealing with suspected disabilities, about pressures of time, money, and family life, about public attitudes toward doctors, about bureaucratic hassles, about their failures and successes. All the doctors I called seemed surprised by my interest in their feelings. Some talked eagerly; others spoke of over-booked schedules and referred me to colleagues. None knew of published work on the subject of doctors' responses to children's disability (in contrast to the voluminous, if moralizing, literature on parents).

Pain and Vulnerability

A child's problem and his parents' pain touch doctors and teachers deeply. They are vulnerable too. Disability reminds people of their own fragility, of the obvious but terrifying fact that all good health fails ultimately. Like neighbors, casual passers-by, or anyone else, a professional feels awkward when confronted with the unfamiliar or stigmatized.

Professionals face other feelings as well—feelings that arise out of their special connection to the child and the role they play in his life. The doctor encounters a family at the point when they agonize most. Often he is the messenger who brings the bad news. He must deal with his own response to a bleak situation, with the parents' confusion and misery, and perhaps with his own reluctance to share pain. The teacher sees the child under other circumstances, in the company of children. He confronts the grim reality of social attitudes toward handicap. He grapples with his own need to help and to make a difference.

Several of the doctors who spoke with me described ways in which a doctor's feelings might interfere with good practice. One described her own experience with a neurologically-impaired baby.

I've looked after three children who are handicapped, whom I've seen since one or two months. One child had really peculiar tone, a lot of eye aversion, a lot of arching, real neurological problems. I was supposed to see her, at the age of one month, on the neurological floor, as a questionable mother-child interaction problem—this mother doesn't handle this baby well. I found it very difficult to tolerate the pain that I knew this child was having. And the mother knew and we talked about it. But I knew that in following up with these parents and trying to work through it, I was very much concentrating on the things the child *could* do. Probably too rapidly! There were things that we should work with, there were things she was showing us, and wasn't it exciting that she was beginning to hold gaze? I was rapidly moving them off the grief of acknowledging the way things were going. I think that I was rushing them through the grief reaction because of my own inability to work through it slowly with them.

I could tolerate acknowledging it, and I could tolerate the pain, and I could tolerate the tears and the gnashing of teeth for one day, and another day, and then a week later, but come a week after that I wanted to start working on, "Well, this kid can do *something*." I wanted them to be able to be as excited about the changes for the positive as I was. But I to some extent lost them in those first few weeks. And this came back on me with a lot of anger and grief. "We hear what you say, but we don't believe that *you* believe what you're saying about the child being so good and so strong. We don't believe that you really think that this child has her own developmental track. You're just saying that."

I thought I hadn't spent enough time acknowledging the pain of it. I was saying, "Hey, forget the pain, let's look at the positive"—I was all bouncy. So I think the intolerance of the long pain reaction can also alienate the physician from the parents. I think I learned through that that you have to take the pace of what you can do when. It isn't okay to break the news, and support them for a week, and then give them an infant stimulation program and everything is fine. Some parents turn around very fast, and some turn around slowly, and you have to repeat things for some parents. And some will say, "Okay, I've heard that, and I've dealt with it to some extent, but I can't take going over and over the pain of it, unless you can tell me something I can do about it." I learned a lot about the pacing. After you've done telling the truth you can't just say, "Whew, I've done that. Now, on with the positive work."

Other people have found in our unit that they've actually followed kids who were iffy, handicap-wise, and literally addressed everything else except their concerns. And found themselves not leaving time to really name the concerns, but spending all the time helping the parent around things he *can* do, as though in covert acknowledgement that something is wrong, but never overt. The parent thinks it hasn't been addressed. The doctor thinks he has addressed it because he has addressed it in his mind.*

A second doctor described his training in a clinic dealing with children's disabilities. He had practiced pediatrics before accepting this fellowship. Nonetheless, anxiety gripped him each time he prepared for a family conference. He wondered how a couple could withstand the news of their child's retardation and worried that they would fall apart as he explained the diagnosis. His fears eased gradually. After several months he learned that most parents are tough enough. Not tough, tough enough. As he grew more confident about their resilience, he learned to listen carefully and make sure that the conference dealt with all the important issues.

These two doctors live at least partly in the world of academic medicine. Perhaps their connections with an elite teaching hospital encourage them to look at themselves with a certain detachment. The physicians who were more involved in ordinary practices talked less explicitly about their own feelings and more about those of parents. They saw themselves as unwilling lightning rods for parents' denial, anger, anxiety, and frustration. As one doctor put it, "We are medicine men. And I am sure that since the beginning of time medicine men have been blamed for the world's ills. It's a hazard of the profession." Illustrating the way this can happen, another doctor described an encounter with a mother who ultimately left his practice:

I had one parent who was very upset with me. She discovered that her child had a hearing loss . . . and needed special help in school. She gave me this [school department] form. There were so many stupid things on the form, I wasn't going to take the time. It would have taken me twenty minutes to fill out the form. I would rather spend it talking to her. . . .

* All quotes from doctors in this chapter are taken from the interviews mentioned above. These conversations were taped, and portions were later transcribed.

I asked whether the mother could obtain services without this paper.

Sure she could. She said she was a teacher, and if I wouldn't fill it out she wouldn't have gotten the services. As I interpreted it she was so upset, and anxious, and angry, and discouraged that she was looking to me to be angry at. I don't think I was as empathetic perhaps as I might have been. I'm sure I have good days and bad days. . . .

At this point he reflected on the way stereotypes blight people's thinking. He felt angry about Senator Kennedy's attacks on the AMA and about the way the press portrays the medical profession. He described some parallel frustrations he had felt with his own father. Then his thoughts returned to the ill-fated form.

I felt, "Screw it. I'll call up your son's teacher and discuss it, but don't give me this shit about a piece of paper." But you know I couldn't say that to her. That's maybe being a little gross, but I'm trying to sketch my feelings. When someone says, "Help me," I'll help you, but don't put me into a [inaudible]. I'm being naive and unrealistic, I'm sure, when I talked about this woman. But I'm trying to see people on an individual basis, not to feel I've *gotta* do anything. I'll do as much as my ego strength and my physical energy can give me, not because the legislature says this is what all doctors should be doing. . . . I take courses for my own pride, not because some idiot in the state house says doctors should.

Clearly, emotions ran high on both sides. The doctor, listening to the mother, guessed that she was "upset and anxious and angry and discouraged." Probably she was. Discovering a hearing loss in a school-age child shocks parents even more than an earlier revelation might. The process of wringing services out of a reluctant school system would exhaust and discourage anyone. A doctor's refusal to complete paperwork might prove the final straw to the lonely disheartened parent.

The mother's request evoked a potent response in the doctor as well. He rebelled angrily against the demand that he fill out a form which seemed meandering, anonymous, and ultimately useless. His reflections suggest that the paper represented more to him than twenty ill-spent minutes. It reminded him of other assaults on doctors: of legislative regulation and media hostility. He speaks as though the referral form were a weapon in the bureaucratic arsenal, as though the real issue was his autonomy, and his resistance to a mindless, alien machine.

Another pediatrician reflected on a different sort of missed connection:

Well, I think in this particular family that I'm thinking of maybe I was a little bit too honest. The child has multiple congenital abnormalities. I've known the family, and followed the older child for many years. This particular child was born and I followed her for about three years. I had endocrine work-ups, neurological work-ups, had a work-up at the L-Hospital, and what I felt to be a very complete work-up. And I guess the fact is that we just kind of stopped there and the answers were just not coming. . . .

And the family, I guess, just weren't willing to accept that particular conclusion. And came to the point of needing information for something or other and got involved with another developmentalist or endocrinologist, and I got a report. Again, I think because of my experience, one thing I work very hard to do is to avoid fragmenting the child's care. There is nothing wrong with having an endocrinologist involved, an orthopedist involved, but someone has to run the show. Otherwise, it's trite but true, the left hand doesn't know what the right hand is doing. Duplication of services, redundance, etc., and at times even antagonism. As it turned out, it did happen. And when I got the report I spoke to the family, I spoke to the father and I said, "Don't do this to your daughter, please. If you want a thousand consults, let me know. I'll send off the information, I'll give them whatever they want." Because as it happened, *very* expensive studies were repeated. Not only repeated, but repeated by the same lab that had done it the first time. But the second doctor didn't know they had been done. I spoke with the family about it, and finally there was something else that had been done. Once again a duplication. And I brought it up to the family. I said, "You know, it makes it very difficult." I don't like to run my practice as though, "Do it my way or I'll take my ball and go home," but I think it does tend to undermine the relationship. And if they are going to pay me for my services I think it's certainly a foolishness for them to come, sit down, get my advice, and then go off and do what they want. And I told them so. And they evidently didn't like that, so they are off seeing someone else.

Maybe in this particular family they're still working through their denial and having to find whatever it is that caused it. They say, "Something must have caused this. So if we can find out what caused it, and find out the cure, then we can reverse whatever it is that took place."

This little girl's failure to develop surely troubled her parents deeply. The doctor's inability to discover the root of the disability frustrated them still further because they believed that diagnosis might provide a clue to treatment. In the sense that they clung to this hope, they had so far failed to "accept."

How does the doctor feel? His clients, people he had known for many years, have sought another opinion behind his back. They have ignored his advice, and shut him out of their search for help. Clearly he is angry; probably he is also hurt. His concern for the child, and perhaps a complex mix of other motives, prompts him to issue an ultimatum: it is foolish for them to get his advice and then ignore it. The family takes its business elsewhere.

Sometimes parents vent anger at doctors that they might more reasonably direct at another target. In our mothers' group, for example, one woman described watching in embarrassment as her husband threatened to hit the doctor who predicted that his son would never walk. Another raged with puzzling intensity at the specialist who had refused to order an expensive diagnostic test as part of her son's work-up. I have cited other examples of unreasonable anger in chapter 2.

Unfortunately, however, the obvious fact that a child's disability hurts parents deeply can blind a doctor to the complexity of his own feelings. Knowing how badly he would feel if this child were his own, he may ignore the smaller but quite real pain he feels as a doctor. Much of what he hears from other professionals confirms his impression that parents often fight pain by denying the disability and complaining about the physician. These often stereotyped expectations lead some doctors to discount parents' reasonable complaints along with unreasonable ones and to overlook the ways their own emotions contribute to an impasse.

Teachers work toward different goals; inevitably, different issues trouble them in their work. Unlike doctors, teachers spend little time with parents. Some manage to ignore minor ripples on the surface of the parent-teacher relationship. However, they spend far more time with the handicapped child than any other professional ever will. The duration and the intensity of this contact force them to attend to problems that another professional might avoid. Their feelings for the child and their responses to his presence in the classroom color their whole teaching experience during the time they are cast together.

Nowadays schools mainstream many handicapped children into ordinary classrooms for at least a part of the day. This practice widens the horizons of both disabled and normal children. It also presents ordinary teachers with some novel challenges. Teachers wonder whether the handicapped child will learn to read, write, figure, and think critically in a classroom designed for more typical needs. They

ponder his effect on classroom d̶y̶
proportionate fraction of their energy
other children or distract them from thei.
handicapped child's social experience: wil.
him? Will they ignore him? Or will they acc.
of factly and respect his strengths?

Academic considerations do matter to teachers
the next section). However, most see their classroom.
as well as a work place. They believe that their jo̶
responsibility for their charges' social learning as well   their
reading and geography skills. Those who welcome a ha̶.dicapped
child into their classroom usually hope that the "mainstream" experience will encourage all children to examine their attitudes and reject
objectionable stereotypes. A teacher may care very much about the
outcome of this process and what she sees of human nature in the
course of it.

Difference disturbs many adults, and they convey some of their
anxiety and embarrassment to children.* Even if they did not, children
would worry about disability or disfigurement for their own reasons.
Paradoxically, adults often hope to find children blind to differences
of all sorts. Sometimes children fulfill that expectation. Perhaps they
sense the adults' hunger for innocence; certainly they look at the
world somewhat differently than adults do. Their feelings are bound
to be complex.

Daily life in a mainstreamed classroom obliges a teacher to grapple
with his own feelings and also with those of the handicapped child
and his able-bodied peers. His job places him in a troubling position:
he must deal both with children's prejudices and fears and with
adult myths about young innocence.

* Vivian Paley's memoir *White Teacher* (1979) examines this issue in an especially thoughtful way. Paley is particularly interested in her own—and other
teachers'—responses to racial heterogeneity, but what she has to say applies to
other differences as well:

> Stuart was in our class that year and he had a bad stutter. Stuttering, like
> skin color, is a characteristic most teachers prefer to ignore. Even after I
> could comfortably discuss color, I could not easily refer to a child's stut-
> tering. I would look intently at the child and not let anyone interrupt, even
> in the natural way children interrupt each other. I felt as though I were
> holding my breath. (Paley 1979, p. 40)

Paley cared so deeply about her children's responses to stuttering and race that
for a long time she could not even mention these differences in class. At the same
time she judged the success of her program partly by the children's willingness to
accept one another.

...at the impact of children's feelings on grown-ups
...a children's book (Sobol 1977) to a graduate class in
...ucation. Less uncompromisingly upbeat than most juvenile
...rature on disability, the book describes the mixed responses of
eleven-year-old Beth to her retarded brother. Beth talks about loneliness, anger, confusion, embarrassment, and fear as well as warmth, pride, and concern. My eight-year-old daughter liked the book "because it talks about the bad feelings as well as the good ones." The graduate students, by contrast, were appalled. One objected, "It's like telling the kid, 'It's okay to have those feelings,' and almost sanctioning those feelings." Another judged the message "horrendous": "I mean even explaining it, I'd have to spend three hours explaining everything she said. There are some pretty powerful issues and complex ones that a little kid isn't going to understand for a minute." A few students cautiously concluded that a skillful teacher might use the book to help children think about mixed feelings, but nearly everyone agreed that it contained potentially explosive material.

Adults accept a special responsibility for the way the young learn about loaded issues. In a way they assume a kind of guilty omnipotence ahead of the occasion. They hope to see a discussion of anger or dislike "resolved" by a final change of heart; sometimes they seem to believe that one listens to a child's negative feelings mainly in order to change them. A sensitive subject like handicap evokes a particularly anxious response.

The teachers in my class wanted Beth to love and accept her different brother. They cared about her feelings because they wanted to see the power of stigma fade, to build a better world for disabled people. The children's book threatened their optimism, their conviction that things are getting better.

Attitudes toward the handicapped are improving, but changes of this sort occur slowly. We cannot expect the younger generation to redeem us all at once, to renounce attitudes that are deeply engrained in most cultures. When we see ourselves turning away from the darker side of children's feelings, we ought to ask whether we are not demanding too much, and whether we might not sometimes allow them some of our own imperfections.

Some parents remember clinging to myths in order to keep themselves going. Many describe a gradual healing process that enabled them to loosen their grip on these half-truths as they gained strength and could tolerate larger doses of reality. Professionals who care about their work may find themselves in a parallel situation. A young man who had taught in a school for autistic children reflects on his own responses to recent changes in thinking about infantile autism, changes that emphasized the organic origin of the problem:

As the diagnosis of retarded began to be applied to children who had formally been classically autistic, I found myself not wanting to acknowledge this change, particularly with the kids in my classroom. Whenever the frequently asked question "what do you do?" was put to me, I replied "I teach autistic (or severely disturbed) children." Never did I say "I teach retarded children." Not only that, but I didn't want to say "I teach retarded children." In believing the children were autistic or psychotic, the door was left open (albeit very slightly) to the hope of a major breakthrough; a sudden, unexpected improvement; possibly even a complete remission. This fantasy was extremely motivating for me; the mystery of this autism, the thought that perhaps at any time one of the children might begin talking allowed me to create a sort of romantic self-image out of this teaching situation.
But if the children were retarded all these hopes were without foundation. Retarded kids made no sudden improvement. . . . The door was shut tight on romantic fantasy in teaching retarded kids, with reality assuming the central position. (Alterman 1978, p. 17)

In professionals as well as parents, disability awakens a childlike need for magic. "Heroes of adjustment," as Erving Goffman calls them, distort our understanding of the disabled: facing disability, we crave miracles. However exceptional the blind man who wins golf tournaments, he is the one in the news. Teachers talk about reading parents' accounts and even journal articles breathlessly, hoping to find the child cured on the final page. At some level each of us yearns to participate in a miracle, to see a disabled child take a giant step toward normality.

Occasionally a remarkable, persistent and fortunate teacher manages to turn a child's life around altogether (see, for example, Hawkins 1979). Such experiences affect the professional almost as profoundly as the child and his family. They affirm him. They sustain him through dark moments of self-doubt. Revisited by the light of new experience, they color a teacher's expectations for other exceptional children.

Helplessness, Incompetence, Inadequacy

Every parent who journeys to a professional with a disabled child hopes to get help. Doctors and teachers are paid to cure and educate.

Successes cheer and reward them. Yet sometimes they can not offer the disabled child any real service beyond care and concern. Such contacts do not fortify their sense of themselves as competent, helpful practitioners: failures leave them unsatisfied as well as sad, unsure of themselves and their calling.

From a certain perspective, the disabled person defines the limit of modern medical science. No doctor can cure his problem, even though it lies within the medical domain. At best, the physician may ameliorate the situation. Often he can only diagnose. Occasionally, he can do even less. In our culture we go to medicine for two things: for cures and for concern. Often the model of technical medicine geared to quick cures gets in the way of giving sustained concern.

This is not to say, of course, that doctors never help disabled people. They often do. An operation saved my son's life. Another operation may have spared him future pain and discomfort. Daily doses of phenobarbitol and dilantin control his seizures. Nonetheless, no medical procedure can restore his vision, give him control of his hands, or allow him to speak the words he understands.

The chasm between the promise of technical medicine—the stories we read in *Time* magazine—and what doctors can offer our own hurt child wounds parents deeply at first. Like every other parent, I asked my doctor—the neurologist on this occasion—"What can I *do*?" He showed me how to put Jody's foot through a range of motion. He warned me, however, that this exercise would not accomplish miracles: "It might make it a little easier to put on his shoes when he gets older."

I could have cried. I wanted to know how I might make my baby better. How could I teach him, or make him less blind, less crippled, less unhappy? And he showed me how to stretch his heel cords so his shoes would go on more easily in a few years (Why would he need shoes, I wondered, if he couldn't walk?).

My doctor was not insensitive. He simply didn't know any way that either of us could help Jody much. The limits of technical medicine sear the parents' heart. They trouble the doctor too. One pediatrician I talked to suggested that in such situations the doctor's frustrations might distort his perceptions of parents: "When doctors say that they are worried that parents will be angry with them, they are really reacting to their *own* anger. They would like to be able to help, to cure, to perform a miracle. They feel angry at their own helplessness." No one enjoys feeling ineffective. The knowledge that others care deeply about our success adds an especially disagreeable barb to the thorn of frustration. Day to day experiences in the hospital and consulting room may prepare the doctor poorly for this sort of encounter. As another doctor points out, the often exaggerated respect of parents and patients for physicians can encourage unrealistic self-portraits:

The other thing is that because some docs get behind the desk they really do believe after a while in what keeps coming across through the transference and that it has something to do with them. It really doesn't; it has to do with the transference.

People's feelings about physicians, upon whom they are so often *very* dependent, sometimes causes such adulation coming across that if the doc believes everything he hears he'll believe he's omniscient and prescient.

Perhaps, as this doctor charges, medical practice gives some doctors an inflated sense of their own power and importance. A child's disability can threaten this sense of power in several ways. I have spoken of its most direct impact: the doctor cannot cure the disability. He cannot fulfill the family's hopes. He disappoints them, and also, perhaps, himself.

The physician may face a further problem: the treatment he *can* provide solves problems that the parents have not even perceived. For example, the child with cerebral palsy or spina bifida may require an operation simply in order to grow normally. The doctor who recommends this surgery creates problems for parents, even as he tries to help. The family that has worried about their child's immobility must now grapple with two new fears: the effect of surgery and hospitalization, and the possibility of future deformity. Their response, however well-balanced, probably will not reassure the surgeon that he has performed a vital, life-giving service.

Even the surgeon who lobbies enthusiastically for the needed surgery sees the frustrating, equivocal nature of his job. There is a big contrast between this brand of medicine and the dramatic cures he saw during training and sometimes achieves with other patients.

When one gets into medicine the whole direction of our upbringing is toward the illnesses that are critical, life and death, where you can put your finger on a particular abnormality, where you see the appendix is inflamed, and you have the ability to go in and cut and remove it and that's it.

We tend to get bogged down and it really can be a definite quagmire.

People tend to avoid that and don't want to get sucked in because you find yourself uncovering an area of concern, and then another and then another, and then another, and it does very often become a quagmire. And it's unfortunate and I'm sure a good part of it happens to be because of the discomfort of the individual and the inability to end up with some positive end result.

The other thing, too, is that the result, the reward, the goal, isn't realized in a manner in which one can say there is a definite cause and effect. It's not a case where the physician does something and the next day, two days later, the fever goes down, the rash disappears, the patient feels better and is up walking around. It goes on and on and on.

Dr. Mel Levine, who has interested himself in the problems pediatricians encounter in coping with disabled children, suggests that the disabled child threatens the primary practitioner in another way. The on-going involvement of other specialists—the otologist, the orthopedist, the endocrinologist, the neurologist—puts him at a disadvantage. He knows that these doctors will do things to the child that he does not completely understand. He knows that parents will ask him to evaluate their recommendations and clarify their diagnoses. Their questions put him on the spot and remind him of how much he does not know.

The disability may raise questions about the doctor's powers in other spheres as well. The doctor who refused to fill out the special education form seems to have been rebelling against bureaucratic efforts to order him about. His client's demand reminded him of the statutory requirements surrounding continuing medical education: both encroached on his personal and professional autonomy. The doctor quoted on p. 191 voices a parallel complaint: this family treats him as a technician, whose advice they may follow or ignore at will.

Parents of disabled children probably do oppose their physician's advice more often than other people. Anger, confusion, and denial shape some decisions. After all, such families play for very high stakes. Even if parents crave their doctor's approval and long to place difficult decisions in his well-trained hands, they may oppose his judgment and seek a second opinion. If another clinician can suggest an operation or therapy program that will restore some normal function, they *must* seek it out. To the doctor, these searches may spell blind folly. To the parent who knows that some families have found real help after an unpromising start, docility may look almost immoral.

Like the doctor, the classroom teacher wants to perform the role he was trained for. A disability can make him feel painfully inadequate.

Having discovered that a little boy does not learn as swiftly as his classmates, that, indeed, he does not seem to process certain kinds of information at all, the teacher would like to help. He tries a new approach. He hopes to find a way around the problem so the child will succeed in class, avoid the "Dummy" label, and pass on to the next grade. Sometimes the teacher succeeds; sometimes he fails. As a first grade teacher, for example, I worried about one of my students, David, who was learning nothing from the phonic reading scheme I was teaching. After weeks of fruitless drill I discovered that although David could not seem to "hear" initial consonant sounds, he could generate rhyming words at an incredible pace. When I finally abandoned work papers on the letter "B" and substituted some games involving rhyming monosyllables, David began to read. Our shared success repaid the hard work of puzzling over David's problems and writing special assignments for him. Encouraged, I turned my energies to eager, obedient Nicole, who tried hard, coloring every worksheet obediently between the lines, while sinking inexorably to the bottom of the lowest reading group. I experimented with each one of the four reading schemes I had learned about in graduate school. I asked Nicole's mother about special interests and family projects, thinking that we could read some appropriate books together. Nothing I did seemed to help. Feeling like a failure, I watched Nicole's bright smile fade with the autumn leaves, as she fell further and further behind her classmates.

Neither Nicole's parents nor I turned to experts for advice. In those days my school system employed one psychologist for every twenty thousand students, and children who needed help waited an average of two-and-a-half years for a consultation. Today a teacher in my position would probably ask the learning disabilities specialist for ideas and materials. She might request a full-scale evaluation. She would be less alone, but she might be equally frustrated. For the classroom teacher, many problems remain after a team of experts has evaluated the child, recommended an individual educational plan, and disappeared into the sunset. The plan is often disappointingly vague about the actual procedures to be used, and yet its carefully specified goals seem to promise that the problems will yield to persistent, intelligently designed treatment. The teacher's experience may suggest otherwise. He wonders whether parents will blame him when a child fails to improve. He knows he could do more if he had more time.

Studies of attitudes toward mainstreaming have found the majority of teachers reluctant to include seriously handicapped children in their classes (Winefield 1979). Sometimes a mainstreaming experience reduces their enthusiasm still further. Considering how little support most teachers get when they try to wrestle with the completely novel challenges of a child with, say, a severe hearing loss, their attitudes should puzzle no one.

Neither the conditions of work nor community social attitudes encourage a teacher to see himself as a skilled practitioner doing valued work. Lay people describe teaching as common sense. Teachers judge their training as largely unhelpful (Lortie 1975). Most say they learn their skills in the classroom, through trial and error. Many parents discount teachers' judgments; school administrators often treat them like cogs in an educational machine.

A teacher's sense of competence is a fragile creation, and it is always being tested. If children misbehave or fail to learn, the teacher questions his own adequacy. So do parents and principals. Naturally teachers welcome the opportunity to do what they feel competent and well-trained to do, and resist being put in a position where they feel ignorant and inadequate.

Often a disabled student's educational plan implicitly disparages what the homeroom teacher has to offer. It specifies the need for outside specialists—psychologist, LD teacher, or whoever—who take the child out of class for particular sorts of help. The scheduling often ignores regular classroom activities, so the child walks in and out in the middle of lessons. The teacher concludes that everyone values the specialists contributions more than they value his, and perhaps even that the parents, the principal, and others see his program as something to occupy the child when the specialists are busy elsewhere. As one teacher asks, perhaps rhetorically, "What are we trying to do for him in the classroom if we're always taking him out of it?" (Fisher 1977, p. 12).

In a special setting like a resource room, both the teacher and the child may stand a greater chance of feeling successful. Expectations are usually scaled down somewhat; the teacher has been trained to meet special needs. Unfortunately special teachers are terribly overworked. Some school systems abuse mainstreaming as a device for expanding their teaching loads. After all, the bureaucrat reasons, if each child spends only one-third of his day in the resource room, the teacher can handle three times as many children. This logic ignores the special teacher's responsibilities for helping classroom teachers to plan each child's homeroom program and for meetings and paperwork.

Finally, both homeroom teachers and special educators must figure out a way to share responsibility. Their training rarely prepares them for this sort of work. The model for most education, especially at the elementary level, is the self-contained classroom—one teacher alone in a room with twenty to thirty children. Although some schools are moving away from this traditional pattern, teachers still train and work in settings which isolate them from other adults. A handicapped child may force them to experiment not only with new teaching techniques, but with new approaches to planning and cooperation. Many of the best teachers love the independence of classroom teaching. For them the necessity for cooperative planning adds another frustration and another challenge to their sense of competence.

Both the teacher and the doctor want to help. Success builds their sense of competence, their confidence that their work is worth doing. The hope of success helps them to get out of bed when the alarm clock goes off in the morning. Very often, however, the child with a disability undermines that confidence by posing problems that they cannot solve.

Professional Training

So far, I have tried to show how the child's disability touches professionals in ways that dimly echo its impact on parents. Professional roles lay the foundation for certain fears, certain sorts of guilt, and most pervasively, for a nagging sense of inadequacy. But professionals, unlike parents, train for their jobs. We might hope that their education would equip them with the skills they need to navigate these tricky waters.

In some ways, of course, it does. Years of medical school, internship, and residency teach the pediatric neurologist a great deal about diseases of the nervous system and allow him to make certain judgments more accurately than a layperson. College courses give the special educator techniques for helping blind children to learn. Parents flock to professionals because they value their special knowledge. Still, valuable as training is, it makes for problems as well.

Experience sets parents and professionals apart from one another.

Parents have never stood in professionals' shoes and tried, for example, to decide how to break the news of retardation to an anxious family. Similarly, few professionals know first-hand the anguish that comes with a child's disability. No course of training can breach these chasms. Sometimes professions magnify the inevitable differences.

Teaching provides a pertinent example. Until fairly recently, many school systems refused to hire married woman teachers. Even in the seventies many insisted that women quit the classroom by the third month of pregnancy (before they visibly join the enemy's ranks?). Rules that make motherhood incompatible with classroom teaching ensure that parents and teachers share fewer experiences than they might otherwise.

All this is changing now. New attitudes and more sensible hiring practices have brought mothers back into the classroom, so more educators now have access to the sort of knowledge that parenting teaches more surely than college. For example, any mother who has survived a child's infancy and toddlerhood knows that children tolerate frustration better after meals than immediately before, and that children and adults operate on different thermostats. I recall that as a young, childless first grade teacher I rarely noticed children's blue lips and hunched shoulders in a poorly heated room. Nervous energy kept me warm even when the mercury sank below sixty.

Although the experience of raising children may inform the vision of an individual teacher, doctor, or social worker, few professions acknowledge or respect them. A woman applying for a job in a school does not include the fact that she has raised four children on her curriculum vita. And people seeking professional work with the handicapped seldom cite their lifelong experience with a disabled family member, even though their resumes may carefully note every volunteer summer job.*

Professions evolve formal training requirements and generate a

---

* A woman who runs a school for emotionally disturbed children noted that nearly every one on her staff had a relative or friend who was different in some way, and yet none of these people mentioned this personal experience in interviews or in their first weeks on the job. She wondered whether they felt in some way guilty about their relationships to these people, but to me it seemed more likely that they saw these personal connections as irrelevant to the impersonal "professional" world. In the same way, she said, women who were re-entering the work world after a long absence would never mention their experience on the PTA or in other voluntary organizations. She had to prompt them to discuss the work they had done without formal training or pay.

vocabulary of recondite terms. In general, the more difficult, time-consuming, and expensive the rites of passage, and the more mysterious the vocabulary, the more respect the profession can command. Teaching, although an exhausting, challenging career, is relatively easy to enter. The training is brief and readily available. It is a relatively low-status profession. Many people doubt that teachers know a great deal more about education than laymen (although most who are not teachers would retreat quickly if asked to establish a pleasant, effective learning environment for twenty-five children and to run it for six hours a day, five days a week). The status of teaching seems perpetually at risk.*

Doctoring is different. Nearly everyone acknowledges that doctors understand certain medical matters better than other people. They endure a long, rigorous training. Their knowledge and skills save lives. The doctor probably needs no reassurances about his specialness.

But doctors acquire more than technical knowledge in the course of their professional education. They learn to look at human problems through special lenses. A recent sociological study of medical decision making in a teaching hospital (Carlton 1978) documents one aspect of this evolution: the acquisition of the "clinical perspective." The clinical view (as Carlton defines it) focuses on the medical dimensions of a case, rather than the complex human and ethical questions it may raise. It asks, pragmatically, what the doctor can do and what results will follow on each course of action. The uninitiated—the layman, the parent, the medical student—attend to a broader range of issues. (The drama and tragedy on a hospital ward offer considerable scope for the imagination.) Thus the medical student, making rounds for the second or third time, notices Mrs. Jones's empty bed and asks about the time and manner of her death. His teachers reply perfunctorily: his curiosity serves no clinical purpose; it is inappropriate to a doctor making rounds.† The student notices that such inquiries are unwelcome and directs his attention elsewhere.

* For a good discussion of this see Lortie 1975.
† One of Carlton's other examples clarifies the distinction between the "clinical" and the "moral"—the medical and the lay—perspective. A nine-year-old boy is admitted to the hospital with kidney failure. The mother refuses a transplant on religious grounds. The medical student concentrates on the clinical issues: "Is a donor available for transplant? Is the boy a candidate for dialysis?" Since the answer to both questions is "no," his recommendations coincide with the mother's wishes. The mother's reasoning, which emphasizes religious considerations, illustrates the moral perspective. The medical student reaches the same conclusion utilizing the clinical perspective (Carlton 1978, pp. 104–105).

Considering the awesome human questions that confront doctors every day, it seems both wise and psychologically necessary to focus the minds of young physicians on what they can actually *do*. Nonetheless, a training that teaches people to see complex human questions through technical lenses will set them off from the rest of the human race and may not equip them for dealing with disability.

Professionals, then, come to an encounter with parents with a very different background of relevant experiences and sometimes with a different set of concerns, or at least a different focus.

Often a professional is trained to see nonprofessional experiences as less valid and less informative than paid professional work. This point of view can lead to a patronizing view of clients. In the past much of what was written about parents of exceptional children in the "scientific" literature intended for students and professionals conveyed a lack of respect bordering on contempt. Things are better now, but even those writing in the last decade tend to explain parent-professional difficulties by gesturing in the direction of presumed parental pathologies. A special education text warns prospective teachers:

Parents of exceptional children have caused many educators hours of discern [sic] because of the problem of providing guidance is not a simple process. A professionally trained individual will probably devote many hours and many repeated efforts before any understanding and acceptance will be made by the parents of an exceptional child. (Van Osdol 1976, p. 125)

Difficulties between doctors and parents are interpreted in much the same way. Nancy Wagner Hart includes a discussion of "the unusual degree of hostility between parents of retarded children and the doctors whom they consult" in an essay on parental responses to retardation. After marshaling three vignettes to illustrate parents' irrationality, she concludes with a few remarks on parent groups:

Their excessive anger has given parents' groups a dubious reputation not only with doctors but among other professional groups as well. Social workers, educators, and public officials who are invited to speak at meetings often find themselves harassed by a barrage of angry questions at the end of the speech. Many of these comments have little or no relevance to the speech but are rather a retelling of some past injustice. A few speakers who have been thus indoctrinated [sic] say they will never again appear before such groups. (Hart 1970)

Most modern writers avoid the patronizing generalizations that marred a good deal of earlier scholarship. However, individual families still fare poorly. I think, for example, of Doreen Kronick's recent study of three families with learning-disabled children. Kronick disclaims any intention of suggesting that family pathology generates learning disabilities and avoids generalizing about the larger population of exceptional children. However, she paints every one of the six parents she observed in an extraordinarily unfavorable light, and she compares the families to those Jules Henry described in *Pathways to Madness*. Although two of the three couples first impressed Kronick as warm and caring, few favorable adjectives survive the forty hours of in-home observation.

Though I was not in a position to assess whether the parents in the sample have academic processing problems, they display the other behaviorisms typically associated with learning disabilities; rigidity, disorganization, unawareness of the impact of their behavior on others, short interest span, lack of in-depth commitment to anything or anybody, and inappropriate handling of feelings. Consequently, though their learning-disabled offspring may have intrinsic deficits in the areas we have examined, the home environment is antitherapeutic in that alternative behaviors are not modeled. . . . These families are in no position to institute therapeutic measures until they learn healthy modes of interaction. (Kronick 1976, p. 83)

If these parents have significant strengths, Ms. Kronick has failed to locate them.

These attitudes are not confined to writers and social scientists. Criticizing parents is a way of life in schools. As Sara Lawrence Lightfoot shows in her excellent study of schools and families (Lightfoot 1978), antagonism between mothers and teachers goes back a long way into American history. The culture reinforces a kind of competition between these two nurturing groups. Although many mothers and teachers manage to cooperate successfully, each group seems too willing to blame the other for a child's difficulties in school.

The idiom of the staff room tends to confirm the entrenched mental health doctrine that the problems children display in school reflect the errors and shortcomings of their parents. When this attitude greets the mother at conference time, it rarely elicits a favorable response. Thus stereotypes confirm one another, with parents and teachers turning their worst faces toward one another.

If the experience of training and early professional work magnifies the distance that separates professionals from parents, it has also failed to teach doctors and teachers the skills that would help them serve atypical children. Up until recently few classroom teachers studied the educational problems of disabled children in college. They learned to teach the modal or "normal" child and to refer his atypical sister to a specialist. Under these circumstances, only the intrepid would welcome a blind, retarded, or epileptic child into the ordinary classroom (see Winefield 1979). A training system that insisted on special personnel for special children sent an implicit message to its graduates: these children are *really* different.

Medical training omits equally critical skills. A recent survey of ninety-seven randomly selected New England pediatricians found the overwhelming majority (79 percent) dissatisfied with their preparation in child development. Few of these doctors viewed clinical experience as an adequate substitute for the courses they did not get (Dworkin et al. 1978). In practice, the pediatrician shoulders the major responsibility for diagnosis even when the specialist bestows the actual label. Inadequate knowledge of development prevents him from helping parents to focus their diffuse concerns about a child who seems subtly different.

In this section I have described some ways in which professional training and conditions of practice contribute to ongoing difficulties in the parent-professional relationship. Doctors and teachers also describe encounters that broadened their vision or forced them to examine old assumptions. Not all of these occur on the ward or in the classroom, but some do:

Part of my residency was spent in S—— Training School. M.R. [mentally retarded] Kids. This was in the early fifties.

I went there as resident for six months—I had no kids of my own at the time. But before I went there I was sent up by my chief of residence in Baltimore who said, "They need someone there for six months. It's part of Yale's program. You will enjoy it. Go up there and see what it's like."

And I walked into a TB ward where I saw a child who was vegetative from TB meningitis being tube fed, being kept alive. Smart-ass resident, I said to the chief, "Why are you doing this? Why are you keeping that child alive?" He said, "If you decide to come here, you'll understand." And I said, "Well, I'm not sure I can vigorously treat that child, if that child gets a pulmonary pneumonia. What if that child gets a pneumacocal pneumonia, how can I vigorously treat?" He said, "I'll be here to treat anybody you don't want to treat, but maybe you'll understand a little more at the end of your residency than you did in the beginning."

We decided to go up. And believe it or not, that child developed a pneumoccocal pneumonia and I vigorously treated her *because* that child had *parents* who drove up every Sunday and sat with her and held her hand. And she responded to them with eye blinks.

I remember when it went click in my head that I was going to treat that child if need be. And I was relieved that I had the opportunity to prove to myself—it was an absolutely eye-opening, amazing life experience for me. I remember every moment of it. I remember coming back to my apartment and saying to my wife, "Let me tell you what happened."

Anyway, it's that kind of experience that I think one has in one's professional life that turns things around in the way you think about life. And death. And people. And what one person gets out of living and another person gets out of living.

There is a lot to pay attention to in this memory, now over twenty-five years old. The amazing coincidence strikes us first, but the real drama takes place inside the young resident's head.

Three factors catalyzed the change which seems so important to him. First, and most obviously, the girl and her family. Noticing the parents' great concern—their regular visits, their careful attention to the little girl's expression as they sat beside her bed—he watched the child closely. His interest allowed him to see something he had missed before: an intelligence intent on communication. The special characteristics of this child and her family allowed him to glimpse the humanity that diagnostic categories occasionally obscure, to understand that a complex web of social relationships gives any life much of its meaning.

The young doctor might not have noticed the eye blinks, or the family, had his teachers not prepared the ground first. He knew that his chiefs *expected* him to grow, he knew they hoped he would learn a different way of looking at retarded people. Their attitudes encouraged him to watch and listen.

The story does not end with the resident's realization that this little girl is more than a "vegetative" (medical terms are sometimes bald) case, or with his decision to treat her then-hypothetical illness. Fate provided him with a chance to *act* on that change of heart, maybe to save her life. The action itself mattered immensely. It allowed him to prove to himself that he had changed; it gave substance to the inner drama. He describes it as an "eye-opening, amazing life experience." He still remembers each moment in vivid detail.

This encounter contains, in fortunate combination, four critical ingredients: a little girl who defied stereotyping; parents who responded with sensitivity and realism to what she had to offer; senior staff who promoted humane values; an opportunity for effective action consonant with the young doctor's vision of himself as a healer.

Making Things Better

Just as parents must attend simultaneously to the wider issues of services and respect for the disabled, and to the particular needs of *their* disabled child, so the professional must live and work in a world molded by "macro" and "micro" issues. Social policies concerning delivery of medical and educational services and cultural assumptions about the role and status of parents and professionals create the context for all work with children and families. The practitioner's own skills, his assumptions about himself and his obligations, and the particular parents and children with whom he works, all decisively influence what happens on a given work day. A professional's efforts to improve services may focus either on society and specific institutional practices or on himself, his own skills and level of awareness.

The macro—the social—contexts of disability have been brilliantly discussed in a recent Carnegie report by John Gliedman and William Roth (1980). The reader should consult this important work directly, but some points deserve reiteration here.

The relationship between parents of disabled children and professionals is imbalanced. An individual family needs a professional far more than the professional needs them. The professional, particularly if he is a doctor, enjoys a higher status than the parent. (Parenthood, alas, confers negative status; only professional training or irrelevant social factors raise the parent to the professional's level.) In consequence of these asymmetries of need and prestige, the professional wields far more power than the parent.

Parents' vulnerability has at least three undesirable consequences. First, it reduces the incentives for certain sorts of professional learning. If a practitioner values a client's good opinion and patronage, he will search for signs of approval or disapproval and modify his performance accordingly.

Second, parents relative impotence allows institutions to treat them as patients. Professionals expect passive acquiescence rather than active participation from powerless clients. As Roth and Gliedman astutely observe, the pathological model that informs so much professional thinking about disability places parents in a double-bind: "Either submit to professional dominance (and he operationally defined as a patient), or stand up for one's rights and risk being labeled emotionally maladjusted (and therefore patient like)" (p. 150).

Finally, the professional who encounters little effective resistance to his claims to dominance often comes to confuse his technical expertise with a broader moral authority. Forgetting the role that values play in most child-rearing decisions, forgetting the fundamental uncertainty in which professionals as well as parents operate, he comes to see himself as an arbiter rather than an advisor; he expects parents to follow his recommendations on a wide variety of matters not directly related to his special training. Consider, for example, the old practice of recommending institutionalization for children born with Down's syndrome. Clearly the pediatrician's clinical experience with similar children both inside and outside of institutions ought to be considered pertinent, but the issue is at bottom moral rather than technical.

The power of parent groups has grown in recent years. Their collective action has forced some changes in social policy and in specific institutional practices. But the relationship between parent and professional remains tipped in the professional's favor. Our policies and assumptions must shift, making parent satisfaction important to the careers of doctors and teachers, if we are to see important change.

In this chapter I have not focused on these essentially political macro issues, important as they are. Here I am concerned with professionals' personal responses to disability. I hope that my discussion of the difficulties that professionals face in their work with families will be an invitation to doctors, teachers, and other professionals to look thoughtfully at their own professional lives, at their training, at their responses to particular parents and children, and at the conditions of their work. I am anxious not to be misunderstood. I do not want professionals to slink into their classrooms and clinics and beat their breasts for past sins. On the contrary, I described the problems of a few doctors and teachers in order to encourage other professionals to look at themselves and their co-workers with a measure of sympathy. Doctors and teachers can support one another in the same way parents do—by sharing memories, dilemmas, and insights.

In general I am more comfortable describing problems than outlining solutions. General principles rarely eliminate specific problems; solutions, when they exist at all, usually emerge from a sympathetic analysis of a particular situation. Nonetheless, I will briefly adopt the didactic voice in these final pages.

It seems to me that professionals can help parents, children, and themselves by learning to listen better. A doctor or teacher's willingness to listen benefits parents in obvious ways. First of all, listening conveys respect. When a doctor attends carefully to a mother's description of her son's skills, when he scribbles rapid notes and extends her line of thought with questions, he communicates two judgments. First, the mother is an intelligent observer who contributes valuable information. Second, the child is a unique, puzzling human being, rather than a member of a substandard category.

Listening is also supportive: much of the value of psychotherapy comes from simply opening up, talking about feelings to an interested outsider. Therapeutic insight is part and parcel of the opportunity to hear oneself. Many parents need more chances to talk than they get. Social scientists who interview mothers of disabled children remark on their informants' eager volubility. During interviews parents comment: "I have never talked over such things with anyone before" (Barsch 1968, p. 28); "No one has ever been interested enough in us or our child before this. You are the first person who has ever asked us to tell what it is like" (Osher 1978, p. 3). Participants in a support group return year after year to talk and to listen.

Most professionals agree that everyone deserves the satisfaction of talking it out. However, individual doctors and teachers often shrink from the role of professional listener. For one thing, they lack time. Sick children fret impatiently in the pediatrician's waiting room, while he tries to concentrate on an anxious mother's concerns. The teacher divides his attention among many children; competing obligations limit the time he can give any individual parent. Listening highlights the inelasticity of time: no one can hurry and listen in the same moment. You can streamline the process of correcting workbooks, setting out easels, or conducting a physical examination, but you must listen at someone else's pace (although not necessarily at their convenience).

Because listening consumes a great deal of time, it is expensive. As services are presently organized, the professional absorbs the cost:

doctors usually bill by the visit, not by the minute. Teachers receive a fixed salary, without overtime for lengthy after-school conferences.

Some professionals devise ingenious strategies for stretching the day. One pediatrician invites concerned parents to bring a sandwich and share her lunch break. This practice does several things: parents and physician talk without the pressure of a busy waiting room; the doctor shows concern simply by inviting the parent at such a time; and eating together creates a bond because it is relaxing and social.

By concentrating on cures and technical skills and de-emphasizing the realm of value and feeling, medical training and the medical model of disability hamper the doctor's attempt to show concern for families through listening. In one way or another nearly all my physician-informants reiterated the charge that "doctors are not comfortable with feelings." Whether this is true on a personal level or not, many doctors do not feel qualified to listen professionally. They see counseling as the province of the social worker or psychiatrist and worry that they will mishandle delicate issues. They quite naturally prefer to concentrate on tasks that utilize their special skills. Teachers also receive no special preparation for listening to parents and share some of the same misgivings.

It is true that listening is a skill, that some people "hear" better than others. The main problem is in recognizing and dealing with your own responses to what is said. Sometimes this can be rough: a disabled child awakens powerful, sometimes desperate, feelings; the rage and pain of a parent call forth a response in the heart of a concerned professional. The Murrays' first baby was born dead; the medical record describes her as an "anencephalic monster." Their second, John, suffered from a degenerative neurologic illness. Emily Murray's journal describes the way two different doctors responded to her grief and bitterness:

We saw the developmental examiner today. He is an idealist, a sensitive young man; he likes working with children because there *is* promise. The cruelest thing, he said, is to see a child cut off and the promise destroyed.

When he spoke to us about adopting, though, I said our luck with children hadn't been too good. He drew back, disturbed by my bitterness. And I felt mad. These doctors ought to be willing to let people express some of their anguish without getting embarrassed or cross. That's part of their job. And it is the only time I have done it, God knows. Dr. Meredith's eyes met ours, and hers were filled with tears. That's sharing it. (Murray and Murray 1975, p. 66)

The examiner and the pediatrician care about John Murray and his parents. The younger doctor recoils from the bitterness that temporarily tinges Emily Murray's grief. Dr. Meredith has practiced longer, and, perhaps, endured some tragedies of her own. She seems to know more about anger and sorrow; she acknowledges her own vulnerability. Her tears pay tribute to John, and to a thread of common feeling.

If listening is expensive, if professional training has failed to equip doctors and teachers with specific counseling skills, why should they put aside time for this sort of thing instead of simply referring parents to a psychiatrist or social worker? Most obviously, because parents will talk about their problems and concerns without much of an invitation anyway. Since doctors and teachers have to listen anyway they might as well learn to listen well. Second, and more important, because careful, curious listening allows them to grow professionally, even humanly, and to solve some of the problems that hamper their work with disabled children.

Sustained conversation with parents teaches the professional a great deal about a specific child and his family. Since parents spend most of each day with the child and coordinate his contacts with schools, medical people, and social services, they know more about him than the doctor or teacher can ever hope to discover by observation alone.

The professional who listens attentively to many patients over a period of years learns cumulatively about the experiences that families share. He learns to see a wide variety of situations from the inside. He becomes a student of families and of the human race. This growing expertise bolsters confidence. Even a pediatrician with an ordinary practice, who will follow very few children with a particular disability, can extend his understanding and overcome the inadequacies of his training through in-depth conversations with one or two families.

Certain principles ought to guide all work with families: be frank; respect the child; honor the parents' desire to heal their son or daughter; listen carefully. Such generalities, while true enough, carry teachers and doctors only a certain distance. Families construe their worlds very variously. Even within a family, each parent sees the disability from a special angle; each nurses somewhat different wounds; each travels a largely uncharted path out of despair.

Because each person sees the disability differently, the doctor or teacher who offers support and guidance often risks being misunderstood. Remarks which would alienate or divide one family lift another up from a quagmire of gloom or self-accusation.

After Ellie Lederman died, Catherine told me she felt incredibly relieved, and terribly guilty about the relief. "I was so frightened by my feelings that one day I called my social worker at the hospital to tell her how guilty I felt about my relief. And then, after I hung up, I became terrified that she would call the police, that they would come and take me away. . . . I was so afraid they would think I caused it, by not giving her her medicine (although of course I did give it to her) or something."

She said that during this difficult period another social worker called her, a woman who had known her for most of Ellie's life. "Feeling relieved, and guilty about feeling relieved?" she inquired. And Catherine responded gratefully "Yes! How did you know?" The social worker then urged her to buy a bottle of wine for herself and Peter, and toast the three long hard years they had survived together.

Telling the story later, Catherine noted that this social worker was always very outspoken. "A lot of people don't like her for that." But she had listened to Catherine to good purpose: she guessed how she would respond to Ellie's death and what sort of help she would need. Her idiosyncratic prescription sanctioned Catherine's relief and lifted her spirits.

Few parents face their feelings as unflinchingly as Catherine Lederman, and few professionals know their clients as well as this social worker. Many doctors must guide families through difficult decisions after a brief, unsatisfactory introduction. Some manage to discern a great deal even under these difficult circumstances. They guess what parents need to hear. They find the courage to go beyond the child's medical status to the human questions that torment mothers and fathers. Before he had known them a week, Dr. Riordan talked to the Murrays about the way Little John's handicaps would change their lives.

"It makes you examine a lot of things in your life. Your religion." (He was dressed in a suit as if he had come straight from church.) "There are three parts to a person—the physical, the emotional, and the spiritual. These children are the same as any others in spirit and personality."

And finally, quite astoundingly: "A child like this is a sacrament."

"A child like this is a sacrament!" Having an abnormal child makes one feel one has failed, one is outcast, doomed somehow to be not normal

oneself. Vistas open out of pain and separation and ugliness. But a sacrament is a partaking of the holy, the truth, the center. Whatever one wants to think of God, even if only to dismiss him, the notion of the sacramental remains, a metaphor with many-layered meanings. To place it in the being of a helpless child—"a hopeless case"—is to offer an entirely different covenant with existence. We saw our life and our child in a new light, not as a source of darkness and misery, but as in some way closer to truth and spirit. We felt, at once and whenever we recalled it in the future, like climbers who unload their packs in the thin air of the peak, released and almost floating, weightless. Suddenly there was order out of chaos. We could never be as hopeless or despairing again. This doctor, who had the courage, seeing our stricken faces, to speak out to us, had given us back our child to love. (Murray and Murray 1975, pp. 62–63)

Words like Dr. Riordan's often strike a discordant note. Spoken to the wrong parent, at the wrong moment, they can sound fatuous and unrealistic. This was the right moment. Dr. Riordan stirred the Murrays and gave them hope. We cannot often touch another person's spirit with such healing hands.

These two encounters remind us that good listeners discover strengths as well as weakness. Because they heard both, these professionals were able to help three unhappy people through some black moments.

Chapter 8

Acceptance

WHEN PEOPLE use the term "acceptance," they usually refer to one of four parallel processes, or sometimes to an amalgam of several. First, families acknowledge the existence of the handicap and its long-term significance. Second, they begin the long, difficult task of integrating the child and the disability into their lives. Third, they learn to forgive their own errors and shortcomings. Fourth, they search for meaning in their loss.

Parents change and grow. They re-examine old verities, searching for a philosophy that fits what they have learned. But each person attacks these immense, baffling tasks with different tools and different goals. Some sturdy parents argue that the whole idea of acceptance is not even desirable, and given the multiple meanings of the term, they have a point. We must look at acceptance in a complex way, focusing on individual lives, recognizing that both the routes and the final destinations will look very different.

Facing Reality

Most people have to face a reality before they can begin to weave it into their lives. But a realistic assessment of a child's limitations may take a long time, since children are complicated and sensible experts are sometimes hard to find. Acceptance, in this sense, means a resolution of the inner dialogue I described in chapter 1, the conversation between the voice that warns of trouble and the voice that tells us that all is well. As long as our observations support contending points of view, as long as we doubt our child's normality but cannot confirm our worst suspicions, we stand transfixed. When time, or medical evaluation, or our own investigations clear up the ambiguities, we move toward our own hard-won version of what others glibly call acceptance.

Usually we must agree to two related realities. First, we acknowledge that our child differs from other children in some significant way. Then we admit that although we can help, we cannot cure. Most of the mothers I know recognized their children's differences readily enough—many spotted the problems before their doctors. The question of prognosis troubles them for longer. They wonder about various treatments, and dream of cures. Magazine articles, T.V. specials, and popular fiction encourage optimism by dramatizing medical breakthroughs and innovative educational programs. Knowing that neither medicine nor education are monolithic, parents hope that somewhere in this vast, sprawling, various country, someone has a solution to their problem. Encouraged by their neighbors and their dreams, many search for some way to remake their child's future.

A few parents succeed. There are cures for some and help for many. Success stories feed the skepticism of other families who still struggle with intractable problems; they also shed some light on a critical part of the meaning of acceptance. Do we have to accept the handicap in order to accept the child? Is it possible to accept on the one hand and, on the other, to move heaven and earth in order to effect change? Does not any form of acceptance imply some diminution of effort? Is acceptance another word for surrender? These questions are important to all families with a difference, miracle cure or no miracle cure.

Neil Kaufman, describing the extraordinary self-designed program through which he and his wife, Suzi, turned their autistic son Raun into a loving and highly verbal two-and-a-half-year-old, explores at great length the question of basic attitude. One feels, in fact, that the book is, in Kaufman's mind, as much about attitude as it is about the child. Kaufman feels he has resolved any possible tensions between acceptance and the exhausting therapeutic program. I am not quite convinced that he has.

Kaufman's philosophy comes from something called "the Option Method"; its guiding principle—the Option Attitude—is articulated as: "To love is to be happy with." To me, this terse, static definition of love highlights the tension between acceptance and rigorous intervention. Why work on changing someone if you are already happy with him? The Option teacher, when queried, suggested that Raun be left alone. "He thought if he could, or wanted to, Raun would come to us" (Kaufman 1976, p. 59). The Kaufmans disagreed. Yet they felt their disagreement to be in no way a rejection of Raun as he was:

What did we know about our son? Distant and encapsulated . . . yes. But he was also gentle, soft and beautiful, happy with himself and the fantasies of his universe. Quiet ,and peaceful with an incredible talent for concentration on objects. Raun was a flower, not a weed. A journey, not a burden. Perhaps a gift, but certainly not an affliction. We would intervene. (p. 59)

In the next paragraph Kaufman reveals *his* resolution of the conflict between acceptance and intervention:

We decided we could have special and different wants for Raun, but that our relationship with him would not be conditional upon them. To be happy and not judgmental . . . this would be the place to begin with Raun. (p. 60)

This equanimity was, inevitably, difficult to maintain. Raun tested it in a particularly heartbreaking way. During the months of intensive work he progressed remarkably. He stopped drooling, made contact with the family, began to play with toys, cried in order to communicate, responded to commands—and finally spoke! Then he regressed, stopped speaking, avoided eye contact and cuddling. He rocked. He cried constantly. As the Kaufmans took stock of the situation, they had to reassess the nature of their acceptance.

Was our loving and feeling good about Raun contingent on his progressing and achieving? Did we expect a guarantee that this forward movement would continue, that he would always keep improving and never return to his original autistic state? And were we now thinking that this day marked the end? That it had all been in vain? That we had lost him behind that invisible and impenetrable wall? Suzi and I worked through all these beliefs and feelings. We could really know nothing for sure. We could only love and keep going. (pp. 187–188)

Their attitude is admirable, even heroic. Under the circumstances, it seems almost inhuman. I myself identify with Maire, the teenage girl who helps with Raun's daily program. Watching Raun withdraw and return to autistic self-stimulation, Maire dissolves into helpless weeping. "I can't stand it. I love him so much and to see him like this after all the progress just kills me" (p. 189). She understood, writes Kaufman, "the trap that she had created . . . she understood her unhappiness. It would not be okay to lose him. And yet, precisely because it was not okay, she understood that in some way, she was now disapproving of his behavior . . . and ultimately, that would lead to disapproving of him" (p. 189).

When one has glimpsed a promised land of improvement and human connection, how can one "be happy with" withdrawal, isolation, and regression? Kaufman's formulations worked for his family, but it seems to me that there are real tensions and contradictions in what he asks.

If the parents who write the "miracle" books do not accept their children's handicaps, there is a sense in which they do accept the total experience. They describe the ways in which they themselves, and other members of the family, have grown and changed through working with their child. The experience is a triumph of love and hard work, a unique education. David Melton's reflections are typical. He tells his son Todd:

"Sometimes God lets things happen to us so we can learn a lesson. This is His way of talking to us. Maybe He is telling us we have to work for worthwhile things. I don't think God gives us more than we can do. He selects us to do these things because He knows we can do them." My voice was a whisper. "I think God saw you were a strong boy who would work hard, and He said, 'Todd and his family are strong enough for a big problem.'" (Melton 1968, p. 153)

He rephrases the point for his readers:

I believe a brain-injured child is a gift from God. This child is a precious gift to a family.

Through Todd our family learned understanding and patience. And, in a deeper sense, we learned love. For in the untouched innocence of this child, we were reminded innocence dwells in every human being. (Melton, p. 154)

The Kaufmans and Meltons, and thousands of other parents, reject the future that their child's diagnosis seems to dictate. What some people would call "denial" actually helps them because it directs and fuels their efforts.

Looking back over a difficult childhood, Robert Myers concluded that his parents' unwillingness to acknowledge his brother's retardation had "created personal confusion and misdirection of purposes." But he also believed it had given Roger the education he needed to cope with the world:

By denying to themselves and others that he was retarded, they unconsciously and indirectly set out to prove he was not retarded, and so gave him as many experiences as a non-retarded person would get. That is just what the experts recommend today. (Meyers 1978, pp. 22–23)

Because the experts disagree about symptoms and prospects, because there is a lot no one knows about disability, and because our more optimistic side recoils from the bleakest predictions, years may pass before two parents arrive at a realistic definition of their child's condition, treatment, and future prospects. During this period the disabled child usually occupies more than his share of their thoughts. The inner dialogue—or efforts to silence it—consumes a great deal of emotional energy. Resolution, when it comes, often liberates people in surprising ways.

Not everyone accepts what experts say, even in the long run. This may not matter. Indeed, defiant optimism may help the child and the family. What does matter is that parents settle on a view of the disability that really makes sense to them, a view that daily experience confirms. We have to live with our ideas. Realistic expectations allow us to talk comfortably to other people, and to enjoy our child. Unrealistic ones add the anxiety of nagging doubt to other difficulties. In order to maintain illusions we may begin to avoid people who ask unnerving questions. We may end up narrowing our lives unnecessarily.

Picking up the Threads

The shock of disability seems to obliterate the life that exists and to dictate the pattern of what will follow. "The world crumbled and fell around us," writes the mother of a girl with Down's syndrome (Canning 1975, p. 11). "In one cataclysmic moment, our world had been shattered," Suzanne Massie remembers (Massie and Massie 1975, p. 12–13). "What began as one of the happiest moments imaginable shattered the life I had so painstakingly built," says Diane Kovacs (1972) of her son's retardation.

Over the years each of us makes patterns in our lives. New experiences take their place in the larger design. Like threads in a piece of weaving, they enhance a detail here, or subtly shift the emphasis there. Time alters the pattern, but slowly—until we experience a major loss.

At the stroke of calamity, our lives look fragile. A child's disability menaces the old life and threatens to define an ominous pattern for the new one. In the terms of my metaphor, we see it as a master design that will determine the place and importance of every thread we will ever use. As the years go by our perspective changes: the disability is only a motif among others.

For a long time the disability dominates not only parents' day-to-day lives but the meaning they give to them. One professional woman, whose deaf son is now nearly twenty, remarked that during the early years she often felt an impulse to introduce herself thus: "Hello, I'm Sara York. I'm the mother of a deaf child." Acceptance means moving away from the narrow confines of this definition of oneself toward another that gives greater latitude and more room to be.

At the most minimal and wintry level, acceptance may begin with a recognition that the child's handicap no longer represents the only obstacle to happiness. I still remember the exact location of my car on the day when I realized—it is a terrible admission—that Jody's death would not solve all my problems. It was many years ago, and Jody was still quite tiny. He cried constantly, and it seemed to me that none of us would ever be happy again.

I had been happy, even smug, when Jody was born. I was young and healthy. I had interesting part-time work that seemed to be leading somewhere, a husband I loved, and a beautiful, bright, lively child. Then there were two, just as I had dreamed. Jody's problems had turned all blue skies grey. Yet on this particular day, driving along the river toward home, I realized that the unhappiness that seemed to have settled over Liza since she started nursery school and my own confused responses to her feelings were making me more miserable than the baby's bleak prospects. At that moment it occurred to me that we make room in our lives for a certain amount of unhappiness, and that if we were not coping with a sick baby, our other problems might expand to fill the void. With this realization I began to look at Jody's disabilities a little differently. They became part of the pattern of my life, rather than the dominant motif.

To those who think in terms of some richer notion of acceptance that takes each human being as equally valuable and awards to each child a love based on his or her appealing qualities, this experience may not seem like much. It is, nevertheless, a step. A step away from the depressed biological fatalism of "Hello, I'm a mother of a deaf child." A step away from life forever defined by someone's disability.

Josh Greenfeld takes a somewhat different cut at the notion of acceptance. His journals show the extraordinary strains—physical, marital, psychological—involved in living with his son. At many points it appears that an institution is imminent: the cost of living with Noah is just too high. No miracle cure exists. Noah improves in some ways as the years go by; neither his father nor the reader expect anything like a normal adulthood for him. The first journal ends with the affectionate reflections of a father who has finally tucked into bed a balky, endearing five-year-old.

But now finally he and Karl are off to sleep. The house is quiet. Foumi's put a pie into the oven, and now she's at her desk writing—lately she's begun a new sideline career, having published two articles in two of Japan's leading magazines. And I've just gone to the bookcase to check on that first sentence of Tolstoy's, and come away shaking my head. "Happy families," I know, "are not all alike." (Greenfeld 1972, pp. 190–191)

Here again we see not some absolute state of acceptance, but a step, a movement. In this case the movement is toward a happy family life that includes Noah, a conviction that the family's difference is, if not for the best, at least not for the worst.

Probably Josh has changed somewhat. Undoubtedly Noah has grown and learned. The changes in Noah, while small by the standards of normal development, make him easier to accept and live with:

he is practically toilet-trained; he is willing to get in the tub alone (rather than requiring an adult in the water with him); he sleeps in a bed like other members of his family.

Josh Greenfeld and I are marking a similar process. We are both saying, in different ways, that our disabled child no longer totally dominates our lives. Barbara Sullivan makes the same observation with less fanfare. She is learning to set boundaries for her son Luke, who has cerebral palsy. One morning she boasted about her achievement of the morning. She had ridden in the cab that takes Luke to school every day because she wanted to attend our mothers' meeting. Seeing her beside him, Luke screamed to be held. She stood firm; the car seat was the safest place for him. Seeing that she meant it, he quieted down. Barbara remembered a time when Luke's slightest whimper sent her running to his side. She was learning to treat him like other children.

As we learn that our child's difference need not entirely define us, we begin to fit it into the images we already have of ourselves and our lives. For we ourselves create the meaning of an event—even as important an event as a disability. We are the ones who decide how to weave this thread into the larger design. Out of the many possible ways we might use it, we choose one or two. To one parent the message of a disabled child is: "Life is harsh, but I am tough enough to survive." To another the disability says: "Everything I touch seems to wilt."

A child's disability means something to each family member. I asked one father how learning of his son's retardation had shaken him. He said it had confirmed his fear that he was a failure. Images of the disabled intertwine with many men's secret fears of not succeeding, of being helpless and dependent—of being a bum. So it was for this father.

Looked at in this way, the impact of the child's disability is both more and less than we first think. Its independent importance diminishes when we realize how much power and meaning it gains from associations with other events. But because the disability becomes part of an intricate pattern of meaning and self-perception, parents have trouble altering the messages they draw from it. It is only a part of the fabric, yet it is woven into the central design.

Recently, I talked with a social worker who has years of experience counseling parents of exceptional children; I asked whether she thought most parents ultimately come to view the whole experience as something positive. She pondered this question for a week, and then we returned to it. She thought not. We discussed factors that help, and she said something that made sense: if the child's disability gives some kind of direction to a parent's life outside the family, it ceases to be a wholly negative force. When people build compensations out of the material of their suffering, they suffer less. Sometimes a child's handicap pushes his parents toward a particular profession or focuses their work a little differently. Her son's deafness had led the social worker into counseling families with a difference. Luke Sullivan's cerebral palsy pushed Barbara into a kind of local politics. She began to organize other parents and circulate petitions protesting budget cuts; she badgered local bureaucrats for better services and encouraged others to do more. The rewards of these activities are quite different, but both link the child's disability to experiences that brought a sense of achievement. So does writing a book or teaching courses on special education.

Learning to Live with Ourselves

Every parent of a handicapped child faces choices he cannot make and feelings he would rather not have. We are all inadequate to the challenge we perceive. Learning to live with our own mistakes and frailties may be even harder than acknowledging a child's limitations and integrating him into the family.

Most of us make difficult decisions between uncertain and unsatisfactory alternatives; few of us find a road that satisfies wholly. We decide, for example, how much space to allow the child's disability in our lives. Will we, at one extreme, leave no stone unturned in our search for cure or improvement? Or will we, as some doctors advise, "Always put the normal children first." Probably neither. Most of us turn over a number of stones and leave undisturbed others that look larger or less promising. We make our decisions as best we can; we are never sure. When someone else follows a different path successfully, their story reawakens our uncertainties and perhaps our guilt.

When Jody was six months old, my aunt gave me David Melton's *Todd* (1968). I read, with growing excitement, of the strides that Todd made on the program at the Institutes for the Achievement of Human Potential. I dreamed of a well Jody, crawling, walking, talking, blind, but still very much a normal little boy. We wrote the Institutes for an appointment. We hoped, but we also doubted. How likely was a cure, really? Could you heal the damage to a baby's brain by moving his arms and legs? Could our family really stand the further stress that this exhausting program would create? We did not know; in the end we came to feel that we were more likely to lose than gain by turning over this particular boulder. I still think we were right, but of course I am not entirely sure. And when I hear about a child who is progressing on the Institutes' program, mixed emotions wash over me.

Parents who have placed children in residential care face similar problems when they meet other parents who have chosen to keep their child at home. One of our friends has a teenage daughter who is retarded and physically handicapped; she has lived in an excellent residential school for many years. Early on our friend urged us to place Jody away from home. He spoke gloomily of his likely effect on our other children. In the long, respectful tug of war that followed, we came to see that he considered our choice to be a judgment on his. Several years passed before he seemed to accept our decision—and we accepted his.

Nearly all exceptional parents make important decisions about treatment sooner or later. Confronting others who have resolved an issue differently can be trying. Until fairly recently parents of profoundly deaf children had to choose between two incompatible approaches to their child's education, the manual and the oral.* Oralists held out the hope of a "normal" child: one who could speak intelligibly, understand through lip reading, and function adequately in a hearing world. These important achievements take time. Since strict oralists forbid the use of sign language, the deaf child often communicates poorly with parents, siblings, teachers and peers for many years—even if he is one of the lucky 4 percent who eventually speak and read lips proficiently.†

Manualists offer the child and his family a common language—a way to talk, settle problems, and explain frustrations. Denying the

---

* The options are somewhat broader now, with "total communication" offering children the benefits of sign communication while continuing to work on their oral skills.

† This figure is from Schlesinger and Meadow 1972, p. 2. Estimates of success of course depend on the definition of "proficient."

oralists' vision of successful integration, they argue that deaf people never feel really at home among the hearing, but that they can learn, grow, make friends, and develop normal personalities if they are allowed their natural means of communication by a family who "accepts" their deafness. Versions of this argument pop up in every field linked to disability. The oralist-manualist dialogue is a variation on the "mainstreaming" vs. special placement controversy. (And that, in turn, parallels arguments among racial and linguistic minorities concerning integration or separatism as a tactic and goal.) The only definitive thing you can say about any of these polarities is that a simple answer is almost bound to be wrong: it all depends.

Obviously two opposed approaches carry different risks and offer different rewards. Probably many parents of deaf children have bad days when they wish they had opted for a different set of problems and benefits. And probably these doubts account for some of the bitterness that has characterized discussions of deaf education for more than one hundred and fifty years.

Other people ally themselves with our inner demons without meaning to. Their choices, their good fortune, their tragedies can upset a precarious balance in our own lives. Yet, paradoxically, a deeper involvement with these others sometimes helps us past a crisis and allows us to move forward once again in the fight to accept our own feelings and our own limitations. Thus, every mother in our group learned, Thursday after Thursday, that other lives offer different possibilities. At times each of us smarted with the pain of acknowledging these differences. Lucy Forrest longed to trade Christopher's retardation for the physical impairments of Laurie, Kevin, and Elise. Rosalyn Gibson envied those who knew more about what lay ahead for their children; uncertainties about Nancy's development tortured her. I felt sad when other mothers brought messages of hope from a doctor or teacher. Nonetheless, we built alliances as we talked, and through our friendships with one another we gained the strength to face the parts of ourselves we liked least. At Ellie Lederman's wake I learned how far we had come, and how well we had learned to give and accept support.

When Barbara Sullivan called to tell me about Ellie's death, a wave of contradictory emotions swept over me. I grieved for the golden-haired daughter of a good friend. I remembered her smile. She was so little, and so beautiful; her death seemed cruel and terribly sad. At the same time I realized that the Lederman's long struggle was over.

Catherine would finally get a full night's sleep. She and Peter would not, after all, have to face the heartbreaking decisions about Ellie's future care. Thinking of the road ahead of us, of Jody's adolescence and adulthood, I felt a stab of envy.

I did not mention these feelings to Barbara; I certainly did not expect them to come up at the wake. In fact they did. Catherine spoke of the relief that mingled with her grief. Another mother described the twinge of jealousy that came to her when she realized that Catherine's family was no longer different. She loved her son too, but in some ways she felt it would be easier if he died. We offered these thoughts shyly (we felt that Barbara would not quite approve). Still we knew we had a forum for speaking what was in our hearts. We talked and took another step toward accepting ourselves.

Discovering Compensations

Parents acknowledge the reality of the disability with resignation rather than joy. As we weave the child and our new identity as parents of a seriously handicapped person into our lives, we usually move toward a more cheerful view of the total situation. Still mourning our loss, we find compensations.

But what compensations could there be? Parents' answers to this question can sound maudlin or plainly wrong. After reading what a number of mothers and fathers wrote about living with a retarded child, Nancy Wagner Hart (1970) observes that parents who publish share "some surprisingly similar illusions which have enabled them to accept a situation that otherwise would have left them desperate." She concludes that parents commonly delude themselves about their disabled child's character and their family situation in order to survive psychologically. Presumably there is some of that: many of us stoke up the fires of our failing mental health by looking for the positive sides of any difficult situation. Sentimentality can, in an odd way, be functional.

It is also true that parents' inside view offers them a unique perspective. Many of the awful aspects of the situation—the hard work, the grim prospects for future care, the child's glaring and occasionally embarrassing difference—are obvious. The gains that parents talk about are in the realm of personal education—important but invisible.

Mothers speak of an enhanced appreciation of learning and development. Lorraine Frank glowed with excitement when her retarded son Peter picked up an empty cup and tried to drink from it (Frank 1951). Sharon Ulrich (1972) waited with almost unbearable anticipation for the day when her blind child would walk. The mothers to two cerebral-palsied daughters (Segal 1966; Killelea 1952) recount the landmarks of their children's intellectual and social growth with enormous pride.

Parents treasure this sense of wonder for all children. Lucy Forrest spoke sadly about its fragility. At three, her son Christopher still functioned as an infant. She told the mothers' group that when her daughter was born, "I swore I'd never just take her development for granted." For the first year each new achievement brought a special pleasure even when it meant more work. As Michelle pulled the pots and pans out of the closet, "I'd scold her, you know, but inside I was thrilled. I was so happy to see her get into things." Now that her daughter is toddling, however, she finds herself casual toward normal development. "It makes me sad to see myself taking it all for granted. I swore I never would."

In one way or another disabled children teach parents the truth behind the cliché about the "miracle of development." Some mothers and fathers also find themselves re-examining feelings about handicap and difference. For me this happened slowly. I did not realize I had changed until I started looking at schools for Jody.

On the way to the first preschool I got lost and nearly ran out of gas. I was nervous. I knew the children would be handicapped and I wondered how they would look to me. I was afraid I would want to turn away in embarrassment.

When I entered the classroom I was astonished. It was not the children's disabilities that struck me. It was their vitality and beauty. I marveled at the miracle of mobility and the achievement of human communication. A little girl hitched herself across the floor to offer me a toy and a smile. I was touched. Driving home I thought, "This was a gift from Jody. If I had visited this school three years ago, I would have recoiled from the kids. Now they look beautiful to me."

Any disability teaches parents new lessons and attitudes toward themselves and the wider world. Sometimes—as with me—the particulars of the disability seem almost irrelevant to learning. In other cases, the child's special problems and a parent's response to them generate a special perception, a new faith that emerges from intense experience.

For years Clara Park laid siege to the walls that seemed to surround her autistic daughter Elly. In time she succeeded in contacting the little girl inside. Her success changed her ideas about all human beings.

I am a teacher, and from Elly I have learned much about students— about normal students, many of high intelligence, who talk and read and understand and go about their business and yet who challenge our ideas of normal and abnormal because they are so like Elly. . . .

Human beings fortify themselves in many ways. Numbness, weakness, irony, inattention, silence, suspicion are only a few of the materials out of which the personality constructs its walls. With experience gained in my siege of Elly I mount smaller sieges. Each one is undertaken with hesitation; to try to help anyone is an arrogance. But Elly is there to remind me that to fail to try is a dereliction. Not all my sieges are successful. But where I fail, I have learned that I fail because of my own clumsiness and inadequacy, not because the enterprise is impossible. However formidable the fortifications, they can be breached. I have not found one person, however remote, however hostile, who did not wish for what he seemed to fight. Of all the things that Elly has given, the most precious is this faith, a faith experience has almost transformed into certain knowledge: that inside the strongest citadel he can construct, the human being awaits his besieger. (Park 1967, pp. 274–75)

We select many of the challenges of our adult life. Most of us do not choose to mother or father a handicapped child. (Although some do, of course: an increasing number of couples adopt disabled children; some women who learn about chromosomal defects like Down's syndrome through amniocentesis choose to continue their pregnancies to delivery.) Necessity presents itself; with no real alternative, we accept. This fate, so different from any we might have sought, exposes new sides of ourselves. With plenty of luck and support, we survive and even grow.

Looking back over three years with Ellie, Catherine Lederman concluded: "Because of Ellie I became a different person. A better person. Coming to the [mothers'] group I was more completely myself than I had ever been anywhere else." She felt that she could be honest with other mothers because they faced the same problems and understood her feelings. She felt she *had* to be honest in order to survive. "Ellie was the worst thing that had ever happened to me."

Before Ellie's birth, Catherine remembered being terribly concerned with appearances. "I put up a big front. I tried to dress perfectly; everything had to be perfect on the outside." Shattered by the news of Ellie's retardation, she learned "to be real." She made fewer snap judgments and gave other people more of a chance. She valued the changes that desperation had forced on her. After Ellie's death she searched frantically for new commitments because she worried that in her new "ordinary" life she would revert to earlier ways.

Pain isolates; it can also create bonds with other people's misery. At the end of the first year of the mothers' group, Patricia O'Conner reflected on the ways her retarded three-year-old had changed her: "When I think of myself four years ago and myself today, I am a little more gentle, a little kinder." She had been down to the bottom, so when someone came to her in trouble, she listened, thinking, "Yes, I know how you feel, I've been where you're at."

Without belying the sadness of the loss, we recognize such changes in ourself as, in some measure, compensations. Jay puts it this way: "If you're lucky, you can take some of the broken pieces of the tragedy and work them into something good for you." In his case, having a severely handicapped son makes him mourn the loss of a normal son deeply. He does not think he'll ever accept the loss. The whole experience has made him hungry for sons, he says, and so, along with his permanent sorrow, he finds himself looking around in the world for sons to adopt and father—not literally, though he thinks of that, but metaphorically. Just as he went looking for fathers when his father died—and found a number—so he now searches for sons, and finds them: as a teacher with his students, with friends' sons, and with boys generally. His loss has made him, self-consciously, a more fatherly person. He wants to insist on both truths, however: the loss is real, and feels permanent, and he has responded by reaching out.

Maybe acceptance means that this disability is part of your life and that, on balance, you accept your life. You see how the child and his disability have contributed to making you what you are, your life what it is. Perhaps, indeed, you would have liked yourself and your life even better if all the children had been healthy—but that would have been a different life, and it is hard to know. Hemophilia defined

Bobby Massie's childhood. He accepts it as a fact of his life, believing that the pain and struggle give him strength he would not otherwise have.

How can I—or anyone—wish that the most important thing that ever happened to me had not happened? It is like saying that I wish I had been born on another planet, so different would I probably be. Put it this way: I wouldn't have it any other way. (Massie and Massie 1975, p. 411)

When I read this passage to a friend, a physician, he replied skeptically, "That's ridiculous. Does he mean that if pushing a button would enable his body to synthesize clotting factor VIII he wouldn't do it?" Of course not. No one would take on hemophilia voluntarily. What Bobby Massie and others like him are saying is that the disability is now woven into their past; it is bound up with what they have lived through and what they are. They could not remove the painful threads without ripping out the whole fabric of their existence. To have the best you must take the worst.

At the end of "a terrible week" with little John, the Murrays reflect:

So often we think the fabric of our lives just temporary threads, colors, patterns, but one day we will wake up to find these were our life itself, inextricable, intrinsic. Without them, not only the pattern gone, the fabric gone too, death. We are not two people waiting until the children grow up and leave, but changed, woven, shaped, sculpted by these children, these stresses, these forces, until they become us—we are no longer ourselves in any secret isolated sense. (Murray and Murray 1975, p. 214)

Perhaps ahead of their time, they echo Erik Erikson's remarks on the fruits of old age—the final stage of ego development: "It is the acceptance of one's one and only life cycle and of the people who have become significant to it as something that had to be and that, by necessity, permitted of no substitutions" (Erikson 1968, p. 139).

Some readers may find Bobby Massie, Clara Park, or the Murrays excessively cerebral and abstract. Jacobs quotes a mother who gropes toward a similar formulation in simpler language:

Doctor Jones asked me a question one day, and it goes like this: "If you could have John turn normal right now, would you want it that way?" And I came out and I said—No. I said it so fast that I wanted to pull the words back in right after I said it, cause I feel like this, and some day I'm going to tell Dr. Jones this. I'm going to answer him in this way, and that is that I wouldn't want John to turn normal just like that, right now, because there are so many things that I enjoy out of John the way he is that I would miss actually, and besides that to just all of sudden have so much time to yourself, it's kind of a shock to you too. I mean, I'm going all the time after John; now if all of a sudden I've just got the time to set and relax, that's going to bother me—just drive me crazy. And so, now I should have really answered, that is I would have liked to see John turn to be normal, but to do it just gradually. Even if it takes five years. (Jacobs 1969, p. 123–124)

We are natural conservatives. We fear change, even when we want it. We live the life we have. We enjoy our pleasures and endure our pain. How do we know what a new life would bring?* Jacobs' informant makes the choice that most parents of retarded children would make, I think: cure him, but do it gradually, so the fabric stays whole and of a piece.

Stages

There is nothing final about acceptance. Whether our children are healthy or disabled, most of us view our life quite differently from one day to the next. Josh Greenfeld, writing on a soft midsummer evening in 1971, concluded that Tolstoy was wrong, that his own family, although different, was a happy one. Five months later things looked far less rosy:

Ever since we've been to Letchworth Village I move in the same cloud of uric-acid-lye stench that permeated the wards there. And I see no way out. I'm boxed into an untenable situation. We must keep Noah at home as

* Ray Barsch's survey data illustrate what I mean here. Barsch and his colleagues administered a handicap ranking scale to groups of students, professionals, and laymen—about twenty-four hundred people altogether, all living in Wisconsin. They found close agreement among different groups: most respondents judged cerebral palsy the most severe problem, followed by mental retardation, mental illness, and brain injury. Parents of cerebral-palsied and retarded children dissented; most suspected that other families faced problems even more immense than theirs. Thus, for example, fathers of children with cerebral palsy rated mental illness and mental retardation more serious than cerebral palsy (Barsch 1968, pp. 329–34). In living with this handicap they had apparently defeated some of its terrors. Other problems now looked more dreadful than the one they had managed to absorb into their families.

long as we can, otherwise we destroy his life. But we cannot keep him at home too long, otherwise we destroy our lives. Poor kid. It's him against us. (Greenfeld 1978, pp. 31–32)

The desolations of late November seem as apt in their way, as the optimism of the summer. True perspective has to honor both, to allow and expect that they can coexist in the same consciousness.

When experts talk about the adjustment to any sort of tragedy, they often identify stages (see for example, Elisabeth Kübler-Ross's [1969] influential work on death.) Stage theories of many kinds abound in the field of psychology today. Those who write about parent's response to a child's disability often speak about stages of adjustment: denial, rejection, and finally the promised land of acceptance. I agree that many families follow similar paths when they move beyond despair, but I am uncomfortable with most stage theories. They carry too heavy a freight of straight-line progress; they also suggest an implausible final harmony. The actual process is not linear, and often it is bought at a high price in human suffering. In the vocabulary of stages, acceptance becomes a kind of high plateau, once out of reach, now felt firmly underfoot. Gone are the fears and self-reproaches of yesterday, the sighs for what might have been. Matter-of-fact realism now guides our efforts. Having struggled out of darkness, we will not have to be afraid any more.

Actually the process is more complicated than this. Contradictory feelings continue to coexist in our consciousness, as Stanford Searl (1978) points out in an autobiographical essay questioning the whole idea of stages. Searl describes the way his own retarded daughter changed him. He welcomed this painful education, which gave him a maturity he might not otherwise have known. He loved his daughter. Nonetheless, he often resented her insistent needs and the restrictions she put on his life. He and his wife became so anxious and depressed that they nearly collapsed. They never did "get over" the bad feelings, he insists. This does not mean they did not accept or adjust to their daughter, but they want to frame this acceptance in a way that does justice to the recurring pain and sadness.

Few parents reach an emotional promised land; most have good days and bad days. They solve one set of problems only to uncover another. Insight comes without blotting out confusion and regret. I know I did not rout fear for all time when I acknowledged the extent of Jody's handicaps. And although I no longer torture myself with useless guilt about his toxoplasmosis, I still reproach myself for writing when I might be playing with him. So it goes. The issues I have talked about all through this book can last a life time. We should not use the notion of stages to grade ourselves on our progress, as though life were a series of examination questions.

For years those who have written about the impact of disability on parents—in the past "parents" has almost invariably meant mothers—have likened the birth of a disabled child to the death of a child. Solnit and Stark (1961) sensibly point out the limitations of this analogy, observing that because parents of a disabled child have neither time nor emotional space for mourning the normal child they have lost, the adjustment to a disability may be even harder than the acceptance of death. A consideration of the differences between these two crises suggests some of the reasons that a simple stage model fails to capture the diversity of family experiences.

First of all, disability is never as clear-cut as death. Grief usually mingles with confusion and uncertainty. Parents of a Down's syndrome child may be told little beyond the label and have no idea what degree of retardation to expect. As they learn more, either through their own research or through professional consultation, the picture changes. And as the child grows, he or she changes too—often invalidating earlier professional predictions. Not knowing what fate to mourn, the parent faces a thousand alternative scenarios.

In the months following the diagnosis of Jody's retardation I tried to consider every unpleasant alternative. Part of this was superstitious: since the baby had proved so different from my expectations, I had convinced myself that to imagine an eventuality was somehow to prevent its occurrence. But in another way my behavior made sense: I wanted to adjust to every possibility so the lump in my throat would one day go away. But I found I could not "face the worst" while it remained hypothetical. I do not think the human heart works that way. Until the truth becomes inescapable, the inner dialogue continues. Disability remains unbearable until you have borne it.

Even an unambiguous diagnosis tells a small fraction of the story. Only experience can show how things will turn out. Suzanne Massie speaks of her own changing perspective: "It was not until he [Bobby] began to bleed in the joints at age six that Bob and I understood that the biggest problem might be, after all, not what the disease did to his body, but what the world was preparing to do to his soul" (Massie and Massie 1975, p. 96). As the years went by her prayers changed. At first: "Other people had advised us to pray and we had prayed. Not for strength to accept, and for wisdom to understand, but for Bobby to be well" (p. 17). Later, in the widespread midnight desperation that Mrs. Massie describes better than anyone, she asked God for another kind of help: "I did not pray for alleviation or cure; I prayed for strength . . . only strength to go on" (p. 192). How could she have known, in Bobby's infancy, what the ordeal would require?

One obstacle to grieving, then, is the ambiguity surrounding the nature of the loss. Another problem is that parents are often unsure of how to speak about the disability to the other children or to the disabled child himself. It is hard to talk to children about tragedy. They are young, alive, full of promise, yet vulnerable. We want to protect them from sadness. It is hard to check the impulse to sound upbeat, to avoid searching out a bright side for every dismal situation. For this reason parents often ask for guidance in talking to children about death—even the death of a pet creates awkwardness. Disability presents far stickier problems. We want children to mourn a dead grandparent or cousin, even though we want to protect them from panic and despair. The proper attitude toward a sibling's disability eludes us. Do we really want them to see it as a tragedy? Grandma is dead and gone, but baby sister is here to stay, and most mothers and fathers hope their other children will love and enjoy her. The conscientious parent aims for some ideal mix of messages: we love the baby, but her limitations sadden us. The ideal is just that—mixed messages. Consequently, parents—and children—mask part of their true feelings. This circumspection complicates and prolongs sorrow.

The most important difference between mourning a death and mourning a disability is that the child in question is not dead at all. Instead of an aching hole—the empty bed, the now-useless baby clothes—parents face the insistent demands of a child who needs even more care than an ordinary infant would. They must shoulder the heavy responsibility of leading this child into life, and love him as though he embodied all their dreams. While death provides a moment's respite from ordinary demands, disability generates new tasks and necessities.

Because people in a family live with a changing, demanding, beloved child and not just an intrapsychic loss, external factors influence their adjustment. Frances Grossman's data (1972) suggest ways that margins of money and time help a child see the good side of a disabled sibling. The same probably applies to parents. If the burden of routine feeding, bathing, clothing, stimulating, teaching, and comforting a disabled child can be shared and if a mother has time alone by herself and with her normal children, her husband, and her friends —two gigantic "ifs"—then many of the problems discussed in earlier chapters become less acute, although they do not disappear. Sadly, lots of families have few margins of any sort. If a mother cares for a disabled child during most of her waking hours, he will probably continue to occupy a central position in her consciousness—possibly crowding out other legitimate interests. If she is constantly exhausted, the good side of the experience will surely elude her. Indeed, there may not be any good side.

Physical space is almost as important as money and help. Large houses and apartments create opportunities for privacy, allowing children and grown-ups to escape one another when they want to. In close quarters minor annoyances turn into federal cases.

Margins do not come in stages. They depend in part on luck and on community services. They depend on the disabled child and his development. They depend on grandparents, neighbors, the job market, and a thousand other imponderables. In most families, margins wax and wane.

Answering Ultimate Questions

Acceptance has an intellectual dimension as well, although it would be artificial to set the intellectual entirely off from its emotional, material, and social contexts. Still it is worth noting some of the profound questions that this sort of tragedy raises in all parents' minds. A child's disability challenges our values—and the more severe the disability the more forceful the challenge. What makes a life worth living? Is one life worth more than another? Why do we value people?

When Jody was fifteen days old we learned that he was blind. Friends, relatives, and friends-of-friends wrote to console us. Many spoke of blind adults they had known: people who, despite blindness, led useful independent lives. We wept for the experiences he would miss—the changing colors of a New England autumn, the splendor of a clear night sky, the faces of the people he would love. Yet we realized how much remained—if he were "only" blind. Most of the activities that gave our lives meaning and importance would still be within his reach. He could read, write, teach, play, and enjoy the fellowship of friends. He could talk and think, give comfort and, in time, go about his own life independently, perhaps with some special understanding born of his disability. Anyway, that is what we hoped. The idea of blindness made us sad. It led us to examine our values: it did not shatter them. However, as the months went by we learned that Jody was not "only" blind. He had cerebral palsy; he was probably severely retarded. During the first eighteen months of his life he cried almost continually from pain that no one could diagnose or relieve. His days and nights were passed in misery; his future looked bleak and limited. Hardly a day passed without our asking ourselves whether his life was worth living. Each of us, separately and together, wished for an end to his ordeal: a peaceful, painless death.

He did not die. He was remarkably tough. Unexpectedly, after the doctors removed an infected shunt, his pain went. He cried less during the day and slept longer at night. He smiled more often, even laughed. Liberated from his inner torments he responded to us. We began to like him. He gave more: his smiles, his laughter, his delighted shrieks. He asked less. He still needed a lot of special care, but we no longer performed our family routines with one hand while patting a wretched baby with the other. Each of us began to feel that Jody's life was worth living, and that he made his own special contribution to the family.

Barring a miracle, Jody will not lead a "useful independent life." He will not read and write; he may never talk to friends in the way that we do. He will always depend on others for his basic needs. Yet he maintains a vital human connection to the people and events around him. He is part of a web of shared experience. He makes us aware of our own fragility and limitations, and of how much we share with people whose interests and circumstances differ dramatically from our own. He "contributes" in his own quiet way.

Jody forces us to ask uncomfortable questions. Our oldest child loves animals. When she was seven she challenged our conviction that human lives are more valuable than those of animals. How, she asked angrily, could we justify such a belief? Some parents would have talked about the human soul. We replied that human beings understood and feared death more, that because of their more developed consciousness, they suffered more deeply. She denied our assertions vigorously—how could we arrogantly estimate the suffering or consciousness of another creature? Our formulations distressed us as much as they irritated Liza, for they seemed to deny Jody's worth and humanity. We had not examined our own ideas. What if the family dog understood more than Jody? Would we value the dog more highly than our son? No. Yet surely our answer led that way.

We asked friends and students why people mattered more than animals. My sister-in-law answered: "We value people because we are people; if we were squirrels we would value squirrels. We love Jody because he is like us." This argument raises as many problems as it settles. It brings us back once again to the whole question of deviance and disability. If we value people because they resemble us, where does this leave the people who are different? Yet I think she is right: at bottom we value other people because the conjunction of difference and similarity reinforces a sense of common humanity. We ourselves are like, and yet not like, others. There is very little difference between one man and another, William James says, but what difference there is, is very important.

Jody's father writes:

The experience with Jody is valuable in part because it makes me more conscious: makes me examine life. Yet the odd thing is that Jody's own life seems more or less unexamined, and, as far as we know, a good deal less conscious than ours. The enhanced consciousness is a byproduct of seeing that he is like us, in ways that he helps bring about, without himself realizing. Consciousness is like a free gift arising out of a bond that is tragic and good. But for him, I guess, and for us, the bond is what comes first.

Every parent asks "why?" searching for a perspective that will bring solace. Unhappily, searching in and of itself can cut you off from other people. The Abbot in *Essene* (Frederick Wiseman's documentary film about a modern Episcopal monastery) strives to heal the divisions within his monastery and create a face-to-face community rooted in brotherly love. Saddened by the schisms all about him, the endless squabbles about whether to use first names and who left the rake on the lawn over night, he reflects, "How meaningless it would all be, if God were not watching." This comforts the Abbot, with his sure faith; it does not help me, because I do not know whether God *is* watching. In fact, the Abbot reminds me that my own faith in the importance of the daily struggle is somewhat unexamined and perhaps even fragile.

So it is with disability or loss. Even when parents share a great deal and offer each other support, sympathy, understanding, and respect (which is a great deal for one human being to offer another), they sometimes find it hard to share the things that keep them going, their private, hard-won, sustaining truths. The loss acquires such different meanings for each. Suzanne Massie agonizes about Bobby's pain and her own. She grows bitter, and considers suicide. In time, she comes to see a divine purpose behind Bobby's hemophilia. She thinks her son's childhood suffering has strengthened him as fire tempers steel. She believes that God has chosen her. She accepts her fate, praying: "I am yours. If it is your will that I should survive then keep me as your instrument" (Massie and Massie 1975, p. 192–195). Although Suzanne Massie's answer moves me, it cannot bring me peace. I do not know the purpose of my son's disability. I do know that suffering does not ennoble everyone, that disability narrows some people's sympathies as surely as it extends those of others. One mother in our group spoke of her own growing intolerance for other people's problems. Overwhelmed and exhausted by her blind daughter, she wishes she could turn off their complaints. Inwardly she responds: "Don't tell me your troubles; I've got my own."

Like some others, I find that my son's disability has brought me closer to other parents of hurt children. We are united by our children's difference, by the feelings and experiences we share. Beyond that, I feel that my child's disability has brought me closer to people all over the world, people whose children may be able-bodied but who suffer in other ways. When I see a newspaper photograph of a family made homeless by fire, I suffer as I did not suffer ten years ago. I know what it is to stand powerless before the gods, to see a child I love hurt by forces I can neither name nor control. The moment we conceive children we become vulnerable in ways we are often too young and inexperienced to understand. "Hostages to fortune" is the old phrase. When children are born disabled, our vulnerability multiplies ten-fold. We are, as they say, at risk. Despite our middle-class homes and our well-stocked refrigerators, Suzanne Massie and I feel a special sisterhood for the young Cambodian mother who weeps over her starving baby. Through no virtue of our own, we are larger people than we were.

In a way, Shakespeare's *King Lear* is a text on this; in his tragedy Lear discovers that at some level what we have in common with other men and women is a kind of nakedness and vulnerability. Social class and variations in wealth and luck can fool us into thinking that some people are different from others. Like King Lear, families with profound disabilities find themselves staring at the final truth—what people are faced with when they lose everything that can be taken away short of life itself. They have to look at life stripped bare and try to decide its meaning. They feel like Lear, when he sees the old beggar: "Is man no more than this ? . . . Thou art the thing itself; unaccommodated man. . . ." (III, iv, 107–11) He tears off his royal robes and joins poor Tom in his nakedness. This act of sympathy for another "poor bare forked animal" is Lear's first strong gesture toward humanity. He was a king; now he sees the connection between himself and another human being. Something has dawned on him that he never really saw before: his kingdom is full of suffering.

> Poor naked wretches, whereso'er you are,
> That bide the pelting of this pitiless storm,
> How shall your houseless heads and unfed sides,
> Your loop'd and window'd raggedness, defend you
> From seasons such as these? O, I have ta'en
> Too little care of this! (III, iv, 28–33)

Now Lear becomes something more than "every inch a King." He becomes a man. The catastrophe that destroys him makes him realize the dreadful vulnerability of our common lot. Too late, perhaps, he has learned to care.

Randolph Bourne was born in 1886. The forceps delivery mutilated his face permanently. At the age of four, he contracted spinal tuberculosis, which twisted his spine, leaving him a dwarfed hunchback. He spent a miserable childhood and youth convinced that weakness of will prevented him from climbing trees and making friends. No one took him very seriously, and no one would hire him. For a time he ground out a wretched living perforating rolls for player pianos. He went to college late, found friends, and made a name for himself writing for the Progressive reform magazine, the *New Republic*. He became a cultural and literary critic and a social reformer, with a special sympathy for the young and a particular interest in education.

From his own hardships, Bourne wrote at twenty-five, he gained "a profound sympathy for all who are despised and ignored in the world . . . for the unpresentable and the unemployable, the incompetent and the ugly, the queer and the crotchety people who make up so large a proportion of human folk" (Bourne 1911). He learned to find the unsuccessful as interesting as the successful, to see the world through the eyes of the struggling many rather than those of the fortunate few, to imagine and work for a social order in which there was more joy and less inequality.

Without minimizing or sentimentalizing his pain, Bourne concluded: "It is hard to tell just how much of this philosophy has been due to my handicaps. If it is solely to my physical misfortunes that I owe its existence, the price has not been a heavy one to pay. For it has given me something I would not know how to be without" (Bourne, 1911).

Our philosophy guides our life, teaching us what to make of people and events. We learn that philosophy from parents, teachers, and books, from artists, poets, and friends, and most of all, perhaps, from experience. If our children's limitations help us to see the universe and our fellows more clearly, perhaps we have gained as much as we have lost.

None of us are Lears and few of us are Randolph Bournes. It seems necessary, however, to close with their message of brotherhood and sisterhood. In the end, as Bourne makes clear, the message is political, for it says something about the kind of society we need to build. This is not a political book, however. It is a book about families and their private worlds of grief and endurance. It is about difference and commonality. My family and other families with a difference are both like and unlike the rest of the families on the planet. Both facts are important; I hope neither has overshadowed the other in these pages.

When Charles De Gaulle's daughter Anne was born with Down's syndrome, his wife Yvonne wrote sadly, "Charles and I would give everything: health, fortune, promotion, career, if only Anne were a little girl like the others." The years passed. De Gaulle proved a devoted father. Often he would put aside the affairs of state to play with his daughter and make her laugh. Finally, she died. At the graveside De Gaulle took his wife's hand saying, "Come, now she is like the others" (Massie and Massie 1975, p. 407).

So she was. But De Gaulle was only partly right. Anne and her family had also been like the others all along.

Afterword: A Note on Sources and Limitations

YEARS AGO I was a student, and then, much later, a teacher, in David Riesman's wonderful Harvard undergraduate course on American social character. Riesman encouraged us to make use of different kinds of data, including our own experiences, to use insight and observation as well as statistics. In writing about families I found myself turning back to the preface to the new edition of *The Lonely Crowd* (Riesman, Glazer, and Denney 1969), where Riesman talks about the origins of this brilliant analysis of American social character. He explains that in the early fifties, while working on the book, he and Nathan Glazer conducted interviews with people of different ages and backgrounds. But they did not use much of this material in *The Lonely Crowd*. "Indeed," writes Riesman, "it should be emphasized that this book is based on our experience of living in America—the people we have met, the jobs we have held, the books we have read, the movies we have seen, and the landscape" (p. lxi). Like Riesman and his colleagues, I have tried to move beyond personal experience and introspection to a wider vision. Like other social scientists, I start with myself.

As many mothers and fathers do, I turned to books almost as soon as I learned my son was handicapped. I wanted to know all about blindness, cerebral palsy, and retardation: I needed guidance in order to help Jody develop. I remember my first trip to the library. The card catalogue led me to six or seven books with titles like "You and Your Handicapped Child." I searched them out quickly and curled up in a comfortable chair. As the hours ticked away I became more and more discouraged. Nothing in these volumes seemed to apply to me. The practical advice was irrelevant: no one had imagined a child with all Jody's handicaps. The homilies about acceptance struck a false note. I remember that the author of one particularly complacent book had discovered a bright side to my son's retardation: when the other children were beginning to weary of old family customs like singing around the piano, my retarded child would still enjoy them. I grimaced at the picture: two teenagers, their noses wrinkled in disgust, muttering, "Oh Mommy, do we *have* to?" while their retarded brother eagerly searched for the sheet music and the piano stool. With compensations like this, who needs problems?

This was what professionals offered parents: injunctions to accept the handicap, embedded in Normal Rockwell images of family life. I did not like what they wrote for other professionals any better. Here they fitted parents into a variety of clinical pigeon holes—overprotective, rejecting, neurotic—through the use of unsophisticated and methodologically suspect psychological tests. I knew a lot of mothers and fathers, but I had not met the hapless, sodden victims these studies described. I am not the only scholar with this reaction. Dr. Allen Roith, a psychiatrist, recollects that after sampling the literature on families, "I sat back and waited for the horde of guilty and aggressive parents to descend on me. But now after eight long years, I am still waiting for them" (Roith 1963).

I am happy to say that these dismal efforts do not represent the sum of present professional understandings of families. Recent studies speak much more respectfully of parents, making more of an effort to include their perspective and, in a growing number of works, their voices. Thoughtful writers observe that most parents manage to cope with a range of tragic and recalcitrant problems (see, for example, Barsch 1968; Hewett 1970; Mitchell 1979; Roskies 1972). As Boles noted even in 1959, psychologists who described parents' of the handicapped as anxious, guilty, unrealistic, and rejecting usually failed to ask the same questions of parents of normal children. Many of their conclusions came from clinical experience with very unrepresentative families. Researchers who had recourse to a control group of families of ordinary children have started to balance the picture. Sheila Hewett, for example, compared what she learned from mothers of young children with cerebral palsy to what John and Elizabeth Newson found in surveying parents of normal four-year-olds. She discovered that more of the mothers of normal children said they sometimes wondered whether they were bringing up their children the right way. Similarly, more of the mothers of normal children disagreed with their husbands about discipline.

It was a long time, however, before I found these more encouraging studies. My earliest safaris into the professional literature merely depressed me. Fortunately the library offered another resource: books by parents. These narratives fascinated me. Few possess enduring literary merit; after some initial popularity most gather dust on the shelves of branch libraries and second-hand bookstores. Nonetheless, they tell stories of extraordinary human interest: they are first-hand accounts of the way ordinary families learn to deal with serious trouble.

From such books and articles, I learned more about the pressures on other families. I found some feelings described eloquently. I learned to expect a certain rhythm in the accounts: serenity, tragedy, turbulence and misery, a plan, and a growing sense of mastery and control, and finally some sort of acceptance.

Published accounts have real limitations, of course. For one thing, their authors represent a tiny fraction of the affected families. Parents who publish share certain attributes. They are sufficiently well educated to write for publication. Their situation no longer overwhelms them completely. Writing requires a certain margin. At the very least, an author must be able to organize his or her life to ensure some time away from both children and paid employment. Many parents would search in vain for the necessary leisure.

Emotional obstacles may loom even larger than practical ones. Parents who begin to write about family tragedies sometimes reopen old wounds. A student in one of my college classes decided to tell the story of her daughter's defection from the family in a long paper. She found the project more harrowing than she had imagined. Near tears she told me as she handed it in, "I wish I had never started. There isn't any point going through it again." Another middle-aged mother began to write about the death of her six-year-old daughter twelve years earlier; her blood pressure shot up and she had to lay the work aside. Few people could bear to write a book-length account of their experience with a disabled child unless they had worked through their most disturbing feelings and arrived at some sort of resolution. This process can take years—in some cases it takes forever.

Probably many such unfinished accounts yellow at the bottom of desk drawers. Those that see the light of day have a particular character: I call them "notes from the other side." Most of these stories describe painful feelings honestly. But the authors speak from a certain distance. They have reached a turning point; often the very act of writing helps them to get there.

Telling our stories in retrospect, we may impose too much order on turbulent feelings. Remembering the changes that occurred over time, we may forget the way that our emotional barometer rose and fell over the course of an ordinary week. The life we live is often more chaotic than the life we remember. The accounts that grow from journals—for example, Josh Greenfeld's (1972, 1978) and John and Emily Murray's (1975)—preserve the record of daily ups and downs and remind us that most people see things differently on different days.

Undoubtedly a complex mix of motives buttresses any decision to write autobiographically. People speak of wanting to get things straight in their own minds. Sometimes words give a curious sort of power over feelings. Writing a book can also help to reshape the meaning of a tragedy. By writing we begin to integrate the experience into the fabric of an on-going life. We forge a new identity—writer—out of an old loss. Many mothers, fathers, sisters, and brothers also speak of a need to reach out to others in the same position. Believing that they have learned something, they want to smooth another family's path.

The hope of helping others encourages parents to tell their story accurately. Nonetheless, everyone has to live with themselves, their families, and their neighbors after publication. Certainly we would expect greater explicitness and candor on some subjects than others. Not surprisingly, for example, few parents who have remained married criticize their spouse or describe serious conflicts, although a few do. Similarly, few explore the full complexity of their children's responses to one another: anecdotes illustrating pride, protectiveness, and affection far outnumber those suggesting anger or jealousy. Pride, natural reticence, discretion, and sensitivity to the feelings of others all require that some events be omitted and others abridged. Every book is written from an angle of vision that is good for some things and less good for others.

Knowing how hard it is to look unblinkingly into your own soul, to expose yourself and your family to public scrutiny, I read these accounts with a sometimes skeptical eye. I believe that, read rightly, they open a valuable window on families. They give more detail than we would ever get in an interview, or even a series of interviews. They offer a chronological, sequential picture not only of the child's progress, but of the ebb and flow of family feelings. Most important, they tell what the authors believe is significant. We need to know that. How do people make sense of this experience? What does it mean to them?

During the spring and summer of 1976 I dug into the professional literature on families and read many books and articles by parents themselves. I reflected on my own experience and went back over the notes in my diary. Gradually an essay began to take shape in my mind, a piece intended to balance the picture of misery and pathology I found in the research literature. It seemed to me that parents were saying that although their child's disability had saddened them, it had also helped them to grow. Through living and enduring one comes to grips with these tragedies and learns to see them in a different light. The message of my own experience, and the message I found in books, was hopeful. I tried, in those early months, to set it down.

Then, in September of 1976, I got a telephone call from the social worker at my son's school. She was forming a parents' group, to meet one morning every other week. Would I be interested in joining? I was. I missed the first meeting because of a family funeral, but rushed eagerly to the second. I was excited to meet other women facing problems like mine (I knew that at a morning meeting "parents" meant mothers), and I was curious to know how these problems looked to them. I was surprised by what I learned.

On the way home from my first meeting, I mentally tore the pages I had already written into little pieces. These women had not spoken about rainbows after the storm, about families drawn closer by tragedy. They were in pain. Their eyes misted over as they struggled to describe the uncertainty of the early months, the despair with which they contemplated the future. These were not voices from "the other side," encouraging the exhausted swimmer. These were voices from the middle of the river, the gasps of courageous women who sometimes felt themselves going under. Some mothers could scarcely believe in, let alone glimpse, another side. I returned to my desk wondering how many people ever make it to the much advertised state of acceptance.

I continued to go to the meetings regularly for two and a half years. These women became my friends. I cared about them; I learned about them and about myself. The membership and the character of the group shifted as the months passed. By the time my job prevented me from going, in January of 1979, most members of the original group had followed their children to other schools. Other mothers joined. They changed the group and it changed them. But these alterations were gradual, and the continuities real.

I did not join the group in order to write about it, and I did not expect to use what I learned there in any direct way. The relevance of our conversations became obvious very soon, but I hated to invade the privacy of my friends and ask for permission to feed their heartbreak into my book. So for a few months I kept my writing and research separate from my participation in the group. Finally, made brave by the social worker's interest in my project, I told the group about my book and got permission to include their experiences while changing their names. After that I kept notes on exchanges and experiences that seem important.

In the second and third years I grew more systematic. I wrote copious notes during the afternoon following each meeting. Much as I would have valued a truer record of our conversations, and a means of telling each woman's story in her own words, I avoided using a tape recorder. The group existed to support all of us in our difficult jobs as mothers of severely handicapped young children. The meetings were a place to speak about troubling thoughts and feelings. For some people they were the only place these feelings could be unwrapped and inspected. I thought that the persistent intrusive presence of a tape recorder would make the setting less comfortable for at least a few people, and maybe for many.* Their need for support

* In January of 1979, I drove to a distant suburb to have lunch with two members of the original group, both good friends of mine. As we ate our egg salad sandwiches, I remarked that I wished I could tell people's stories in their own words. Barbara Sullivan laughed and said, "Yes, you should have hidden a tape recorder in your sleeve." Shocked at the suggestion, I reflected silently that social scientists have, over the years, earned themselves rather a bad name. But Barbara turned serious, and said that she doubted that anyone would have minded my taping the meetings. Catherine Lederman disagreed: she would have objected strenuously, "Because it was the one place where I could be completely honest. And I really needed it."

obviously took precedence over my scholarly desire for a record of what was said.

It is not hard to get mothers of handicapped children to discuss their experiences. Many welcome the chance to talk and be listened to. However, most people approach certain topics rather guardedly, particularly with comparative strangers.* Couples, for example, often present a united front in public, even while negotiating serious differences privately. After getting to know other group members, some mothers and fathers test more frightening waters, raising issues they usually avoid. Common experience, trust, and a commitment to giving as well as taking, support an impulse toward fuller exposure.

Those who attempt to learn about the impact of a disabled child on a family through interviews often complain of the difficulty of obtaining a representative sample of parents and siblings (see, for example, Hannam 1975, and Grossman 1972). When Charles Hannam asked the seventeen families in the training center his retarded son attended to talk to him, only three couples assented; all of these were middle-class and, in his judgment, coping well. Parents still struggling with recalcitrant feelings and insoluable problems may shrink from this sort of confrontation. Over the long run of a handicapped child's preschool experience, a group offers more rewards for candor.

The parents in my group are no more representative than those studied by other investigators. They are simply atypical in somewhat different ways. First, all were raising very young disabled children. Our school served multiply handicapped boys and girls ranging in age from nine months to seven years. My own son was four at the time the first group began to organize. Even then I had been at the business of "exceptional mothering" for longer than any of the other women except the social worker. All of us had faced problems like adolescence and public schooling in our imagination, but none had yet grappled with the long-term realities.

Second, the children in the school were, on the whole, more seriously handicapped than most children receiving special services. In the wider world, children with learning disabilities or mild mental retardation far outnumber those who are blind, deaf, or severely re-

* McMichael, for example, describes differences in data gathered by an interviewer who knew the parent well and one who did not: she found that distressed parents talked far less freely when the interviewer was a stranger (1971). Charles Hannam, who taped his conversations with mothers and fathers of retarded children, observes that couples began to speak more eagerly as soon as he turned off his machine to terminate the interview (1975).

tarded. Although parents of these children face many of the same problems, they see them from a different viewpoint.

Third, every woman who attended the group regularly was married and living with the father of her disabled child. This does not make them unusual: many Americans still live in two-parent families. However, a very significant minority are divorced. Some studies indicate that marital disruption occurs even more frequently in families with disabled children. (I have not seen any statistics that seem definitive. Hewett (1970) argues rather persuasively that professional pessimism may derive from small studies of unrepresentative families.) In any case, a sizeable minority of handicapped children grow up in households run by a single parent. I cannot say very much about the special point of view of these families, although I would be interested in finding out more about their special perspective.

My group's families fell along the middle of the economic and social spectrum. None were rich, and none were really poor. They lived in the suburbs; the men worked as policemen, truck drivers, and CPAs. A few of the women held part-time jobs. Like the other members of the group, I am the mother of a fairly young, seriously disabled, child and two normal children. Like them I am married. Thus in many ways the limitations of my sample reinforce the limitations of my experience.

I hope my reading and teaching have helped me to transcend some of these limits. Family members write books, articles, and letters about their encounters with all sorts of disabilities, ranging from fatal degenerative illnesses to fairly minor learning disabilities. Some tell a very short story: their children are still young. Others trace the family saga through a handicapped person's childhood, adolescence, and adulthood. But even more important for my own education than this wealth of published material have been what Clara Park calls "the others": the people you meet everywhere. At the food coop, at work, at dinner parties, in the line at the supermarket, in doctors' offices, and in the graduate school and adult education classes I teach, people tell me about their handicapped sisters and brothers, sons and daughters, and grandchildren. Every day of our lives most of us talk to, ride with, or shop beside someone whose life has been altered by another person's disability. More of these people talk to me about their experiences because they see that I walk a similarly shaded path. Although I have not used many of the experiences of these "others" in this book, they have taught me that the same themes run through very different lives.

This book describes the way a child's disability touches those who love him. It does not paint the experience of all family members equally vividly. Its limitations reflect mine, but also those of the culture. Any adult who chooses to listen can soon learn a great deal about the strains and rewards of motherhood. At every level of society, the twin topics of children and parenting enliven women's conversations. I observe this interest in child development and family dynamics among mothers who share every household and child-care chore with their husbands as well as among full-time housewives. Even conscientiously liberated men reflect less audibly on their experience as fathers—at least when I am around. I do not mean that women are slaves of biology, that children absorb all, or even most, of their mental energy; I mean only that women who happen to be mothers usually talk more than their husbands about how the experience feels. Whether this is good or bad, it means that I have learned an immense amount about the pressures and pleasures of mothering simply by being a woman in America, and that I have learned a lot less about the way men feel about fatherhood. Fortunately more men are beginning to talk about the way parenthood shapes their lives, and many have written about their disabled children.

After meeting regularly for more than a year, mothers in the group began to talk about their husbands' need for support. In order to bring the men together the social worker scheduled some evening meetings and invited all interested couples to attend. From these meetings, and from many conversations with fathers, I concluded that mothers and fathers share many of the same concerns, although I never got to know the men as well as I knew their wives.

A child's disability touches every family member—brothers and sisters as well as parents. The evolving perspective of able-bodied children interests me deeply. However, my information on this topic is limited: I have listened to Liza and Cait talk about Jody over the years; I have listened to other parents, especially those in my group, talk about their healthy children; I have talked to able-bodied siblings; and I have read what I could find by and about brothers and sisters. These glimpses into young lives have left some vivid impressions. They have convinced me that a good deal remains unsaid in most households and that, within a family, the fallout from a disability distributes itself quite unevenly across children. Understanding one child's—or one parent's—perspective is not the same as understanding the family as a whole.

I have said almost nothing about the way the family's difference looks to the disabled child. The children I have known most intimately were in no position to communicate these feelings or reflect on their families' difference. The disabled adults I have talked to were quite circumspect in what they said, although several felt their disability had strained family relationships in one way or another. Their own stories suggest that disabled people may travel a road quite like that of mothers, fathers, brothers, and sisters. Certainly they too are afraid, angry, lonely, and guilty. Certainly they have difficulties with parents, brothers, sisters, and professionals. Certainly they fight toward some sort of acceptance. I wish I could say more about their struggles. Fortunately, the disabled are now telling their own stories, just as they are beginning to act on their own behalf as part of an important human rights movement. This book, however, is really about families.

REFERENCES

Alterman, S. 1978. "Influences on Labelling and Diagnostic Practices at The League School of Boston: 1973–1978" Unpublished paper, Harvard University.

Axline, V. M. 1964. *Dibs in Search of Self.* New York: Houghton Mifflin.

Barsch, R. H. 1968. *The Parent of the Handicapped Child: Study of Child Rearing Practices.* Springfield, Ill.: Charles Thomas.

Baruch, D. 1952. *One Little Boy.* New York: Julian Press.

Bassin, J., and Drovella, D. 1976. "Parent Outreach." *Exceptional Parent* (June).

Baum, M. H. 1962. "Some Dynamic Factors Affecting Family Adjustment to the Handicapped Child." *Exceptional Child* 28: 387–92.

Bennett, Mrs. H. 1974. Letter. *Exceptional Parent* (May/June).

Bennett, J. 1974. "Proof of the Pudding." *Exceptional Parent* (May/June).

Berg, K. 1973. "Christina Loves Katherine." *Exceptional Parent* (March/April).

Bettelheim, B. 1967. *The Empty Fortress.* New York: Free Press.

Birch, H., and Chess, S. 1965. *Your Child Is a Person.* New York: Viking Press.

Blatt, B. 1973. *Souls in Extremis: An Anthology of Victims and Victimizers.* Boston: Allyn and Bacon.

Boles, G. 1959. "Personality Factors in Mothers of Cerebral Palsied Children." *Genetic Psychology Monographs* 59:159–218.

Boston Women's Health Book Collective. 1978. *Ourselves and Our Children.* New York: Random House.

Bourne, R. 1911. "The Handicapped." *Atlantic Monthly* 108 (Sept.):320–39.

Breisky, W. 1974. *I Think I Can.* Garden City, N.Y.: Doubleday.

Brown, H. 1976. *Yesterday's Child.* New York: M. Evans.

Browning, E. 1972. *I Can't See What You're Saying.* New York: Coward, McCann, and Geoghegan.

Buck, P. S. 1930. *The Child Who Never Grew.* New York: John Day.

Buscaglia, L. 1975. *The Disabled and Their Parents: A Counseling Challenge.* Thoroughfare, N.J.: Charles B. Slack.

Canning, J., and Canning, C. 1975. *The Gift of Martha.* Children's Hospital Medical Center.

Carlton, W. J. 1978. *"In Our Professional Opinion . . .": The Primacy of Clinical Judgment over Moral Choice.* Notre Dame and London: University of Notre Dame Press, 1978.

Carr, J. 1975. *Young Children with Down's Syndrome: Their Development, Upbringing, and Effect on their Families.* London and Boston: Butterworth's.

Cleveland, D. W., and Miller, N. 1977. "Attitudes and Life Commitments of Older Siblings of Mentally Retarded Adults." *Mental Retardation* 15:38.

Collins, M., and Collins, D. 1976. *Kith and Kids: Self-help for Families of the Handicapped.* London: Souvenir Press.

Connors, F.; Kirk, S.; and Blatt, B. 1977. "Special Education Yesterday, Today, and Tomorrow." *Exceptional Parent* (August).

Crocker, A. 1979. *The Involvement of Siblings of Children with Handicaps.* Boston: Developmental Evaluation Clinic, Children's Hospital Medical Center.

de Vizia, J. 1974. Letter. *Exceptional Parent* (Nov./Dec.).

Diaz, S. 1974. Letter. *Exceptional Parent* (July/August).

Drabble, M. 1972. *The Needle's Eye.* New York: Popular Library.

Dworkin, D. H.; Shonkoff, J. P.; Levitan, A.; and Levine, M. D. 1978. "Training in Developmental Pediatrics: How Practitioners Perceive the Gaps." Paper presented before the Society for Pediatric Research, April 28.

Edgerton, R. B. 1967. *The Cloak of Competence: Stigma in the Lives of the Mentally Retarded.* Berkeley: University of California Press.

Edgerton, R. B., and Berconci, S. M. 1976. "The Cloak of Competence: Years Later." *American Journal of Mental Deficiency* 80, no. 5, pp. 485–97.

Egg, M. 1964. *When a Child Is Different.* New York: John Day.

Ehlers, W. H. 1966. *Mothers of Retarded Children: How They Feel; Where They Find Help.* Springfield, Ill.: C. C. Thomas.

Eisenpreis, B. 1972. "The Silence of Steven." *Exceptional Parent* (Oct./Nov./Dec.).

Erikson, E. H. 1968. *Identity: Youth and Crisis.* New York: W. W. Norton.

Farber, B. 1959. *Effects of a Severely Mentally Retarded Child on Family Integration.* Monographs of the Society for Research in Child Development 24, no. 2 (Serial no. 71).

Farber, B. 1960. *Family Organization and Crisis: Maintenance of Integration in Families with a Severely Mentally Retarded Child.* Monographs of the Society for Research in Child Development 25, no. 1 (Serial no. 75).

Farber, B.; Jenne, W. C.; and Toigo, R. 1960. *Family Crisis and the Decision to Institutionalize the Retarded Child.* Council for Exception Children, Research Monograph no. 1.

Ferree, M. M. 1976. "Working Class Jobs: Housework and Paid Work as Sources of Satisfaction." *Social Problems* 23, no. 4 (April).

Fisher, H. 1977. "Notes from the Underground: Teachers on Mainstreaming." Unpublished paper, Harvard Graduate School of Education.

Fotheringham, J. B.; Skelton, M.; and Hoddinott, B. A. 1971. *The Retarded Child and His Family: The Effects of Home and Institution.* The Ontario Institute for Studies in Education, Monograph Series 11.

Fox, R. C. 1957. "Training for Uncertainty." In *The Student Physician*, edited by R. K. Merton, G. G. Reader, and P. L. Kendal. Cambridge: Harvard University Press.

Fraiberg, S. 1974. "Blind Infants and Their Mothers: An Examination of the Sign System." In *The Effect of the Infant on Its Caretaker*, edited by M. Lewis and L. A. Rosenblaum. New York: John Wiley.

Fraiberg, S. 1977. *Insights from the Blind: Comparative Studies of Blind and Sighted Infants.* New York: Basic Books.

Frank, J P. 1951. *My Son's Story.* New York: Alfred A. Knopf.

Gauchat, D. 1976. *All God's Children.* New York: Hawthorn Books.

Gibson, A. 1972. Letter. *Exceptional Parent* (August/Sept.).

Gliedman, J., and Roth, W. 1980. *The Invisible Minority: Handicapped Children in America.* New York and London: Harcourt Brace Jovanovich.

Goffman, E. 1963. *Stigma: Notes on the Management of Spoiled Identity.* Englewood Cliffs, N.J.: Prentice-Hall.

Golden, S. 1974. Letter *Exceptional Parent* (July/August).

Golden, S. 1975. "New City, New Doctor." *Exceptional Parent* (Dec.).

Green, M. 1975. "Loving a Special Child." *Exceptional Parent* (June).

Greenfeld, J. 1972. *A Child Called Noah.* New York: Holt, Rinehart and Winston.

Greenfeld, J. 1978. *A Place for Noah.* New York: Holt, Rinehart and Winston.

Gregory, R. W. 1972. Letter. *Exceptional Parent* (August/Sept.).

Grossman, F. K. 1972. *Brothers and Sisters of Retarded Children: An Exploratory Study.* Syracuse, N.Y.: Syracuse University Press.

Hamilton, J. 1977. "The Dark Side." *Exceptional Parent* (June).

Hannam, C. 1975. *Parents and Mentally Handicapped Children.* Baltimore, Maryland: Penguin Books.

Hart, N. W. 1970. "Frequently Expressed Feelings and Reactions of Parents Toward Their Retarded Children." In *Diminished People*, edited by N. R. Bernstein. Boston: Little, Brown.

Harth, R. 1977. "Attitudes and Mental Retardation: Review of the Literature." In *Mental Retardation: Social and Educational Perspectives*, edited by C. J. Drew, J. L. Hardman, H. P. Bluhm, and B. Blatt. St. Louis: C. V. Mosby.

Hawkins, F. P. 1979. "The Eye of the Beholder." *Outlook* (Summer).

Hayden, V. 1974. "The Other Children." *Exceptional Parent* (July/August).

Helsel, E.; Helsel, B.; Helsel, B; and Helsel, M. 1978. "The Helsels' Story of Robin." In *Parents Speak Out: Views from the Other Side of the Two Way Mirror*, edited by A. P. Turnbull and H. R. Turnbull. Columbus, Toronto, London, and Sydney: Charles E. Merrill.

Hewett, S. 1970. *The Family and the Handicapped Child: A Study of Cerebral Palsied Children in Their Homes*. Chicago: Aldine.

Hundley, J. M. 1971. *The Small Outsider: The Story of an Autistic Child*. New York: St. Martin's Press.

Jacobs, J. 1969. *The Search for Help: A Study of the Retarded Child in the Community*. New York: Brunner/Mazel.

Joel, G. 1975. *So Your Child Has Cerebral Palsy*. Albuquerque: University of New Mexico Press.

Junker, K. S. 1964. *The Child in the Glass Ball*. New York: Abingdon Press.

Kanner, L. 1949. "Problems of Nosology and Psychodynamics in Early Infantile Autism." *American Journal of Orthopsychiatry* 19:416–26.

———. 1954. "To What Extent Is Early Infantile Autism Determined by Constitutional Inadequacies?" In *Genetics and the Inheritance of Neurological and Psychiatric Patterns*, edited by D. Hooker and C. C. Hare. Baltimore: Williams and Wilkins.

———. 1973. *Childhood Psychosis: Initial Studies and New Insights*. Washington, D.C.: V. H. Winston and Sons.

Kastein, S., and Trace, B. 1966. *The Birth of Language: The Case History of a Non-Verbal Child*. Springfield, Ill.: C. C. Thomas.

Katz, A. H. 1961. *Parents of the Handicapped*. Springfield, Ill.: C. C. Thomas.

Katz. K. J. 1975. "Precious Days." *Exceptional Parent* (August).

Kaufman, N. 1976. *Son-Rise*. New York: Warner Books.

Kelley, C.; Mullins, P.; Caliendo, G.; and Sweet, N. 1978. "Parent-Professional Communication." *Exceptional Parent* (April).

Killelea, M. 1952. *Karen*. New York: Dell.

Klaus, M., and Kennel, J. 1976. *Maternal-Infant Bonding*. St. Louis: C. V. Mosby.

Klebanoff, L. 1971. "Parent-to-Parent." *Exceptional Parent* (June/July; Aug./Sept.; Oct./Nov.).

Klein, S. 1972. "Brother to Sister, Sister to Brother." *Exceptional Parent* (June/July; Aug./Sept.; Oct./Nov./Dec.).

Kleinfield, S. 1979. *The Hidden Minority: A Profile of Handicapped Americans*. Boston: Little Brown.

Korsch, B. M., and Negrete, V. F. 1972."Doctor-Patient Communication." *Scientific American* 227, no. 13 (August):66–74.

Kovacs, D. 1972. "Josh: The Lonely Search for Help." *Exceptional Parent* (April/May).

Kronick, D. 1976. *Three Families: The Effect of Family Dynamics on Social and Conceptual Learning*. San Rafael, Calif.: Academic Therapy Publications.

Kübler-Ross, E. 1969. *On Death and Dying*. New York: Macmillan.

Lasch, C. 1976. *Haven in a Heartless World: The Family Besieged*. New York: Basic Books.

LaShan, E. 1973. "Who Cares What Happens to Miriam?" *Exceptional Parent* (March/April).

Lazarre, J. 1976. *The Mother Knot*. New York: Dell.

Leaf, L. 1975. "Our Arnold." *Exceptional Parent* (Jan./Feb.).

Levine, J. 1976. *Who Will Raise the Children? New Options for Fathers (and Mothers)*. Philadelphia and N. Y.: J. B. Lippincott.

Lightfoot, S. L. 1978. *Worlds Apart: Relationships Between Families and Schools*. New York: Basic Books.

Lonsdale, G. 1978. "Family Life with a Handicapped Child: The Parents Speak." *Child Care, Health and Development* 4:99.

Lortie, D. 1975. *Schoolteacher*. Chicago: University of Chicago Press.

Love, H. D. 1970. *Parental Attitudes toward Exceptional Children*. Springfield, Ill.: C. C. Thomas.

McCracken, M. 1973. *A Circle of Children*. New York: New American Library.

McMichael, J. K. 1971. *Handicap: A Study of Physically Handicapped Children and Their Families*. Pittsburgh: University of Pittsburgh Press.

Mannoni, M. 1972. *The Backward Child and His Mother: A Psychoanalytic Study*. Translated by A. M. Sheridan Smith. New York: Pantheon Books.

Massie, R. and Massie S. 1975. *Journey*. New York: Alfred A. Knopf.

Matina, J. 1977. Letter. *Exceptional Parent* (October).

Melton, D. 1968. *Todd*. Englewood Cliffs., N.J.: Prentice-Hall.

Meyers, R. 1978. *Like Normal People*. New York: McGraw Hill.

Michaelis, C. T. 1974. "Chip on my Shoulder." *Exceptional Parent* (Jan./Feb.).

Minuchin, S. 1974. *Families and Family Therapy*. Cambridge, Mass.: Harvard University Press.

Mitchell, W. 1979. "Fathers of Retarded Children." Doctoral dissertation, Harvard Graduate School of Education.

Mnookin, W. M. 1977. "Choosing Motherhood." *Radcliffe Quarterly* (March).

Murray, J. B., and Murray E. 1975. *And Say What He Is: The Life of a Special Child*. Cambridge, Mass.: M.I.T. Press.

Nemzoff, R. 1977. "A Tale of Two Perspectives: The Development of the Pleasant Valley Workshop for Retarded Citizens." Qualifying paper, Harvard Graduate School of Education.

Olafson, M. 1978. "Falling Through the Spaces." *Exceptional Parent* (October).

Olshansky, S. 1962. "Chronic Sorrow: A Response to Having a Mentally Defective Child." *Social Casework*. 43, no. 4 (April).

Osher, T. 1978. "The Experience of Parenting a Severely Handicapped Child in the North Country of New Hampshire." Unpublished paper, Harvard Graduate School of Education.

Ouellett, A. 1976. "Michelle—Questions and Answers." *Exceptional Parent* (February).

————. 1977. "Michelle—Growing through Camping." *Exceptional Parent* (February).

Paley, V. G. 1979. *White Teacher*. Cambridge, Mass.: Harvard University Press.

Park, C. C. 1967. *The Siege*. Boston: Little, Brown.

Pendler, B. 1975. Letter. *Exceptional Parent* (January).

Pieper, E. 1976. "Grandparents Can Help." *Exceptional Parent* (April).

Pieper, E. n.d. *Sticks and Stones: The Story of Loving a Child*. Syracuse, N.Y.: Human Policy Press.

Rank, B. 1955. "Intensive Study and Treatment of Preschool Children Who Show Marked Personality Deviations or 'Atypical Development' and Their Parents." In *Emotional Problems in Early Childhood*, edited by G. Caplan. New York: Basic Books.

Rhodes, M. J. 1972. "Invisible Barrier." *Exceptional Parent* (April/May).

Richmond, J. B. 1973. "The Family and the Handicapped Child." Clinical Proceedings 29, no. 7 (July/Aug.):156–64.

Riesman, D.; Glazer, N.; and Denney, R. 1969. *The Lonely Crowd*. Abridged ed. New Haven, Conn.: Yale University Press.

Robinson, H. B., and Robinson, N. M. 1965. *The Mentally Retarded Child: A Psychological Approach*. New York: McGraw Hill.

Rogers, D. E. 1953. *Angel Unaware*. Los Angeles: Fleming H. Revell.

Roith, A. I. 1963. "The Myth of Parental Attitudes." *The Journal of Mental Subnormality* 9:51–54.

Roskies, E. 1972. *Abnormality and Normality: The Mothering of Thalidomide Children*. Ithaca, N.Y.: Cornell University Press.

Ross A. O. 1964. *The Exceptional Child in the Family: Helping Parents of Exceptional Children*. New York: Grime and Stratton.

Schild, S. 1971. "The Family of the Retarded Child." In *The Mentally Retarded Child and His Family*, edited by R. Koch and J. C. Dobson. New York: Brunner/Mazel.

Schlesinger, H. S. and Meadow, K. P. 1972. *Sound and Sign: Childhood Deafness and Mental Health*. Berkeley: University of California Press.

Schrag, P., and Divoky, D. 1975. *The Myth of the Hyperactive Child and Other Means of Mind Control*. New York: Dell.

Schult, M. 1975. "I'll Never Do That." *Exceptional Parent* (October).

Schult, Mr. and Mrs. H. 1975. Letter. *Exceptional Parent* (June).

Searl, S. J. 1978. "Stages of Parent Reaction." *Exceptional Parent* (April).

Segal, M. 1966. *Run Away, Little Girl*. New York: Random House.

Sobol, H. L. 1977. *My Brother Steven Is Retarded*. New York: Macmillan.

Solnit, A. J., and Stark, M. H. 1961. "Mourning and the Birth of a Defective Child." *Psychoanalytic Study of the Child* 16:523–537.

Stern, E. M., and Castendyk, E. 1950. *The Handicapped Child: A Guide for Parents*. New York: A. A. Wyn.

Stern, V. W. 1972. Letter. *Exceptional Parent* (August/Sept.).

Strickland, J. 1974. "Camping Is for Everyone." *Exceptional Parent* (March/April).

Thomas, A.; Chess, S.; and Birch, H. G. 1968. *Temperament and Behavior Disorders in Children*. New York: New York University Press.

Thornburg, D. G. 1978. "Siblings: Making Sense of Handicap." Unpublished paper, Harvard Graduate School of Education.

Ulrich, S. 1972. *Elizabeth*. Ann Arbor: University of Michigan Press.

Van Osdol, B. 1976. *Special Education*. Dubuque, Iowa: Kendall/Hunt.

Wakefield, T. 1978. *Some Mothers I Know: Living with Handicapped Children*. London: Routledge and Kegan Paul.

Wilson, L. 1968. *This Stranger, My Son*. New York: G. P. Putnam and Sons.

Winefield, R. 1979. "Examining Teachers' Attitudes toward the Practice of Mainstreaming Handicapped Children." Unpublished qualifying paper, Harvard Graduate School of Education.

Ziskin, L. K. 1978. "The Story of Jennie." In *Parents Speak Out: Views from the Other Side of the Two Way Mirror*, edited by A. P. Turnbull and H. R. Turnbull. Columbus, Toronto, London and Sydney: Charles Merrill.

INDEX

daily activities, 76–80; and explanation of handicap, 72–76; and parental omnipotence, 80–82; and praise/blame, 83–85; and rationality, 76; and rebuilding, 86–90; and secrecy, 175; and self-esteem, 85; in siblings, 82–83, 140, 143, 144; and unhappiness of child, 12

Hamilton, J., 46
Hannam, Charles, 8n, 56, 88, 98n, 99, 117, 180, 247
Hart, Nancy Wagner, 204, 226
Haven in a Heartless World (Lasch), 113
Hawkins, F. P., 195
Hayden, Victoria, 46, 47, 60, 61, 141, 148, 160, 161, 164, 171
Helsel, Marge, 145
Hemophilia, 8, 28, 111, 229, 238; communication of diagnosis of, 38; and fear, 18
Henry, Jules, 205
Hewett, Sheila, 159, 163n, 180n, 242, 243, 248
Hoddinott, B. A., 93n
Howe, Samuel Gridley, 183n
Hundley, Joan M., 145, 156
Hurler's syndrome, 21
Hydrocephalic condition, 4, 27

Identification with handicapped and vulnerability, 148
Infants and personality development, 73
Institutes for the Achievement of Human Potential, Philadelphia, 35n, 119, 224
Institutionalization, 24; anticipatory fears of, 17; as decision, 63
Itard, Jean, 183n

Jacobs, Jerry, 7, 25, 182, 231
James, William, 237
Jealousy, sibling, and guilt, 144
Jenne, W. C., 93n
Joel, G., 150n
Junker, Karin, 14, 98, 104, 105, 155

Kanner, Leo, 71–72, 73n, 90
Kastein, S., 45, 179
Katz, A. H., 185, 185n
Katz, Kay, 41, 57
Kaufman, Neil, 216, 217, 218, 219
Kaufman, Suzi, 216, 219
Kelley, C., 182

Kennedy, John, 31
Kennedy, Ted, 190
Kennel, J., 10
Killelea, Marie, 95, 96, 97, 111, 227
King Lear (Shakespeare), 238, 239
Kith and Kids, 172–73
Klaus, M., 10
Klebanoff, L., 80, 89
Klein, S., 143, 147, 164, 167
Kleinfeld, S., 69
Korsch, B. M., 180n, 183n
Kovacs, Diane, 14, 94n, 220
Kronick, Doreen, 205
Kübler-Ross, Elisabeth, 10, 232

Language development: delayed, 179; preschool problem with, 45
Lasch, Christopher, 113
Lazarre, Jane, 64, 104n
Leaf, L., 34
Learning disability, 97, 180
Lederman, Catherine (mothers' group), 66, 67, 86, 88, 121, 122, 132, 133, 148, 180, 181, 213, 225, 226, 228, 229, 246n
Levine, Mel, 198
Life cycle, 230
Lightfoot, Sara Lawrence, 184, 205
Lip reading, 3, 16, 224
Loneliness, 10, 50–69; cutting oneself off, 58–60; and family dynamics, 54–57; isolated parents, 62–63; and mechanics of daily activity, 52–54; onset of, 51–52; and pain, 50–51; resistance of, 65–69; and search for support, 63–65; in siblings, 60–61
Lonely Crowd, The (Riesman), 241
Lonsdale, G., 163n
Lortie, D., 200, 254n
Love: insecurities about, 20–22; selfish aspect of, 21

McCracken, Mary, 17n
McMichael, J. K., 164n, 247n
Magical thinking in children about disabilities, 143
Mainstreaming, 16, 68, 193, 225
Manualist approach to deafness, 224–25
Marital stress, 10, 91–136; and anger, 97–98; and anxiety, 96; and coping, 131–36; and disagreements, 117–30; and equilibrium, 92; and faith in marital bond, 102–8; and fatigue, 98–101; and fear, 94–97; and organization of the family, 108–17; and privacy, 91–92; sadness and division within marriage, 94–101

Massie, Robert, 8, 18, 33, 37, 85, 110, 111, 220, 230, 233, 234, 238, 240

Massie, Suzanne, 8, 18, 25, 28, 64, 65, 79, 85, 111, 220, 223, 230, 234, 238, 240

Meadow, K. P., 224n

Medical model, limitations of, 113. *See also* Physicians

Medical terminology, 178–80, 180n

Melton, David, 218, 219, 223

Meningitis, 74, 143

Mental retardation, 4, 8n, 162; and autism, 195; communication of information on, 180; denial of, 59; and disruption of family, 162n; and excitement from modest gains, 227; and family dynamics, 162n, 167; fears of, 25–26; and institutionalization, 17; as label, 40; and parental self-image, 76, 88; patterning for, 119; recognition of, 148; relative seriousness of, 231n; residential facilities for, 36; and siblings, 7, 81, 144–45, 148, 174–75; social cruelty towards, 21; and socio-economic class, 165–66

Meyers, Robert, 148, 160, 161, 169, 170, 171, 175, 176

Michaelis, C. T., 39, 148

Microcephalic condition, 32

Miller, N., 164n

Minuchin, Salvadore, 108, 109

Mioclonic seizures, 123

Miscarriage, 88

Mitchell, W., 242

Mongoloidism: acceptance of, 164n; as term, 180

Mothers, vulnerabilities of, 71

Murray, Emily, 8, 101, 106, 120, 211, 212, 214

Murray, John B., 8, 101, 106, 120, 211, 212, 214, 230, 244

My Son's Story (Frank), 48–49

National Association for Retarded Citizens, 66

Negrete, V. F., 180n, 183n

Nemzoff, R., 29n

Nervous breakdown, 63

Newson, Elizabeth, 243

Newson, John, 243

Nightmares and anxiety, 18

Norms, cultural: and children, 115; as supportive to family, 122

O'Conner, Patricia (mothers' group), 59, 88, 229

Occupational therapy, 77, 113, 184

O'Donnell, Michael, 175

Olafson, Mary, 127, 128

Old age and ego development, 230

One Little Boy (Baruch), 72n

Option Attitude, 217

Oralist approach to deafness, 224–25

Orthopedic handicaps, 89

Osher, T., 182, 210

Ouelett, Annette, 33, 54, 79

Ourselves and Our Children (Boston Women's Health Collective), 93n

Pacific State Hospital, 25

Pain and isolation, 229

Paley, Vivian, 193n

Parents: effectiveness training for, 77; information needs of, 178, 181–82; personal accounts of, 8; responsibility in disability, 56; and siblings, 141, 152–57

Park, Clara Claiborne, 8, 44, 45, 47, 71, 73, 114, 152, 153, 228, 230, 248

Pathways to Madness (Henry), 205

Patterning for brain-injured, 119

Pediatricians on behavior disorders, 72

Pendler, Betty, 79, 81

Physical therapy, 57, 135, 184

Physicians: on acceptance of disability, 230; advice on special education from, 185; communications from, 179–80, 183; interaction with parents, 210; limitations of, 196–98; respect from, 182; training of, 204, 206; vulnerability of, 187, 189–91

Pieper, Carl, 127

Pieper, Elizabeth, 34, 127, 150, 151, 183

Placenta, infected, 4

Pneumonia, 84; pneumococcal, 207; pulmonary, 206

Potter, Clare (mothers' group), 150

Predictions, realism in and fear, 24–25

Pregnancy, fears of, 17

Prenatal rubella, 23

Preschooling, 6

Professionals: anger of, 36–39; confrontations with, 186; cultural roots of advice, 126; empathy of, 7, 177; and families, 10; and fear creation, 24–25, 29n; and information, 178–82; and male competition, 126–29; on marriage stress, 93n; power of over family, 113; respect from, 182–84; services of, 184–86; training of, 201–7

Psychiatrists on behavior disorders, 72

Psychoanalysis, 71

Psychologists: perspective of, 7; respect from, 182, 183
Psychotherapy: and loneliness, 65; and parental responsibility, 126

Rage, emotional concomitants of, 30
Ramos, Nancy, 97
Rank, B., 72
Rape, fears of, 17
Rebuilding, 86–90
Regression and acceptance, 218
Rehabilitation Institute of Montreal, 185
Religious conviction and anger, 33–34
Respirators, 74
Retardation and communication, 51
Rhodes, M. J., 94n
Richmond, J. B., 10
Riesman, David, 67, 241
Roith, A. I., 242
Roskies, Ethel, 7, 178, 181, 186, 242
Roth, William, 208, 209
Rubella, 143

St. Rita's Hospital, 62
Schizophrenia, 96, 162; biochemical factors in, 73
Schooling. See Education
Schlesinger, H. S., 224n
Schrag, Peter, 97
Schult, M., 53, 56
Searl, Stanford, 232
Segal, Marilyn, 74, 75, 113, 152, 227
Seguin, Edouard, 183n
Self-concept and disability of children, 228
Self-esteem: in families, 222; and guilt, 85; parental, and adequacy of children, 71–72, 76; rebuilding of, 87
Sensory loss and emotional development, 79
Sesame Street, 69
Sexuality, anticipatory fears of, 17
Shunt for fluid on brain, 5
Siblings, 46–47, 137–76; coping of, 163–76; and family life, 157–62; fantasies of, 137–41; fear in, 23–24; guilt in, 82–83, 140, 143, 144; and handicapped, pressures on, 10; loneliness in, 60–61; and mental retardation, 7; and parents, 141, 152–57; responses of to disabilities, 142–51
Sisters. See Siblings
Skelton, M., 93n
Sleep patterns: disturbances of, 5, 98–99; regularization of, 101
Sobol, H. L., 194

Social psychologists on marital stress, 93n. See also Psychologists
Socio-economic status: and male interaction, 129; and mental retardation, 165–66
Solnit, A., 233
Special education: coursework in, 9; and parent-teacher interaction, 29n; preschool, 185–86; reciprocal nature of, 6. See also Mental retardation
Spina bifida, 58
Spinal cord: defects of, 16, 58; tumor of, 152
Spock, Benjamin, 14, 76
Stage theories: difficulty in, 232; simplification problems in, 10
Stark, M. H., 233
Stereotypes, cultural, as supportive of maternal anxieties, 122
Stern, E. M., 81 ·
Stillbirth, 88. See also Childbirth
Strickland, Jo, 53
Suicide and loneliness, 64
Sullivan, Barbara (mothers' group), 36, 40, 66, 67, 84, 86, 122, 123, 124, 222, 225, 226, 246n
Supplemental Security Income payments, 170
Symbols and faith in marriage, 102

TABs (temporary able-bodied), 69
Tay-Sachs disease, 41
Teachers: on behavior disorders, 172; on community in classroom, 193; competition with parents, 184–85, 186; interaction with parents, 209; limitations of, 199; as parents, 202; respect from, 182; skills of, 203; vulnerability of, 187. See also Education
Temperament: and behavior, 72; and expert advice, 125
Thalidomide, 7, 178, 181
Thomas, A., 73n
Thompson, Maureen (mothers' group), 157
Thornburg, Devin, 47, 153–54, 166
Todd (Melton), 223
Toigo, R., 93n
Toilet training, 20, 77, 222
Total communication approach to deafness, 224n
Toxoplasmosis, 4, 32, 38, 233
Trace, Barbara, 45, 47, 179
Tranquilizers, 179
Tuberculosis, 206, 239
Tuberous sclerosis, 55